T0319465

Luminos is the Open Access monograph publishing program
from UC Press. Luminos provides a framework for preserving and
reinvigorating monograph publishing for the future and increases
the reach and visibility of important scholarly work. Titles published
in the UC Press Luminos model are published with the same high
standards for selection, peer review, production, and marketing as
those in our traditional program. www.luminosoa.org

The publisher and the University of California Press Foundation
gratefully acknowledge the generous support of the
Eric Papenfuse and Catherine Lawrence Endowment Fund
in Film and Media Studies.

Producing Feminism

FEMINIST MEDIA HISTORIES

Shelley Stamp, Series Editor

Producing Feminism

Television Work in the Age of Women's Liberation

Jennifer S. Clark

UNIVERSITY OF CALIFORNIA PRESS

University of California Press

Oakland, California © 2024 by Jennifer S. Clark

Suggested citation: Clark, J. S. *Producing Feminism: Television Work in the Age of Women's Liberation*. Oakland: University of California Press, 2024.
DOI: https://doi.org/10.1525/luminos.180

Library of Congress Cataloging-in-Publication Data

Names: Clark, Jennifer Susanne, author.
Title: Producing feminism : television work in the age of women's
    liberation / Jennifer S. Clark.
Other titles: Feminist media histories (Series) ; 6.
Description: Oakland, California : University of California Press, [2024] |
    Series: Feminist media histories ; 6 | Includes bibliographical
    references and index.
Identifiers: LCCN 2023040997 (print) | LCCN 2023040998 (ebook) |
    ISBN 9780520399297 (paperback) | ISBN 9780520399303 (ebook)
Subjects: LCSH: Women in television broadcasting—United States—
    History—20th century. | Feminism and mass media—United States—
    History—20th century.
Classification: LCC PN1992.8.W65 C54 2024 (print) | LCC PN1992.8.W65
    (ebook) | DDC 791.45082/0973—dc23/eng/20230919

LC record available at https://lccn.loc.gov/2023040997
LC ebook record available at https://lccn.loc.gov/2023040998

Manufactured in the United States of America

33   32   31   30   29   28   27   26   25   24
10   9   8   7   6   5   4   3   2   1

CONTENTS

Introduction

In December 1971, production assistant Carolyn Wean wrote a memo to express her frustration about the workspace at *For Women Today* (1970–75), a locally produced show that aired on Boston's WBZ-TV. In the memo, Wean reported to the station's executive producer of programming and to the general services director that the "disappearance of things from the *F[or] W[omen] T[oday]* office continues" and requested that steps be taken to "insure that this stops."[1] Wean noted that in the previous week half a dozen books purchased for show research had gone missing and insisted that the station provide secure storage for their office. In other memos to station executives, Wean related more problems with the day-to-day functioning of the program's production spaces: no one was assigned to clean the set before tapings, so the assistant director had to take on the task; dressing rooms were not maintained; and no one was free to answer phones while the production team was busy taping the program.

A second set of memos between management and workers at WBZ further illustrates difficulties at the station. On December 22, 1970, program manager Mel Bernstein issued a memo in which he asked five men on staff to help him accompany nine women, four of whom worked on *For Women Today*, to a "'Harem' luncheon." "Since most of them are shy in public," wrote Bernstein, "rendezvous at my office around Noon and we'll chauffeur them," and warned, in closing, "Behave yourself!"[2] The same day, *For Women Today* producer Raysa Bonow, associate producer Claire Carter, production assistant Carolyn Wean, and associate producer Connie Sanders issued a response to Bernstein. They signaled their confusion at the "harem" moniker used to describe them and cited three different definitions of the word from *Webster's Dictionary*: a secluded part of a Muslim household reserved for women, "a group of women associated with one man," and a polygamous group of animals.[3] The next portion of the women's memo matches the "humor" of the original correspondence, indicates refusal of sexist treatment, and sardonically dismantles its flawed logic:

> Since we find it difficult to place ourselves with great enthusiasm into any of these categories, we find against our better judgment and desire for a pleasant lunch that we will have to decline the invitation. However, if one pushes a little, I suppose that we could sneak into category 2., providing then that the memo be sent with only "CC" to all those listed and none to receive a memo addressed "TO." Perhaps, O Mighty Sultan of the Harem, you could send us a new memorandum more succinctly delineating our position.[4]

The tone of the memo subtly shifts in the close when the women call for dignified and respectful treatment and request a revised, professional plan for the lunch: "The staff of *For Women Today* cannot speak for all those who received carbons of your original memorandum, but *we* anxiously await further word (anything that will enable us to attend the luncheon with some smidgen of dignity)."[5] As they each signed off as "a.k.a. woman," the production team reclaimed the gendered identities that made them subject to the indignities of a sexist workplace.[6]

Correspondence generated around *For Women Today* characterizes the challenges women faced as they expressed feminist ideas within the television industry. It therefore typifies the concerns of *Producing Feminism*. First, it relates how television workplaces become gendered through commonplace, even banal, circumstances: the security and maintenance of spaces, the many tasks that exceed official job titles and descriptions, and the cultivation and management of relationships among coworkers and management. Second, it reflects the growing involvement of women in television, in "creative" (directly involved in production) and "noncreative" (support for the various needs of production) roles, during the 1970s. Third, it illustrates the demands and refusals women were making in light of untenable work conditions and sexist attitudes in the industry. Finally, it demonstrates the evidentiary value of workplace communications to concretize and chronicle how women experienced television work.

As one of the first television programs to reflect the impact of the women's movement, *For Women Today* (later named *The Sonya Hamlin Show*) signaled its commitment to feminist principles by employing an all-woman production team and by altering traditions of women's television to align with movement politics. When in 1970 Sonya Hamlin was offered the job of hosting WBZ's morning show for women, executives' disregard for women's television was obvious. Hamlin recalls coming into a room with eighteen men seated around a big table who assured her that she could retain her position as a cultural reporter for the station while she hosted the morning show because of the formulaic and simplistic nature of programming for women. "It's easy," they told Hamlin, since she would have "dodo birds for viewers" and the labor required by the program would involve only "a little make-up, a little hairdo, a chef you can cook with, and from time to time there will be a star coming through." Hamlin initially refused the offer but, after consulting with her husband, came back to the table with a counteroffer: the freedom to "hire an all-woman staff, producer, director . . . everybody" and to program what she wanted. To her surprise, WBZ management immediately agreed to these terms, something Hamlin credits to the influence of "the beginning of the uprising of the women's movement."[7]

With "what at the time was the unusual goal of treating women who watched daytime television as intelligent viewers," *For Women Today* featured feminist leaders and ideas as well as a range of forward-thinking topics.[8] Hamlin recollects programming *For Women Today* "in a very different way," with the show focusing on a single topic in order to "look at every facet of it for a week," which resulted in presenting the audience with "very revolutionary things," "very novel things," and "in-depth" assessments of topics previously deemed unsuitable for daytime television.[9] When Hamlin left the show in 1975, the *Boston Globe* described the program's impact through a number of "Firsts" in Boston television: "Homosexuals first appeared on the air with Sonya and publicly discussed their lives. *Ms.* magazine was introduced on her show a full week before it was released nationwide to newsstands. Sex, of all kinds, was discussed openly, frankly, explicitly, and sometimes with illustrations."[10] A list of show topics from 1970 to 1972 attests to the progressive nature of *For Women Today* and included abortion (for at least three episodes), pornography, homosexuality (a two-part series), premarital sex, sex in marriage, birth control and the law, menopause (female and male), pregnancy, unwed mothers, venereal disease, natural childbirth, rape, and sex education.[11]

According to *Broadcasting*'s 1972 report on the "new shake" television was starting to give women viewers, *For Women Today* "won plaudits from feminist groups" and nonfeminists alike.[12] Along with the expected female demographic reach, *For Women Today*'s audience also included 20 percent male viewership. Cross-gender viewership, along with the capture of a politicized as well as a traditional female audience, would have made the show viable to potential advertisers and buyers outside of the typical daytime market.[13] Given its audience, *For Women Today* was a successful regional program, yet the show was never picked up for syndication, even though Hamlin was approached with a syndication offer. Hamlin left the program under disappointing circumstances, and the program was soon canceled after that, never to reach an audience beyond local Boston viewership. *For Women Today*'s contributions to women's television have been overlooked in feminist television studies and television histories of the 1970s. With the exception of a book on Boston television that mentions the show briefly, there are no scholarly accounts of the program.[14]

Recalling the innovative qualities of *For Women Today* presents an opportunity to assess both why and how such a program can be reevaluated. From its very inception, feminist television studies has demonstrated that "genres and forms previously seen as 'minor' because they were produced and/or consumed by nondominant groups may have even more to teach us about how culture operates and

FIGURE 1. Sonya Hamlin (left) hosts (from left to right) Senator George McGovern, along with actor Joyce Susskind and producer David Susskind, on *The Sonya Hamlin Show* (formerly known as *For Women Today*), WBZ, October 16, 1972. (Getty Images)

how ideology is enforced than the traditional canon."[15] This perspective sidelines the issue of whether *For Women Today*, given its status as a daytime program for women with limited resources and a restricted, regional audience, is worthy of discussion. The question then becomes one of gauging the impact of the program for women and identifying where and how this impact occurred. Content and viewership provide grounds for evaluation, as do its many innovations in television for women. Yet *For Women Today*—like the other television programs included in this book—also merits exploration because of the gendered operations of its workplace and feminist interventions by workers in those operations.

Producing Feminism's primary objective is to understand the relationship between women's liberation and television in the US through the means by which women got their feminist visions to air and into the workplace. This project assumes that television production cultures are created, sustained, and challenged through material, logistical, and interpersonal dynamics as much as they are through economics, policies, and industrial trends. From this perspective, the television workplace operates as what Daphne Spain calls a "spatial institution," in which "the properties of a social system express themselves through daily activities at the same time those activities generate and reproduce structural properties of the social system."[16] Women's encounters with patriarchal regimes of power in television often happened in commonplace ways in the day-to-day functioning of the television workplace. When, during the 1970s, women were employed in greater numbers and occupied new and evolving positions in television, they disrupted the industry's spatial institutions and corresponding social systems. Consequently, the sites and working conditions of television production—in addition to television's on-screen products—offer invaluable opportunities to understand the impact of the women's movement on television.

PRODUCTION STUDIES AS AN EVALUATIVE TOOL

Production cultures are inextricably tied to identity and power. It follows, then, that feminist production studies show how interpersonal, invisible, and undercompensated labor falls disproportionately to women workers, particularly immigrant women and women of color. Scholarship on female-centered occupations, such as costumers and clerical and secretarial workers, and women who broke into male-dominated occupations, such as stunt doubles, focuses explicitly on these issues.[17] But as Miranda Banks argues, we might also understand production studies in general as fundamentally feminist. Feminist inquiry, with its analysis of discriminatory systems and its "recuperation of narratives long devalued," proves instrumental in production studies scholarship, which is invested in marginalized labor and industries in their transitional moments.[18]

Given the feminist priorities of production studies, locating histories of women's liberation in television production cultures is scarcely surprising. Yet as much work as has been done on the relationship between the US women's liberation movement and television, surprisingly little scholarship has taken a production studies approach to the topic. Instead, landmark scholarship tends to belong to two categories: (1) mediated images of liberated women designed to "update" television content and engage politically progressive, lucrative viewers and (2) media reform efforts from feminist groups that operate outside the industry. These foci have helped explicate why commercial media would be attracted to feminism and how feminist activism attempted to shift television's sexist traditions. They also have established analytic frameworks for representation and audiences, provided in-depth explorations of television programs, and constructed histories of media activism. Other concerns in the meeting of women's liberation and television, however, fall outside these two dominant categories and warrant further attention.

In focusing on the worker herself, *Producing Feminism* looks beyond the on-screen image and activism from outside the industry to consider other ways that the women's movement made inroads in television. This reorientation recognizes multiple types of feminist television reform, extends the timeline of the women's movement's influence on television beyond a short-lived existence as a media-worthy spectacle, and acknowledges feminists not typically or centrally featured in histories of television and the women's movement. Issues of the mediation and co-optation of feminist politics shift as well in a production-oriented analysis, as this approach considers processes enacted by agentive women who actively challenged and reformed television workplaces and production protocols.

Assessing women's gains in media industries requires multiple evaluative means, as scholarship by Natalie Wreyford and Shelley Cobb, Miranda Banks, and Vicky Ball and Melanie Bell demonstrates.[19] By the early 1970s, with changing employment laws and regulatory pressure to hire more women, television stations across the country were compelled to hire women in greater numbers, and network television promoted women to executive positions. Program content also changed and included an archetype for a "new implicitly feminist woman coping with her everyday world."[20] While the industry used these actions to announce a newfound awareness of feminism through quantitative (statistics on employment) and qualitative (program content) means, neither dataset on its own provides compelling evidence of feminist influence over television. Rising employment numbers for women at stations were manipulated by recategorization of jobs; promotions at networks involved newly created job titles without corresponding increases in prestige, power, or compensation; and progressive on-screen content was not necessarily tied to women working on its production.[21] Therefore, an uptick in screentime for women characters, "improved" representation for women, and increased employment and promotions for women do not necessarily evince achievements of feminist goals.

A production studies approach to the advancements of women in television tells us what employment statistics or image analysis alone cannot. Workers' perspectives and documents internal to the television workplace reveal how women actually experienced supposed or real opportunities. This evidence augments and complicates the "objective" information conveyed in industry press releases, formalized policies, and statistical reports. It also showcases how workers themselves enacted important political changes in television through logistical decisions, interpersonal dynamics, and the everyday operations of making television, as formative production studies scholarship demonstrates.

People who worked on innovative programs of the late 1960s through the 1980s offer particularly rich insights into how transformative moments in television happen. In her analysis of *Soul!*, a public television show of the late 1960s and early 1970s produced by and for Black Americans, Gayle Wald recognizes the plans made about set design, interviewing techniques, camera angles, and editing as vital contributions to the program's "intimacy and connection with viewers."[22] In his carefully considered ideas about running the show, producer Ellis Haizlip cultivated "black cultural self-definition that refused to accept white aesthetic standards and, in so doing, contributed to the emotion and spiritual well-being of the collective."[23] Despite proclamations by the show's producer that 1980s female-cop drama *Cagney & Lacey* was not a vehicle for feminism, Julie D'Acci charts how the production team crafted "explicit general feminism" for the show.[24] D'Acci's research of communications and planning internal to the production reveals that "commentaries and memos on various drafts of the scripts actually bespeak efforts to be blatantly and 'correctly' feminist" and counter public statements to the contrary.[25] Jennifer Keishin Armstrong's production history of 1970s single-girl workplace sitcom *The Mary Tyler Moore Show* locates the opportunities presented to women on the production team in small, interpersonal moments. Show cocreator Allan Burns promoted Pat Nando from secretary to writer when he walked her to her car and encouraged her to write for the show, saying, "I think you can do it."[26]

These accounts make it clear that progressive changes in the television industry take place not just through regulatory measures, industry-wide reform economic incentives, or other large-scale, systemwide factors. These changes also, and perhaps more often, transpire in the granular details of planning and logistics, conversations both personal and professional, and minutiae of behind-the-scenes relationships. In corresponding fashion, *Producing Feminism* calls upon interviews, memoirs, and primary documents generated in the workplace, just as it cites statistical data about employment numbers, ratings, salaries, and profits.

Throughout the book, I turn to multiple narratives generated by women workers, as well as qualitative evidence from sources that were not public-facing and that counterbalance data used for industry self-promotion. Using interview transcripts, journalistic interviews conducted by others, and my own interviews with workers, I relate firsthand accounts of the changing nature of television labor across a wide array of occupations, including producers, hosts, actors, reporters, writers, researchers, consultants, creative directors, and executives. I call upon materials housed in archives—including memos, workplace communications, meeting schedules and minutes, production plans, workplace memos, floor plans, diagrams of sets, and employee newsletters—to further contextualize policies within experiential and informal aspects of their execution. These materials are housed in a range of collections focused on television (Mass Media and Culture Special Collections, University of Maryland; Norman Lear Script Collection, Emerson College; University of Wyoming, Heritage Center; and Howard Gotlieb Archival Research Center, Boston University), women's political and cultural history (Schlesinger Library, Radcliffe Institute for Advanced Study; Sophia Smith Collection of Women's History, Smith College), state government (Commonwealth of Massachusetts State Archive), and corporate broadcasting (CBS News Reference Library). Collectively, these resources spotlight women who experienced and intervened in the gendered politics of television and reveal the operations of television workplaces as important sites of feminist reform.

TELEVISION RESPONDS TO THE WOMEN'S MOVEMENT

With the growth of the US women's movement at the beginning of the 1970s, television was compelled to take notice. To capture an emerging demographic of women viewers and to capitalize on popular ideas about liberated women, fictional programs deployed what Bonnie J. Dow and Katherine Lehman identify as "lifestyle feminism."[27] This consumerist-friendly mediation of feminist politics, according to Patricia Bradley, was inevitable, as "the movement's goals would be met only in ways that were consistent with the values of commerce."[28] Lauren Rabinovitz's assessment of feminist-inflected sitcoms leads her to a similar conclusion. "A generic address of 'feminism' became an important strategy," she argues, "because it served the needs of American television executives who could cultivate programming that could be identified with target audiences whom they wanted to measure and deliver to advertising agencies."[29]

When feminists, like other activist groups, demanded that television be pressed to uphold its responsibility to the public, television tried to contain the impact of those demands. In 1969, WLBT-TV, a television station in Jackson, Mississippi, had its broadcasting license revoked when it refused to air civil rights perspectives and violated the Fairness Doctrine, the Federal Communications Commission (FCC) policy adopted in 1949 that stipulated equal airtime be given to opposing viewpoints on an issue. The case provided precedent for media reform groups to file similar petition-to-deny cases. Local stations needed to respond to such action, but they "regularized their relationship with activist groups in their communities," as Kathryn Montgomery explains, and satisfied their demands by providing these groups with low-cost, low-impact programming; such tactics "placated the groups, without cutting into the stations' profits."[30]

Even though television reacted to the women's movement through containment, co-optation, and superficial appeasement, feminist scholars identify triumphs and gains that were made despite such responses. While Bonnie J. Dow concurs with prevailing narratives about the feminist protest of the 1968 Miss America pageant as the source of "image problems that have plagued feminism ever since," she also regards the event as a "success in terms of energizing the radical wing of the second wave."[31] Montgomery's scholarship on advocacy groups notes that reform efforts paid off when the National Organization for Women (NOW) began targeting network-owned stations and prime-time programming and identified them as "vulnerable" to protest.[32] Regardless of the efficacy of NOW's licensing challenges, Allison Perlman recognizes that the organization's petitions-to-deny demonstrated feminism's legitimacy as an organized political movement. By engaging in television reform, feminists insisted on their "consumer or economic power as viewers" and defined themselves as "active citizens" who warranted recognition through federal policy.[33] Bernadette Barker-Plummer demonstrates how feminist groups were able to exploit a "dialogical" relationship between themselves and commercial news outlets.[34] As such nuanced scholarship on the meeting of the television industry and feminism in the 1970s makes plain, any analysis of this relationship must acknowledge the complexity of the dynamics involved. By focusing on women workers and their feminist influences on their respective television workplaces and production cultures, *Producing Feminism* adds further fissures to accounts of the industry's co-optation of, or blanket hostility toward, feminism.

To exemplify this point, I turn briefly here to network television's engagement with the Women's Strike for Equality, a momentous public action of the women's movement. NOW organized the strike, which took place on August 26, 1970, and involved a number of events across the country, including church sermons conducted by women, boycotts of products deemed demeaning to women, women refusing to provide unpaid domestic labor in their own homes, mothers bringing children to fathers' workplaces to demonstrate the need for childcare, and radio stations giving over broadcasting to women staff and listeners for the day's programming. A broadside published by Women's Coalition Strike Headquarters encouraged women, "*CONFRONT* your own unfinished business of equality at your office, on your job, or at home," and exhorted them to join the march on Fifth Avenue.[35] Anne Ladky, women's workplace activist and president of the Chicago chapter of NOW (1973–75), describes the strike as "a big, big, big deal" that "launched Chicago NOW," "brought all sorts of members in," and "really did scare the forces of the status quo."[36] When NOW "invited women from across a range of activist organizations to overlook their differences and unite for womankind," it proved a successful call to action.[37] The New York City march included "radical feminists, lesbians, Black Power advocates, pacifists," women of all ages, and some men, and the "diversity of the crowd astounded even the NOW organizers."[38]

Given the scale, coordination, and political significance of the strike, television's response to the event was both surprising and disappointing. Barbara Walters, who was working at *Today* (NBC 1952–) at the time, recognized that the collective action of the over fifty thousand women who marched in New York City's Strike for Equality was a newsworthy event. But when she urged NBC president Reuven Frank to increase special coverage of the protest and to air informational reports on the women's movement, the network did not respond favorably. Frank rejected Walter's pitch for a one-hour special, telling her, "Not enough interest."[39] Ultimately all three networks ended up covering the strike, but when they did, their treatment of the event, according to Patricia Bradley, "had not been sympathetic."[40] Coverage of the event reified the sexist representational practices of commercial television. In Bonnie J. Dow's assessment, all three networks framed the strike for the "visual pleasure" of an imagined male spectator and deployed "sheer spectacle," "absurdist entertainment rather than reasoned protest," and anxiety-fueled concerns about "femininity under attack" in their reportage.[41] The investments of television and feminists in depictions of the strike were, according to Dow, fundamentally antithetical: "Although the feminists who created the strike were attempting to exert control over the image of the movement—by making it visible, by demonstrating widespread support for it, and by dramatizing its demands—television's framing of the action within dominant cultural representational norms undermined those purposes."[42] Feminist reaction to television reports on the strike was not favorable, and their "anger at network coverage was profound."[43]

Television coverage of the Strike for Equality marked an inauspicious start to the relationship of the women's movement and television and seemed to forestall hope that feminism could make meaningful inroads into television. Yet responses to worker involvement in the strike suggest another way in which television could, and did, respond to feminist activism at this stage of its development. If on-screen images repurposed, diluted, and trivialized something as formative in the women's movement as the strike, women workers at the networks experienced a different response to the very same event. This difference suggests the more successful impact of feminist activism from within, rather than from without, the television industry. In anticipation of the event, CBS acknowledged that its employees might participate in the day's activities and offered them the option of taking either unpaid time off or a paid vacation day. NBC and ABC had "no enunciated policy" but instead "left it up to department heads" to determine how to deal with absent workers on the day of the strike.[44] In contrast to on-air treatment of the Strike for Equality, network management's policies about worker participation—even if only a nonpunitive response—marked acknowledgment of, and a degree of respect for, the event.

The single example of the Strike for Equality (something I discuss further in chapter 1), suggests a broader pattern of television's responsiveness to feminism in workplace matters, which often operated independently from the industry's decisions about on-screen depictions of the women's movement. By uncoupling television's decisions about how to depict feminism from its internal responses to workers' feminist politics, we can consider the impact of the women's movement on television's practices beyond representation. This perspective allows us to see, regardless of the messages about feminism that ultimately made their way to viewing audiences, the presence and efficacy of feminist influence within the television industry.

To extend considerations of feminism's impact on television beyond the screen, I call upon more-than-representational and material feminist frameworks. This approach helps locate feminist political activity inside the industry and through experiential aspects of the workplace. "More-than-representational" theorization reorients analysis from assumptions about the fixity and finality of images to considerations of "how life takes shape and gains expression in shared experiences, everyday routines, fleeting encounters, embodied movements, precognitive triggers, practical skills, affective intensities, enduring urges, unexceptional interactions and sensuous dispositions."[45] In critical geography studies, this approach fosters scholarly emphasis not on landscapes that are texts to be read but rather on sites that are experiential, embodied, and affective. In its concerns with "actions and processes" and with the fluidity and mobility of prerepresentational moments, a "more-than-representational" framework translates well to studies of workers, labor, and experiences in image-producing realms.[46]

Although my project investigates feminist activism within the labor and spaces of production, it is not a refutation or rejection of the immense value of representational analysis. With an emphasis on the "more than" rather than the "anti-" or "not- representational, *Producing Feminism* does not entirely disregard the correlation between production cultures and their output. In instances when workers' feminist practices resulted in meaningful changes in television content, I tend to the planning involved in creating images and the hoped-for impact on audiences. Creating images, however, is but one of many in the labors of television production, and I consider representations not as primary indicators of feminist influence in television but as a correspondence with numerous other feminist efforts in production.

Indeed, representations matter to this project because they reveal something to us about the nature of production. This perspective reverses traditions of television histories, in which industry issues offer a means by which to understand what happens on screen. Maya Montañez Smukler's work on women film directors of the 1970s offers a helpful model for this approach. While film content and biographies are part of her examination of women directors, "textual analysis is not the framework for the project as a whole." Instead, Smukler utilizes these texts to consider "a crucial historical juncture during the 1970s" that afforded women greater inroads into the film industries."[47] By regarding labor practices and the places in which they occurred, I am able not just to look at the product of women's work in the television industry but to see the processes by which they created that product and the conditions that afforded that creation. This perspective gets at critical engagements and experiential qualities of television that exist alongside—and sometimes apart from—on-screen representations. This perspective also situates feminists as active and strategic agents in the production of television rather than only reactive critics or passive fodder for sensationalized media coverage.

SCOPE AND ARRANGEMENT OF *PRODUCING FEMINISM*

Producing Feminism focuses on the 1970s, with a start at the beginning of the decade. While the existence of the women's movement preceded this time period, its popularization and everyday presence in American life reached critical mass in 1970. Feminist historian Sara Evans describes that year as one during which "'women's lib' was on everyone's lips."[48] In its assessment of feminism's growth, *Newsweek* identified 1970 as a watershed moment, "the year in which American women became intellectually aware of the modern feminist movement," and predicted that, in the years to come, women's liberation would "become part of [women's] everyday lives."[49] This was the point at which feminism achieved visibility in legal and political realms and made significant inroads into popular culture. New York State liberalized abortion laws; the House of Representatives passed the Equal Rights Amendment (ERA); and the aforementioned Women's Strike for Equality in New York City became the "largest demonstration for female equality in American history."[50] *Sexual Politics, The Dialectic of Sex*, and *Sisterhood Is Powerful* all became bestsellers, and activist interventions in popular culture, such as the occupation of *Ladies Home Journal*'s corporate office with demands for a "liberated issue of the magazine to be done by women," were highly publicized events.[51]

The year 1970 also marked television's engagement with the women's movement and feminist interventions in the industry. NOW established its Media Task Force and successfully lobbied the FCC to include "sex" as part of Equal Employment Opportunity rules. Bonnie J. Dow maintains that this was the time when network news "gave their most sustained attention to the second wave *as a movement.*"[52] On May 25, 1970, ABC aired "Women's Liberation," a news report aimed to inform viewers about the "unfinished revolution of American women."[53] Marlene Sanders, writer, producer, and on-air reporter for the program, served as a "feminist sympathizer" who was "self-conscious" in her attempts to "represent the movement fairly."[54] Sanders's involvement marked a significant opportunity for a woman to helm coverage of the movement and influence how television news would pay attention to it.

While the relationship between television and women's liberation has a clear origin point in 1970, the end point of the relationship is less certain. By and large, commercial television found feminism attractive when it provided compelling stories and easily digestible images and conveyed relatively conservative liberal feminist ideas. This limited perspective not only overlooked the complexity of the movement but also hastened a premature end to its media coverage. According to Patricia Bradley, workplace equality overshadowed concerns of the movement articulated early in its existence that "sought to put on the public agenda issues of how women's secondary nature in U.S. society adversely reflected attention to women's health, child support concerns, rape and legal protections, and domestic abuse—issues that were discrete problems to be corrected well as related to the overall pattern of culture."[55] Events like the high-profile televised tennis match between Billie Jean King and Bobby Riggs in 1973 helped confirm the narrative that women's equality had been achieved. By 1975, this perception had solidified, and full-scale media interest in the movement had effectively come to an end.

By comparison, production cultures reveal more sustained investments between feminism and television. The investments and endeavors of women television workers extended the impact of the women's movement on television beyond the 1975 expiration date that Bradley establishes. Women's careers exceeded short-lived media interest in the movement, and their understanding of feminist issues surpassed the single issue of workplace equality with which television coverage was preoccupied. In tending to women whose career arcs continued throughout the 1970s and beyond, *Producing Feminism* acknowledges their continued energies and identifies the ways that feminist investments operated in television years after the industry's initial interest had waned.

The first chapter of *Producing Feminism*, "Women's Groups and Workplace Reform at Network Television's Corporate Headquarters," explores women's groups that formed at the headquarters of all three networks in the early 1970s, with a focus on the Women's Advisory Council (WAC) at CBS.[56] This chapter considers the impact of women's workplace groups on corporate media culture. These groups gave voice to feminist concerns at network television's corporate headquarters, a sector of the industry that was notoriously inhospitable to activist reform efforts. As a workplace collective, the women's groups organized across occupational divisions and focused on employment concerns for all women workers employed at the corporation. WAC, in particular, harnessed the will of the collective to successfully modify policies and practices at CBS that ranged from reproductive health care, the sexism of the network's office culture, and conscious-raising measures in the workplace to more expected issues of equitable promotion and job training.[57]

By starting *Producing Feminism* with workers often employed at a remove from television production, conventionally defined, I signal the project's investment in the breadth of labors women undertook and reformed in television throughout the course of the 1970s. Secretaries and support staff, researchers, and accountants, as well as "creatives," participated in the network women's groups and collectively agitated for improved workplace conditions. This community of media workers bridged hierarchical divisions of the corporation and recognized unpaid and undervalued labor as central to the operations of the network. In doing so, WAC provides an instructive model of successful, if atypical, feminist television reform. By focusing on the workplace and operating from within the industry, WAC was able to introduce eclectic feminist principles into network television at the very heart of its operations.

Producing Feminism's second chapter, "From 'Jockocratic Endeavors' to Feminist Expression," explores television's role in expressing the feminist potential of women's sports. In a context where feminist leadership and female athletes were ambivalent, at best, about the need to join forces, commercial television provided an environment in which women could demonstrate the productive correspondence of feminism and athleticism. This chapter focuses on two figures who helped actualize this dynamic: tennis pro, television celebrity, and sports commentator Billie Jean King and Eleanor Sanger Riger, the first woman producer at ABC Sports.

King's famed Battle of the Sexes match with Bobby Riggs in 1973, her advocacy for legalized abortion and equal pay for women, and her sports celebrity made her one of the most visible and effective ambassadors for women athletes in the 1970s. Her celebrity translated to a television career as a commentator for ABC Sports, a position that Riger helped broker. Riger was hired as a direct result of feminist protests against ABC's sexist employment practices and spent her career at the network championing female athletes as viable on-air talent, mentoring and training women to take on the role of on-air announcers, and creating new types of programming for women's sports. She challenged assumptions about voices, announcing styles, and color commentary that were implicitly and powerfully gendered and biased against women. Riger also created a cooperative and collegial workplace in sports television, which welcomed more women into its production and helped ensure their success there.

As a producer in a highly competitive, male-dominated preserve, Riger faced considerable challenges to her career advancement and to the changes she wished to bring to television. Despite these obstacles, Riger helped usher in a new era of women's televised sports. When ABC invested in sports in the early 1970s, Riger helped modernize its aesthetics and outreach. She envisioned women's sports in new ways, particularly through storytelling, training for on-air talents, and techniques of camerawork, which redefined women's sports as a viable part of television programming and helped establish ABC as a leader in the genre. This chapter considers how Riger's efforts to showcase women in sports television—evinced in her detailed scripts, shot setups, and correspondence to executives and colleagues—successfully leveraged the industry's economic self-interest to improve its treatment of women in sports, both in coverage and in the hiring and treatment of production staff.

Chapter 3, "Working in the Lear Factory," turns to Tandem Productions, the influential independent production company helmed by producers Norman Lear and Bud Yorkin. The notion of Tandem as a factory, as alluded to in the chapter's title, circulated in popular coverage of the company at the height of its success and was deployed to both praise and critique the rapid, seemingly inexhaustible output of the company. A concept that Lear himself roundly rejected, the factory serves as a useful descriptor that decenters Lear as the singular, auteurist producer and makes room for the contributions women made to Tandem's success. This perspective also acknowledges the workload women shouldered in keeping pace with the company's output and the feminized skills—such as writing efficiency and high levels of productivity honed in work on soap operas—as central to the creation of Tandem's renowned "relevant" television. Although Lear is credited with revolutionizing television in the 1970s, this chapter supposes that he was but one element in Tandem's innovation and centers the multiple feminist forces and players who were also responsible for the groundbreaking nature of the company.

To better understand the impact women had on the making and selling of Tandem's programs, I consider women who played key roles in creative and executive capacities. Their output included the much-beloved cult series *Mary Hartman, Mary Hartman* (syndicated, 1976–77), as well as shorter-lived and lesser-known programs, such as *All That Glitters* (syndicated, 1977). While the feminist sensibilities of these programs reflect the outlook of the women who worked on them, they also influenced Tandem's production and employment practices that privileged unlikely decision-making by and around women. Whether hiring physicist Virginia Carter as director of creative affairs on the basis of her credentials as a feminist activist or creating a new distribution model necessitated by the networks' reluctance to pick up provocative programs, Tandem's business practices challenged prevailing industry models. To do so, it relied on the presence of women and feminist politics both on- and off-screen. The chapter concludes by tracing how women at Tandem translated their work experience there to other career accomplishments, to heightened creative control, and to increasingly feminist programs.

As the women's movement gained momentum and visibility, the US television industry developed programs that challenged long-standing traditions in women's television. Chapter 4 looks to television's "serious sisters," as a 1972 *Broadcasting* article called them, programs made for women that were produced for local, syndicated, and public television.[58] Unlike commercial, network television, these programs were supported through modest financial backing, employed large numbers of women, and articulated a wide range of feminist politics both on-screen and within the spaces of television production. In this chapter, I focus on *Woman Alive!* (1974–77) and *Yes, We Can* (1974), notable examples of television's "serious sisters." Coproduced by *Ms.* magazine and public television stations in Dallas and New York City, *Woman Alive!* employed a majority-female production team and used decidedly feminist approaches to making television for women. Coordinated with a woman's fair by the same name, *Yes, We Can* aired on Boston station WBZ. Jointly produced by area feminists, women employees at WBZ, and members of the Governor's Commission on the Status of Women, the program was broadcast for sixteen hours on a single day, interrupted only by the local nightly news.

In this fourth chapter, I consider how the "serious sisters" managed educational outreach to their audiences and pragmatic and political issues involved in making their programs. The women on the production teams employed adaptive feminist politics to meet unique production challenges, from negotiating resources and workflow informed by sexist traditions in the industry to balancing highly trained media acumen with antielitism and accessibility for viewers. Their innovative production practices resulted in distinctive aesthetics, storytelling devices, and production spaces that signaled a feminist ethos to those who worked on the program, to public and private funding agencies, and to audiences.

Collective cultural memory celebrates the impact of the women's movement on television through programs and characters from the 1970s but largely overlooks women who worked behind the scenes in the industry to enact feminist change. While this tendency has shaped popular and academic understandings about recent history, it also has serious consequences for contemporary media reform. In a brief epilogue, I explore this concern within the context of the #MeToo movement and its aftermath. As women's experiences of exploitative and abusive conditions in media industries came to light yet again in the 2010s, little was ultimately done to systematically overhaul the workplaces that fostered such abuse. This is true, in part, because of the paucity of well-funded, high-visibility organizations dedicated to feminist media reform. Those that do exist, such as the Geena Davis Institute on Gender and Media and its corporate and academic partners, have defined the agenda of contemporary media reform with a focus on representation. *Producing Feminism* concludes with the suggestion that we should broaden our understanding of the legacies of the women's movement and television beyond representation. In doing so, we could see how women workers engaged the television industry's sexism in the past and learn important lessons about how to remedy the unacceptable conditions of media industries for women and other minoritized workers today.

Producing Feminism elucidates a range of relationships between television workers and television content. It begins with workers who were least involved with television production and moves to those who were increasingly identified with television content that they helped create. By ending with productions that were directly under the control of women and that most evidently signaled feminist politics on-screen, the book's organization suggests an arrival at the most successful examples of feminist reform of television in the 1970s. To be sure, women's influence over representations was and still is a hallmark of feminist mediamaking, and the book celebrates highly integrated relationships between feminist workers and feminist content. But rather than seeing the book's narrative arc as one of progression that culminates in the epitome of feminist achievements in television, I understand the multiple nodes of women's interventions in television explored in each chapter as operating in concert with one another. And, ultimately, I hope this project relates stories of women television workers who utilized feminist principles to alter production cultures and workplaces, regardless of whether they directly brought feminism to light for viewers.

As a 1970 *TV Guide* article, "Is Television Making a Mockery of the American Woman?," makes clear, the problem of sexism in television was, by that point, becoming part of the public consciousness and was no longer a concern confined to feminist political groups. That such an industry-friendly publication would ponder the problem is an interesting enough development, but their solution to the problem proves even more surprising. In response to the question, "Is there any chance that the feminists—still a tiny minority of American women—will actually succeed in influencing TV if they keep up this barrage?" the answer was, "Yes, there is." While feminist organizations outside the television industry, such as NOW with its various media reform campaigns, seemed likely candidates for affecting change, *TV Guide* argued that television workers themselves offered the best hope for challenging the sexism of the industry. With "the entire communications world . . . studded with feminist Trojan horses," *TV Guide* predicted that it would be "feminist borers from within" who would revolutionize television's gender politics.[59]

The notion of "feminist borers from within" grounds *Producing Feminism*. It signals a mode of activism that came from the ranks of television workers, including writers, producers, on-air talent, clerical and administrative staff, executives, community volunteers, and below-the-line personnel. It indicates how feminist action shaped commercial and public broadcasting, corporate network headquarters, and independent production companies. It suggests the scope of influence women had over television formats ranging from situation comedy to sports to news and other factual programming and the workplace cultures that enabled their production.

Rather than a project of recuperation or retrospective analysis in which feminist action must be interpreted or read into the past, *Producing Feminism* highlights the deliberate, coordinated efforts of television's feminist Trojan horses. These workers enrich histories of women's gains in and impact on television in the era of women's liberation. By telling their story, *Producing Feminism* affords discussions of more and different types of women involved in feminism and television during the 1970s.

1

Women's Groups and Workplace Reform at Network Television's Corporate Headquarters

On Tuesday, January 20, 1970, Judith Hole, a researcher, and Josephine Indovino, who worked in accounting, wore pants to their jobs at the CBS Broadcast Center in New York City. They were just two of thirty women across the company in creative, clerical, technical, and operational positions who wore pants to work that day. This action defied the company dress code policy for women and merited the attention of the *New York Times*, which published pictures of the women in the newspaper's "food, fashion, family, and furnishings" section. With this placement, news of women wearing pants at CBS appeared on the same page as the budget for First Lady Pat Nixon's home decorating plans, advice on children's activities in the city, and a Bloomingdale's advertisement for face moisturizer, thereby characterizing the protest as yet another lifestyle choice or fashion statement for women. The "Pants Ban" article reinforced this perspective by taking care to describe the physical appearance of the women workers involved and the sartorial choices each of them made.

Despite framing the day by conventionally feminine and arguably superficial elements, the article also relates the significance of the one-day protest. Along with descriptions of "a delicately-boned blonde in navy pants and a sweater" who "could have stepped out of the pages of *Mademoiselle* or *Elle*" and an array of fashions—tweed bell bottoms, beige cuffed trousers, gray twill trousers, a white silk shirt matched with an orange cardigan, and a "flowing brown print scarf"—the article provides a useful accounting of the "radicalized" women involved in the protest.[1] Regardless of how tongue-in-cheek the description of "radicalized" women may be, given the rather dismissive tone of the article, the day's action attests to the collective will and organizing potential of women at CBS. In addition to Hole and Indovino, participants in the pants-in included Irina Posner, assistant producer of documentaries; Angelika Oehme, who worked in the local operations department; Grace Diekhaus, unit manager for news specials; Merri Lieberthal, secretary for journalist Mike Wallace; Jean Dudasik, secretary for news anchor Harry Reasoner; and Mara Posner, secretary for science reporter Earl Urbell.

Although Indovino herself described the one-day "pants-in" as "laughable," she identified the protest's value in the communal awareness it generated. "If it's a way to bring a lot of women together," Indovino noted, "maybe one day it'll bring us together for something important."[2] Indovino's assessment acknowledges the number of women involved in the pants-in and a community of CBS women who had, by the time of their protest, come into feminist consciousness. Soon after the protest, Indovino's hopes were realized. The kernel of activism embedded in the pants ban protest of 1970 grew into full expression as women started to organize formally at the headquarters of all three US networks and lobbied for politically progressive workplace conditions and practices.

From 1971 to 1973, women workers founded what generally came to be known as "women's groups" at NBC, ABC, and CBS. Composed of creative and clerical personnel, the groups represented the interests of workers who provided support for network executives and on-air talent, created programming and content, and helped conduct the wide-ranging business of the corporation. The groups called out sexism at the networks, helped change company policies on a range of issues affecting women, and built collective political action among women workers across organizational divisions and occupational hierarchies. This chapter focuses on the in-house reform efforts of these women's groups throughout the early to late 1970s with an emphasis on the most successful of them, the Women's Advisory Council (WAC) at CBS. WAC changed labor conditions for women within the corporation and, in doing so, articulated priorities of the women's movement at the very center of the broadcasting industry. This was a feat that no feminist group formed outside of media organizations had accomplished to the same degree or in the same fashion. To consider WAC, then, is to broaden considerations of feminist media reform and to identify strategies for progressive political change within corporate workplaces.

To relate WAC's story, I draw on interviews with group members and CBS leadership, as well as archival documents—including communications within women's groups, memos, policy notes, newsletters, and intraoffice correspondence about workplace practices—the majority of which are located at CBS's News Reference Library in New York City.[3] These resources track multiple expressions of feminist media reform beyond the domain of liberal feminism, locate feminist activism at the epicenter of the network television system, and identify otherwise anonymous women production workers who did not appear in front of the camera or occupy higher-visibility "creative" work. WAC's activities at CBS bring to light not just an unorthodox aspect of feminist media reform but also the internal operations of a major media corporation. Accordingly, this chapter contributes to commercial broadcasting history, which, as Michele Hilmes, Shawn VanCour, and Michael Socolow demonstrate, is notoriously difficult to reconstruct.[4] More particularly, it centers on a broadcasting company whose industrial inner workings remain relatively inaccessible. Unlike the robust NBC archives, which have provided research resources for vital scholarship in television and broadcasting histories, the CBS archives, to the degree that they exist, are housed at the corporation without finding guides or transparent public access.[5]

The archival materials generated around WAC's existence reflect the group's influence on formalized company policies (e.g., health care, hiring and promotion, and pay scales) and everyday, experiential aspects of the workplace (e.g., spatial configurations, behaviors, language, and interpersonal dynamics) in which myriad gender inequities were rooted. This archive thus enables elements of a "critical media industry studies" approach that, per Timothy Havens, Amanda Lotz, and Serra Tinic, "examines the micropolitics of institutional operation and production practices" rather than regulation and economics.[6] Consequently, these materials make visible elements of CBS's corporate culture via its relationship to women and its selective acceptance of feminist politics by way of its workplace. They also illuminate how and with what effects women-led and women-oriented media reform influenced a powerful broadcasting entity at the time of the women's movement.

FORMING THE WOMEN'S GROUPS

In the fall of 1971, women at NBC began organizing as the Equal Opportunity Committee. They were followed by ABC women, who started the Women's Action Committee in the summer of 1972, and CBS women, who founded the Women's Advisory Council in 1973. Each group began with informal meetings and from there developed into more formal organizations. At NBC, according to one group member, women started "marvelous clandestine meetings" in which women would "meet in closets—literally in closets" and "scurry around secretly at lunch" in the hopes that no one would see them convene. The NBC group grew from three production assistants in November 1971 to a group of eight until they "were ready to go public" and meet with the personnel department in January 1972. But they would not meet with top management until nine months had passed. While women at NBC had little success in dealing cooperatively with the network, they broke ground that helped the other women's groups. They inspired women at ABC and CBS to form their own groups and mobilized women within and beyond the networks. When the NBC women filed a lawsuit against the network, their legal efforts were supported by "personal contributions from women at the other two networks," "all kinds of women['s] groups," and other women who worked in various media companies. The NBC group also helped ABC and CBS groups access their respective management much more quickly. Alice Herb, one of the original members of ABC's

NEWSLETTER

FIGURE 2. The newsletter of ABC's Women's Action Committee circulated information about the group and its actions and reported on problematic departments and behavior. (Eleanor Sanger Papers, Sophia Smith Collection of Women's History, Smith College, SSC-MS-00286)

Women's Action Committee, recalls that the group started in the summer of 1972 during the Republican National Convention and by either "the end of August or the beginning of September," began meeting with management.[7] The CBS women met with company president Arthur Taylor soon after they formalized their complaints about company policies.

The alacrity with which both ABC and CBS responded to their respective women's groups suggests that the networks were increasingly aware of the disruptive potential posed by organized workers and the validity of their complaints. WAC, in particular, benefited from management's growing awareness of feminist activism that included actions taken by the NBC and ABC women's groups. News of a lawsuit from ABC women and plans by the National Organization for Women (NOW) to file suits against all three networks prompted CBS to take a proactive stance. As a result, according to NBC's Equal Opportunities Commission cofounder Katherine Kish, CBS was "the most receptive of the three networks" to input from its women's group. WAC also benefited from strong in-house support from workers in departments across the company's holdings. Priscilla Toumey, one of the original members of the CBS women's group, estimated that—in comparison to the formative meeting for ABC's Women's Action Committee, attended by an estimated thirty-five to forty women—"upwards of three, four hundred women" participated in WAC's election for committee members, and four to five hundred women attended meetings in the early days.[8]

The formation of women's groups at the US networks coincided with the rise of women's workplace groups that expressed feminist-oriented media reform during the 1970s. Research by Jeannine Baker and Jane Connors on the Australian Broadcasting Commission, by Marama Whyte on the New York Times, and by Anne O'Brien on Irish newspapers illuminates a global movement of women worker-activists across a range of media industries, occupations, and national contexts.[9] While these groups deployed different strategies and privileged different priorities, to varying degrees of success, they all shared advantages as industry insiders: professional expertise of group members; relationships with workplace leadership; and knowledge of their respective media industry's culture, protocols, and priorities.

Like their contemporaries, the women's groups at NBC, ABC, and CBS benefited from their status as industry insiders. The nature of their workplace, however, distinguished them from other media worker groups. First, unlike public sector broadcasters in other countries, US networks managed their obligations to the public in ways that protected their commercial interests. This limited the impact of activism from outsiders and in matters of programming. Second, corporate broadcasting headquarters were neither focused on a single media product nor dedicated exclusively to media production. This shaped their workforce, which was both sizable and dispersed. Workers were employed across multiple divisions and, in addition to media production, purchased and managed media content and conducted and supported the business operations of the company. These conditions shaped the composition and actions of the women's groups at broadcasting headquarters: they needed to represent the interests of women workers who were not unified by occupation and to contend with their employers' resistance to particular modes of media reform.

Initial Presentation by The CBS Women's Group To CBS President Arthur R. Taylor Thursday, July 19, 1973

CBS Response to Women's Group Presentation August 17, 1973

CBS WOMEN IN ATTENDANCE: Rene Burrough, Sylvia Chase, Judy Hole, Jane Tillman Irving, Anita Kopff, Ellen Levine, Barbara Lomholt Lingel, Marie Mahecha, Chin Mahieu, Nancy Perov, Lily Poskus, Susan Quigg, Janet Roach, Inge Schmidt, Lynn Sherr, Joan Stewart, Cheryl Taylor, Mary Gay Taylor, Priscilla Toumey, Louise Waller

AGENDA

1. Mutual Introduction of Women's Group and Management
2. Introduction of Presentation
3. Labor Grade Problems
4. Secretarial Problems
5. Promotions, Opportunities, Training Programs and Salary Differentials
6. Benefits
7. Women Counselors
8. Image of Women at CBS
9. Affirmative Action Plan and Conclusion
10. Question and Answer Period

INTRODUCTION OF PRESENTATION

We represent CBS women in New York. We were chosen in fully publicized general meetings where every CBS division in New York was represented.

We appreciate this opportunity to meet with you. We know you are aware that women face discrimination at CBS. Since we are closest to the problem, we would like to work with you. We expect that this and subsequent meetings will lead us to solutions that will benefit CBS as a whole. Your policy notes indicate to us that you're willing to confront the situation and intend to change it.

We will talk about some of the most pressing problems women encounter as CBS employees and will make some initial recommendations.

LABOR GRADE PROBLEMS

Fifty-one percent of the CBS work force is female.

The women of CBS are concentrated in labor-grade positions where the pay is low and the possibilities for change or advancement extremely limited.

Think of a switchboard operator. Does a man's voice come to mind? Think of a secretary. Can you picture a young man with a good education hitching his wagon to that star? And picture yourself living on their pay.

The vast majority of CBS women are employed in non-exempt jobs as secretaries, telephone operators, billers, clerks,

At the meeting held on Thursday, July 19, 1973, we had agreed to respond promptly and fully to the many points raised in the presentation submitted at that meeting. While there are some issues on which we are not completely in agreement with your views, there is no question that the area of agreement is more significant and extensive than the area of disagreement. We want to continue to discuss our disagreements; meanwhile, the fact that there is such broad agreement is a very important consideration for the future.

As has been pointed out in the President's Policy Note on Women, there is no dispute that over the years women have not progressed in the same manner and to the same extent as men and that, in consequence of this, serious inequities exist. This is, of course, a national problem, existing extensively throughout business and industry as well as government—a problem really only focused on in the last couple of years. We think that most fair-minded people would concede that CBS's record to date has been significantly better than that of others. Nonetheless, there is still much to do.

We believe that the drive for the equality of opportunity for women in business and industry has reached the point where there can be no turning back, where it has an inevitability and momentum of its own. All of business, CBS included, obviously has a lot of catching up to do. However, not a great deal of purpose will be served by either excusing or condemning the past; the key standard for all of us is our present and future commitment and whether programs are developed and carried out effectively to give meaning to that commitment.

One important disclaimer: No one should expect instant perfection. Many of the problems and inequities raised in your presentation, even with the best will in the world and with maximum effort, will take time to correct; that is inherent in effecting change in any large organization. It is true whether we are dealing with issues relating to women, men or minorities, or even non-personnel issues that do not so intimately involve the human equation.

Suffice to say that CBS has always cherished its role as a leader in an environment of change; in the same way, we expect to provide constructive leadership in finding solutions to the flood of problems being identified by the women's movement. You should bear in mind, however, that those who lead the way on uncharted paths are precisely those who are most likely to stumble from time to time. We hope, therefore, that if we occasionally seem to be groping for our way, you will not mistake our intentions. We also hope that you will not reject ideas simply because they come from management. The management of CBS—even if it is composed predominantly of

FIGURE 3. A transcript of the first meeting between the Women's Advisory Council and CBS president Arthur Taylor and CBS's response to the Council's concerns were published in a multi-page report made available to employees. (CBS News Reference Library)

In recalling the origins of WAC, researcher Judith Hole highlights the abilities of workers to utilize corporate resources and their professional expertise to their advantage. A policy note issued to executives on February 13, 1973, proved to be the catalyst for women organizing at CBS. The document claimed that the company did not discriminate on the basis of sex, race, or national origin. Skeptical of this account, Hole and her colleagues called upon their training and researched CBS's claims. "We went to the CBS internal phone book, which in the back of it had every department and the director of that department, the manager of that department," Hole recollected, "and there was not one female anywhere."[10] Priscilla Toumey, CBS Radio Network publicist, also remembers that evidence of a male-dominated organization provided WAC with leverage to meet with CBS president Arthur Taylor. In Toumey's account, a small group of women "disagreed" with some of the points Taylor made in the February 13, 1973, policy note.[11] On the basis of discrepancies between Taylor's statement and findings from their own research, they requested a meeting with Taylor to "discuss the areas of disagreement."[12] The women's request for a meeting was "granted quickly," and Taylor issued a formalized response to the concerns presented in that meeting within three weeks' time.[13] At that point, the women suggested that they have an "ongoing method of communicating with top management regularly on a more organized basis," to which Taylor agreed.[14] WAC's access to Taylor marks its success among the network women's groups. But although WAC effectively pushed CBS to acknowledge the "flood of problems being identified by the women's movement," the corporation was not always amenable to feminist politics and reform pressures, particularly when they originated from women outside the company.[15]

CBS AND FEMINISM

"We do not dislike women." So said CBS board chair William S. Paley in 1970 at the company's annual board meeting. The meeting proved unexpectedly eventful when the feminist group Women's Liberation Front (WLF) disrupted the proceedings. In comparison to NOW's legislative path to righting sexism, WLF's radical feminist approach involved consciousness-raising for women and activism directed toward "changing societal structure, informational efforts, and shock tactics."[16] The WLF demanded that the company improve employment opportunities for women, allocate half of all jobs and half of the seats on its board for women, provide airtime for feminist ideas, and remove sexist programming and advertising from the air. These actions compelled Paley to weigh in on the network's attitude, or its lack of "dislike," toward women. Paley's ambivalent statement reveals the fundamental gender problems of the television industry. That network leadership would respond to feminist protest in such underwhelming fashion indicates the magnitude of the struggle feminists faced in changing the television industry and the unpreparedness of industry leaders to respond thoughtfully to feminist demands, particularly when these came from industry outsiders. CBS was so affronted by the WLF that at its next annual stockholders meeting in 1971, the network took "extra security measures" and hired eight plainclothes L.A. police for the event.[17]

Industry publications supported the CBS board's resistance to the activists' demands, amplified Paley's tepid response, and were disinclined to treat these women with respect or to take their activism seriously. Lest this seem like a matter of typical journalistic attitudes of the time, the *Wall Street Journal*'s coverage offers an instructive difference. Overall, the *Wall Street Journal* struck a more objective, dispassionate tone than the leading media industry publications. The *Wall Street Journal*'s article title, "Ten Women Disrupt CBS Meeting, Assert Daytime Network Shows Turn Them Off," draws upon the rhetoric—being "turned off"—that the feminists themselves used to protest CBS's sexist language in advertising.[18] In comparison, *Variety*'s title, "'Liberation' Women Explode, Finally Get Bounced," places scare quotes around "liberation" and characterizes the protesters as out-of-control, emotional women.[19]

Beyond title choice, the *Wall Street Journal*'s coverage avoids sexist language and describes WLF's actions in political terms. The article leads off with WLF's action. It goes on to relate that once the WLF women left the meeting, they encountered a protest against the Vietnam War, which they greeted with a "clenched fist" and shouts of "Right on!"[20] Details of political legitimacy and solidarity do not appear in *Variety*'s or *Broadcasting*'s coverage of WLF's actions. In *Broadcasting*, the activists were not even mentioned in the article title, "CBS Strides into the 70s," and their actions constitute relatively little of the article. When industry publications did mention the feminists, they invalidated the political character of their group. *Broadcasting* described WLF women by their "unwelcomed strident tones" and seemed more concerned with the activists' violations of Robert's Rules and gender norms than with the merits of the criticisms they lodged against the network.[21] *Variety* did little better. It described the activists as a "covey of quarrelsome, cursing women" who "broke up" the board meeting with their "complaints."[22] When the "largely male board" yelled at these "loud lasses," WLF women responded with "certain profanities." With an incredulous tone, *Variety* noted that, upon exiting, the protesters "even refused to talk to male reporters—speaking only to newshens [*sic*]."[23]

Both *Variety* and *Broadcasting* characterized the protest as an unwelcome disruption to the real business of television. Despite *Variety*'s teasing news about "explosive" women getting "bounced" from the meeting in its sensationalized headline, WLF's protest essentially was used to frame the business report of the meeting, which constituted the majority of the article. *Variety*'s article opened with a two-paragraph description of the activist disruption and then moved to the scheduled business of the meeting. Four out of the article's twelve paragraphs dealt with the women's protest; the remainder reported on the network's concerns about the ban on cigarette advertisements and Federal Communication Commission

(FCC) restrictions on the network's station ownership.[24] Like *Variety*, *Broadcasting* presented CBS business as the centerpiece of its coverage and assured readers that, against the "backdrop" of "the unscheduled cacophony," "CBS leadership . . . managed to get its message across."[25] In both articles, Paley was cast as a sympathetic figure trying to keep order, someone who, in *Variety*'s report, was "finally forced to stop the session until the women could be bounced from the building."[26]

Though feminist activism from outside the industry provoked anxious and defensive reactions from the network and industry publications, feminist activism expressed by CBS workers garnered a markedly different response. Soon after the infamous April 1970 board meeting and Paley's apathetic statement about not disliking women, CBS formulated a more cogent stance on its relationship with women and with the women's movement. In August 1970, just four months after the WLF interrupted the CBS board meeting, *Variety* noted in front-page coverage that "CBS ha[d] come a long way, baby," when it "extended formal recognition to the Women's Liberation Movement" on the eve of the Women's Strike for Equality.[27] In anticipation of the strike, CBS executive vice president John Schneider provided employees with a background on the women's movement and argued both publicly and within the company for the need to take feminism seriously. Schneider warned that "'embattled women'" would "'not be prepared to wait'" for rights, anticipated a forceful and long-lasting feminist movement, and argued that feminist demands "'deserve[d] calm, respectful and understanding consideration.'"[28] As Schneider's reaction to the strike indicates, CBS was more inclined to acknowledge the relationship of its own workers to the women's movement than it was to respond to feminist activism from outsiders. The confirmed and potential involvement of the CBS workforce in feminist actions proved a significant catalyst in changing the corporation's attitudes.

As the discussion of the August 26, 1970, Women's Strike for Equality in the introductory chapter of this book indicates, the networks recognized that their workers would participate in the action in New York City. Workers at the networks were at worst not punished and at best given leave to participate in the Strike, and CBS led the way in its response to its workers. Unlike NBC and ABC, which came up with an ad hoc policy on employee absences on the day of the strike, CBS formulated a coherent, company-wide policy that offered women the option to take unpaid time away or to use a paid vacation day in order to attend the action. *Broadcasting* regarded CBS's policy on the Strike as exemplifying the company's overall outlook; CBS now understood that the women's liberation movement was, in Schneider's words, "'serious business.'"[29]

The dissimilar ways that CBS treated its own workers and outsider activists could easily be attributed to the groups' distinctive approaches to feminist reform: WLF's direct action and demands for change as opposed to WAC's researched responses to policy notes and requests for meetings, for example. Yet the distinction between CBS women and overtly politicized feminist groups appears more complex when one considers the political leanings of CBS women who joined feminist protest on the streets or the commonalities between the points of reform WLF demanded and the ones that WAC expressed to CBS. It is productive, then, to see that CBS women were not wholly divorced from feminist organizations and that WAC's goals were similar to those of feminist groups, even radical ones. How WAC achieved gains for women at CBS was not so much a question of political investments or engagement with media reform. Rather, WAC's almost exclusive focus on workplace reform, its knowledge of CBS culture and relationships with company executives, and its expertise in engaging company policies account for the group's successes.

OUTSIDER VERSUS INSIDER MEDIA REFORM

In the US, media reform has been defined by media advocacy traditions and by campaigns mounted by political activist groups. In the early 1970s, NOW, the "largest organization of feminist grassroots activists," coordinated challenges to FCC broadcasting license renewals, which was one of the most significant media reform efforts associated with the women's movement.[30] NOW's petitions-to-deny, as documented by Patricia Bradley, Kathryn Montgomery, Anne W. Branscomb, Maria Savage, and Allison Perlman, positioned women as an underserved public to whom media industries were beholden.[31] WAC does not easily align with prevailing traditions of feminist media reform. It was a group neither composed exclusively of like-minded feminists nor engaged with public-oriented impact. Nonetheless, its efforts affected the labor conditions of women media workers and altered a media industry workplace, thereby contributing to the feminist media reform movement of the time.

WAC's purpose at the corporation and their obligations to all women workers meant that WAC was not, strictly speaking, a feminist organization. This was the case with many women's workplace groups of the time. In her exploration of the Women's Caucus at the *New York Times*, Marama Whyte addresses a limitation in prevailing understandings of feminist movements. Rather than looking only to "women who self-identified as feminists or participated in activism coordinated by feminist organizations," scholars must also consider how to assess and recognize "women who undertook feminist actions while actively not identifying as feminists."[32] There is clear evidence that, while WAC was not a feminist organization, its membership included active feminists and women familiar with the strategies and ethos of the women's movement. For instance, group members Judith Hole and Ellen Levine took an approved leave from CBS to research and write *Rebirth of Feminism* (1971), a "comprehensive survey of the modern women's movement based on extensive interviews and painstaking research into the mound of recent feminist literature."[33] And, while some WAC women clearly identified with the women's movement, there were others who likely did not. This does not, as Whyte helpfully argues, preclude a group from undertaking actions with feminist consequences. It does, however, require a nuanced sense of how feminism operates in nonfeminist groups and/or groups with nonfeminist members. It also complicates how feminism appears and registers in group actions.

Perhaps counterintuitively, CBS shaped WAC's capabilities to take on the work of the women's movement and provided the group with certain advantages in its relationship to feminist politics. Unlike the univocal reform efforts of NOW to challenge license renewals, WAC was able to—indeed, compelled to—engage in eclectic strategies and forms of feminist thought to meet the needs of a variety of women workers at CBS. It defined its operations and agenda according to multiple practices and values of the women's movement: consciousness-raising, antiracism and anti-ageism, recognition of private sphere concerns in employment, and identification of gendered power imbalances in cultural and economic forms. Although WAC was not a feminist group, its ethos and impact underscore Myra Marx Ferree and Patricia Yancey Martin's idea that organizations bear feminist value not just through the orthodoxy of "ideal" political affiliation and identity but also through "the places in which and the means through which the work of the women's movement is done."[34]

Workplace reform, as Yvonne Benschop and Mieke Verloo point out, frequently utilizes liberal feminism, as it "meshes well with the political ideals of free market labour and the meritocratic workplace, and uses those ideals to critique existing gender inequities like those in wages and positions of authority."[35] Given the profit-driven and hierarchically arranged organization of the networks' corporate operations, WAC called upon tenets of liberal feminism to identify "structural impediments to women's progress" and ways that women could fairly compete with male coworkers.[36] While its use of liberal feminist approaches may seem unsurprising, WAC complicated a univocal approach to improving workplace conditions. It drew upon an assortment of feminist practices and priorities, including consciousness-raising, antiracist measures, recognition of private sphere issues in employment, and exploration of affective and interpersonal aspects of labor and power. The eclectic feminism deployed by WAC demonstrates the adaptability of the women's movement, the ways that feminist politics influenced the business of television, and the transformative possibilities of feminist activism within the staunch conservatism of corporate culture.

Commercial television was disinclined to respond to activist pressures when they threatened what CBS reporter Marlene Sanders called the "sacrosanct" nature of "program content."[37] The inviolable nature of programming meant that, at best, activists who tried to influence on-screen content would be "placated if possible but not at the cost of changing programming."[38] When advocacy groups protested objectionable content, as Kathryn Montgomery demonstrates, the networks developed strategies for "managing" advocacy groups, primarily through its standards and practices department.[39] Arthur Taylor made CBS's position on the matter clear in August 1973 in a special issue of Columbine, the CBS company newsletter, that reported on the corporation's relationship to a newly formed WAC. "'The question of programming," he wrote, "is an area in which CBS has historically resisted pressure from all groups outside its programming organization: government, religious groups and countless other entities that wish to influence programming decisions.'"[40] Even as Taylor supported women's advancement in the workplace and proved receptive to the majority of WAC's demands, his stance on programming portends the ways that the networks would treat calls from their own women's groups to reform televisual representation.

When pressure to reform on-air content came from within the industry, via the network women's groups, the networks responded even more directly and defensively than they had with outsider activists. While it is clear that the Equal Opportunity Committee at NBC faced resistance from management because it was the first of the women's groups to form, it also encountered refusals from NBC because of the nature of its complaints against the corporation. Along with improved opportunities for women in the workplace, NBC women also pushed for improved representations of women. This agenda "added to their difficulties" in negotiating with management, so much so that negotiations grew "hostile" and "legal intervention became necessary."[41] In 1973, after a year of stalled negotiations, twenty-two women at NBC filed a class action suit against the network. Charged with "across-the-board sex discrimination" by the Women's Committee for Equal Employment, NBC lost the lawsuit. As a result, it was forced to pay out a cash settlement to employees and to institute a series of policies to ensure an equitable workplace for women.[42] But, even with this victory for NBC workers, issues of programming remained unaddressed.

Although it expressed less hostility than NBC did, CBS took an unapologetically protectionist stance when dealing internally with critiques of programming. CBS women were warned against "seeking a voice in CBS program content," which was deemed by John Schneider, president of the Broadcast Group, to be a "highly controversial issue, touching as it does on First Amendment (Freedom of the Press) considerations."[43] When WAC members did request that CBS address the issue of representation, which appears only once in transcripts of their presentations to management, they were careful to link the issue to that of workplace investments, an area that proved less controversial to company leadership. In anticipating gains in women's promotions, WAC argued that a woman in power at CBS would require improved programming for her "self-respect": "Any executive will be proud to say that her company was in the vanguard, was first to determine that something should be done to portray the new woman as she really is."[44] Tellingly, CBS did not respond directly to this presentation point. Instead, Taylor made a statement that he was "in agreement that the public image of women was another area in which CBS would provide leadership" and welcomed "comments and suggestions" from CBS women.[45] But Taylor ultimately insisted that the company retain its authority, with himself and the president of the Broadcast Group as the representation of that authority, over programming.

John Schneider, the same executive who, in response to the Women's Strike for Equality, circulated information to CBS employees about the women's movement and called for respect for the movement, also cautioned CBS women against seeking influence over programming. In a 1974 *Columbine* article, "Broadcasting: The Issue of Influence," Schneider opined that if CBS women oversaw changes to programming, "practical and philosophical problems" would arise, including issues of what content would best represent women's interests and elitist assumptions that CBS women were positioned to tell women audiences what they "'should' rather than want to see."[46]

On representational issues, CBS struggled to represent the women's movement. It did fare better when dealing with its workforce and the culture of its workplace. To be clear, CBS's internal responses to feminism were not without disappointment and compromise. Yet its responses included legitimate attempts to reform sexism in the corporation, primarily through education of its workforce and cooperative policymaking between management and women workers. The variability with which CBS addressed feminist issues confirms what Kylie Andrews identifies as the "paradoxical" nature of media organizations. In her study of women workers at the Australian Broadcasting Commission, Andrews views the broadcaster not as a monolith but as an entity constituted by human interactions, drives, and engagements. By looking to broadcasting history through workers and the conditions of labor, as Andrews does, it becomes "possible to recognize the competing factions and personalities, motivations and missions of its participants, to contextualise the individuals who affect the policy and processes of broadcasting and to historicise how broadcasters imagine the social function of their work."[47]

ARTHUR TAYLOR, ACTIVIST EXECUTIVE

While CBS president Arthur Taylor fell in line with network television traditions in terms of outsider activism and programming reform, in other ways he proved a significant force for progress. Hired in 1972, Taylor was hailed as an "Activist Executive" and positioned among "an increasing number of corporate heads" in the early 1970s who took "aggressive roles in improving the status of women in business."[48] WAC credited various members of management, including CBS vice president Sheldon Wool, with a willingness to meet with the group to hear their concerns. But no one was acknowledged more readily or frequently as an ally to the group than Taylor, who was invested in equitable employment opportunities, which he saw both as ethically correct and good for the performance and standing of the company. Taylor's support was so vital to future WAC members that they called themselves "the Taylor Committee" when they first organized.

While so-called activist executives were viewed as a new breed of leaders, they were not the first to operate according to what counted as principled politics in business. In the 1950s and 1960s, as Lynn Spigel points out, "corporate liberalism was a general mentality of the era," and television executives, along with other business leaders, "put faith in the idea that corporate growth would create not just a stronger economy but also a better world."[49] Taylor retained aspects of corporate liberalism in his business philosophy, but he adapted to the political unrest of the time and its role in the labor conditions of the workplace. This aligned him with a style of corporate leadership that emerged in the 1970s. In 1971, *Harvard Business Review* polled 3,453 of their subscribers to find that one-sixth to one-half of them were "willing to encourage activist elements in a company."[50] The study also indicated that executives were particularly receptive to an "employee insurgent group" if the issues it raised were "less controversial, less related to public pressure, and more related to everyday standards of decency, honesty, and ethical behavior."[51]

Soon after he took the job as president, Taylor countered CBS's sexism by correcting gender disparities in job promotions, which he characterized a "terrible situation." "You had women who had worked there for many years," explained Taylor. "A good many of them had advanced degrees as secretaries because everyone wanted to get into the television industry. And they had passed these men in through their offices to other offices who have now become executives and they're still sitting there as secretaries and assistants." When William S. Paley, then-board chair and former president of CBS, took a vacation early in Taylor's tenure, Taylor moved swiftly and without Paley's permission to rectify the problem. Taylor promoted every woman who had worked at CBS for five years or more. By Taylor's estimation, this included around fifty women. "So everyone got promoted," recalled Taylor, "And then we had all kinds of new policies which would allow women to advance as quickly as men."[52]

While promotions demonstrate a commitment to women's advancement on business ledgers, in annual reports to investors, and as compliance with federal laws on equal employment, titles alone did not guarantee corresponding gains in power, prestige, and workplace conditions. In an oral history for the Academy of Television Arts and Sciences, Ethel Winant recounted her promotion to vice president of casting and talent at CBS in 1973, the first for a woman at any US television network. Winant explained that, with her groundbreaking promotion, there was no discussion of a salary increase or any negotiation of benefits that would come with the title. Once promoted, she encountered a lack of accommodation, quite literally, for her presence as the sole woman in the executive ranks. When she started using the executive dining room, Winant realized that she would have to take an elevator to a lower floor each time she needed to use the bathroom, since there was only one facility, which the men used. One day, after deciding, "I'm not going to do this anymore," Winant used the men's room, which did not have a lock on the door, and left her shoes outside to signal her presence and prevent men from walking in on her.[53]

While Winant's promotion was groundbreaking in the early 1970s, women's advancement to vice presidential positions accelerated soon after. Unfortunately, these appointments signaled a corresponding devaluation of the job. Anne Nelson, whose sixty-eight-year career at CBS saw her advance from a temp to the vice president of business affairs, was first passed over for a promotion to vice president in 1950. She regarded the slight as expected, not only because of the prevalent gender discrimination of the era, but also because of the relative worth of the position at that time. Nelson was well aware of the sexism at CBS, having experienced it in full force when television and radio split in 1952. When, after three years of combined divisions, television and radio became separate, "naturally the old boys' club got the good jobs" in television while Nelson was rehoused in the less-prestigious radio division.[54] There Nelson trained several men for the job she wanted, the director of business affairs in radio. When she repeatedly asked for a promotion, she was told that a "girl" could not be a head of a department until she finally landed the job in 1954. To Nelson, CBS's repeated refusal to promote her was indicative of the importance of the job. "At the time," she remembers, "the vice president in charge of the West Coast was *the* vice president. It wasn't a matter of being passed over as vice president, it was a matter of getting a job to run the department." Over time, the job title took on less significance when, according to Nelson, vice presidents "proliferated only because it was a way to make it look like they were doing something for the women."[55]

Within the context of devalued vice presidencies, Taylor's decision to promote women en masse raises questions about its impact and Taylor's motivations. Certainly, Taylor understood the business sense that promoting women made. By addressing gender issues, CBS garnered positive public relations and gained a competitive edge in the broadcasting industry. With headlines like "CBS Aims High on Equality Side" and news of women's promotions to management, industry publications relayed CBS's new political awareness and granted the company newsworthy status.[56] Taylor amplified positive PR for CBS in talks at corporate gatherings and interviews in trade and business publications. He repeatedly affirmed CBS's commitment to women workers and asserted that the company would "assume national leadership in providing equal opportunities for women."[57] With Taylor's framing, CBS signaled a laudatory commitment to the women's movement through the reformation of its workplace. And in this laudatory commitment to women, CBS could position itself as a vanguard of the industry.

But Taylor's interest in women's progress at CBS was not just opportunistic. His mass promotion of women preceded any widespread trend, and, notably, his presidency saw the promotion of Ethel Winant to vice president. When Winant became vice president, the position still wielded considerable power and prestige. In a 1996 interview, Winant expressed an assessment similar to Nelson's when she reflected on the differences between a vice presidency at the time of her assumption of the title in 1973 and that of the contemporaneous moment. According to Winant, at the time of her promotion, there were only seven vice presidents at CBS. "You became an officer in the company," recalled Winant. "It wasn't a title. You had to be elected by the board of directors. . . . There were not fifty-three VPs and twenty-five presidents as there are now in every network." Winant identified her promotion, which came at the time of Taylor's presidency and his promotion of numerous other women, as one that preceded the relatively meaningless promotions criticized by Nelson. Rather than providing mere window dressing, Taylor's actions can therefore be understood as good-faith ones. Winant confirms that Taylor, who "looked upon [her] fondly," along with the influence of the women's movement, was a key force behind her career-changing promotion.[58]

While the issue of women's career advancement was Taylor's high-profile cause, it was part of his broader commitment to social responsibility. Taylor felt that CBS needed to "operate in a socially constructive manner" and "encourage its employees to be guided by the same principle."[59] Informed by this philosophy, he instituted a Social Service Leave Program in November 1975, under which employees were granted three months' paid leave to work for a "worthy social service organization," including "private and voluntary education, health, welfare, cultural and civil rights organizations."[60] Taylor also instituted measures that addressed racial inequalities: elections for an advisory committee that met regularly with "key management executives," improved training programs geared to the needs of Black personnel, and active recruitment of employees at historically Black colleges and universities.[61] Taylor established seminars meant to help Black employees with career advancement and to provide CBS department heads with "a continuing updating of our knowledge concerning conditions which face Black employees in terms of career development and to find additional ways as to how the situation can be improved."[62]

Under Taylor's tenure as president, CBS adopted a rhetoric of responsiveness to inequalities in employment, which also served WAC. Memos and policy notes internal to the company document a number of improvements Taylor implemented to address gender discrimination. Anecdotal evidence also illustrates the support Taylor provided women at CBS, particularly as he was coming to terms with gender discrimination on a personal level. Judith Hole recalls that Taylor began to understand feminist perspectives, or what Hole describes as "other nickels dropping," by witnessing the sexism his own four daughters faced. Without these personal revelations, according to Hole, "it would have been a tougher road" for WAC.[63]

ASSESSING WORKPLACE GAINS

As Taylor and CBS utilized the workplace to signal their commitment to the women's movement, WAC pushed the corporation beyond mere self-promotion and superficial solutions to women's issues. The group stipulated that company policies have measurable and meaningful impact. In some instances, WAC's interests aligned with CBS, particularly in assessing progress for women workers through quantitative data on salaries and promotions. These statistics were easily calculated and circulated as evidence of women's progress and required few structural changes to the corporation. It is unsurprising, then, that WAC successfully pitched these measurements of improvement to CBS. After the first meeting between Taylor and WAC in 1973, CBS agreed to a review of salaries and resulting corrections that guaranteed "equal pay for equal work," as well as transparency in hiring and advertisement of job openings.

In addition to the relatively straightforward issue of women's access to equal employment, WAC's plans for meaningful accountability engaged CBS leadership in nuanced discussions about institutionalized gender issues. In their initial presentation to the company, WAC leaders highlighted the reasons why women occupied lower-paying, less prestigious, and less powerful jobs in the company. Women possessed the requisite interest, training, and talent, WAC argued, but they were "conditioned to accept" being passed over for promotion.[64] WAC cast light upon ageism as well as sexism facing older women, who were often passed over for promotion and pay increases, and asked for redress. Given these circumstances, WAC maintained that it was not enough for CBS to provide only equal access to job opportunities. The company also needed to actively recruit women for higher-paying positions and to rebuild the culture of a workplace that had normalized women's inferiority. To substantively change this culture, WAC proposed that all employees understand their own roles in perpetuating workplace inequities. To this end, the group recommended "consciousness-raising sessions," clearly based on the concept within the women's movement, that brought workers to an understanding of "all the ramifications of sexism and how to eliminate it from the day-to-day working environment."[65] In response, CBS referenced a pilot program of "awareness sessions" aimed to correct "deeply ingrained male attitudes" that posed "an obstacle to the progress of women" and agreed to expansion of the program "as rapidly as practical."[66] WAC also requested that CBS not just alter its own practices but also use its widespread influence to challenge multiple blockage points in women's career aspirations. One way it suggested CBS do this was to pressure unions that barred women's involvement to allow women to join them and consequently qualify for the many unionized technical jobs in television, radio, and recording. CBS cited a low turnover rate in union jobs as an impediment to the plan but indicated that it would support the initiative and would express to the technical unions its "desire to see women candidates" for union jobs.[67]

To further gauge the impact of workplace reform and to hold management accountable for reform efforts, the position of "woman counselor" was created at CBS in early 1973. Women counselors performed a number of tasks: they expressed workers' needs to management, "provid[ed] better access for women to management for redress of individual grievances," and kept employees informed "on a day-to-day basis" of management's "actions" that would "improve the situation of women."[68] While counselors provided a conduit for CBS management to address women workers, they also brought to management perspectives from women on how policies affected them so that CBS would be "better cognizant of those women's thoughts and needs."[69]

In its initial presentation to Arthur Taylor in July 1973, WAC asked CBS to revise language in their communications that described women's complaints to women counselors as "gripes."[70] Instead, CBS should utilize conventional language used in organized labor that identified worker complaints as "grievances."[71] To do otherwise, WAC argued, was offensive and suggested that CBS failed to "consider the status of women at CBS a serious labor problem."[72] WAC also pushed CBS to expand the number of women counselors and, in order that counselors would no longer spend personal as well as company time in their role, to convert the role of counselor to a full-time position. This newly enhanced position should also include management training as one of its benefits. In its August 1973 response to this WAC presentation, CBS agreed—albeit rather begrudgingly—that the "gripes" wording would no longer be used. It also acknowledged the value of women counselors and the demanding nature of the position: "The contributions made by the Women Counselors have been inadequately recognized. Perhaps most importantly, they have influenced management in its thinking; it is hard to visualize how we could have made such progress between February and August without them."[73] In January 1974, CBS started to adequately compensate the labor of counselors and converted the positions to full-time, permanent ones. The new job categorization provided counselors a place on the "first rung of management employment," increased salary, and the possibility of "performance bonus plans."[74] Women were appointed to the newly enhanced counselor positions from a wide assortment of departments and jobs. Among them were a former secretary and current community relations coordinator, an audience services manager, and assorted project managers.[75] The egalitarian advancement of lower-level employees to counselor positions safeguarded against already-established women using the opportunity to advance their own careers rather than agitate for "upgraded female employment."[76]

In addition to the gains it procured for counselors, in its first year WAC had accomplished several of its other goals. By fall 1974, job postings were made available in common spaces at CBS before they were publicized beyond the company, and the personnel department was "required to conduct a conscientious search for women and minorities to fill these jobs."[77] Women were appointed to a variety of management positions. CBS offered tuition remission for continuing education, hosted educational workshops, and provided management training for women. Yet even with these successes, WAC remained vigilant in applying pressure on management for expanding and diversifying workplace rights for women. To mark the one-year anniversary of their first presentation to Arthur Taylor, WAC leaders made another presentation to Taylor, a number of corporate staff, and group presidents on July 11, 1974. In this presentation, they documented lapsed commitments and endorsed an evolving need for new policies. They noted that there was still an "insignificant number of women vice-presidents" and that there were "still far too many women whose jobs do not use even a portion of their skills."

WAC also called for new actions ranging from open job posting to increased training programs to seminars on gender-specific career challenges for women. WAC once again stressed company accountability by asking that all management attend training sessions for compliance with new company policies and that management's raises and bonuses be tied to "concrete implementation" of these policies.[78]

Overall, CBS responded favorably to the initiatives the CBS women presented to them in 1974. The corporation agreed to improvements to women counselor positions; expanded health care and childcare benefits; increased appointments of women to management positions; and increased funding for tuition remission, educational workshops, and management training for women. However, it is also worth noting that the ambitious requests of the 1974 committee presentation were met with some refusals. CBS cautioned against the "mandatory" nature of awareness sessions for all CBS management, indicating that compulsory participation would "result in resistance rather than awareness." CBS's response to quantifiable hiring practices was mixed; it agreed to additional research but did not want to set "numerical targets" that would "take on the aura of quotas" and "would result in a change in the atmosphere we have of working together."[79] These setbacks indicate the constraints WAC faced. Yet even in its negative responses, CBS focused on issues of efficacy rather than outright rejection of, or hostility to, the committee's proposed changes.

WORKER COLLECTIVITY AND THE VALUE
OF MARGINALIZED LABOR/ERS

Much like any bureaucratic entity, a media corporation like CBS was purposely designed, as Kathy Ferguson argues, to be "sufficiently large so as to prohibit face-to-face relationships among most of their members." This serves the needs of the organization rather than the worker since it ensures the isolation of workers and the rationalization of tasks that are central to the organization's "continuity and stability."[80] Before their first meeting with Taylor in 1973, WAC had to grapple with the organizational logistics of the corporation in order to ascertain and represent the concerns of all CBS women. By organizing across siloed departments and hierarchical job titles, WAC challenged axiomatic corporate divisions of labor that thwarted worker solidarity and valued labor unequally.

When CBS women first started to organize, differential treatment among them was a key issue. During the pants-in action of January 1970, the New York Times reporter Marylin Bender related an observation from "one of the many secretaries who c[a]me to work in blue jeans and timidly change[d] to dresses" that the "privileged" women in the news division were allowed to wear pants, which violated existing dress codes for women Bender noted that women who worked at Columbia Records—"creative types"—were permitted to wear jeans to work, another violation of company policy.[81] Uneven enforcement of workplace rules regarding "professional" attire signaled larger and more significant divisions among women at CBS, which hindered workplace equity for all women and reinforced hierarchical relationships between clerical and creative workers. If WAC were to succeed, it had to confront the divisions among women at CBS, so the group was guided by principles of collectivity.

Starting with their clandestine meetings in closets and bathrooms, group women refused bureaucratic protocols and engaged one another through face-to-face contact. They took measures, similar to those implemented in the women's movement, to limit the negative impact of organizational structures of their corporate workplace and within their own ranks.[82] When WAC became operational, CBS employed upwards of twenty thousand people and comprised nineteen divisions, including broadcasting and records, and, to a lesser extent, publishing and other assorted media. To contend with corporate sprawl and worker dispersion among divisions, WAC established subdivisions at the broadcast center; corporate headquarters; and the subsidiary publishing company of Holt, Rinehart, and Winston in order to represent occupationally specific concerns within the larger collective.[83] Membership was available to all women, regardless of job title; group leadership was elected from all ranks of workers; leadership roles rotated; membership was antihierarchical; and governance was shared among the widest range of workers possible. Elected WAC representatives, meant to "cover the spectrum" of women working at CBS, came from a variety of positions that included personnel department employees, food service workers, secretaries, and television producers.[84]

By encouraging all CBS women to join the group, WAC worked to bridge divisions between relatively privileged "creative types" and those who carried out largely invisible and undervalued labor. Workplace issues involving clerical workers, secretaries, and support staff were as much a part of the group's concerns as those of promotion to executive ranks and high-level jobs in television and radio. This recognition reconceptualized who counted as production workers and which labors constituted media production work. In addition, by enfolding bureaucratic aspects of corporate work into the production culture of the network, WAC signaled that all women's work at CBS was burdened with inequitable, gendered expectations that cut across occupations.

In acknowledging all workers as contributors to media-making, WAC recognized labor that fell outside of the business and creative positions conventionally identified as central to the making of television. Its comprehensive understanding of where media work happens aligns with production studies scholarship that, according to Miranda Banks, expresses "anti-auteurist" tendencies and illuminates "production at the margins."[85] Participants in WAC and the other network women's groups occupied not just above- and below-the-line positions but also ones that operated beyond either category. Erin Hill's work on women employees in the Hollywood studio system illustrates the invisibility of these workers and their contributions. The classification of workers in systems of media production as either above or below the line, as Hollywood filmmaking does, "overlooks many others, because, for example, secretaries were usually considered parts of studio overhead operations rather than members of any particular production."[86] Likewise, women who worked as secretaries, support staff, researchers, accountants, and marketing staff at network headquarters served the operations of the corporation rather than the creation of a single television program.

In addition to their contributions to the creative aspects of the television industry, women in support staff roles were essential to the industry's corporate workings. Ethel Winant understood and relied upon these contributions as essential both to the culture of the network and to her career. Because of her relationship with informal networks of information sustained by secretaries, Winant gleaned vital information at CBS. When her promotion to vice president was kept a secret from her, only to be revealed in a surprise announcement in 1973, Winant considered the plan's success completely atypical of her experience at CBS. "They kept it a secret from me," she recalled. "Now that's really hard to do because nobody'd ever kept anything a secret from me at CBS. Because I went to the ladies' room with all the secretaries, and they knew everything. And so they always told you everything. And so I always knew what was going on. And if I didn't know, my secretary could find out." Winant continued to rely on this culture in her executive position. As the sole woman in such a position, Winant had a "great relationship with a million secretaries" that provided her with information that her male colleagues did not have access to. Therefore, Winant's unique status as a woman vice president, according to Winant, "was actually sort of an advantage."[87]

Just as they did in countless other offices, the secretarial and clerical staff at CBS worked under circumstances that rendered their labor feminized, disrespected, and unrecognized by waged compensation. In addition to the technical or logistical support they provided, these workers produced what Arlie Russell Hochschild famously describes as "emotion work," or the type of labor that "*affirms, enhances, and celebrates the well-being and status of others.*"[88] In exploring the labor function of women in Hollywood during the studio era, Hill argues that "all women's work" within the studios served the "larger purpose of absorbing routine tasks and unwanted emotion around men's creative process," and therefore qualified as emotion work.[89] Within a presumably noncreative support function, studio women's work consisted of "*both the explicit labor they were assigned on the basis of gender—typing, sewing, inking, and painting—and the implicit 'shadow' labor—the interpersonal competencies, gender performativity, and emotion work their jobs required.*"[90]

WAC identified gendered burdens of labor for women at CBS in the 1970s similar to the ones Hill calls out in the Hollywood studio system. This demonstrates the applicability of Hill's assessment to many, if not all, women across media industries and historical periods. WAC underscored the problems of women's labor on both the explicit and shadow fronts and made it clear that women's work at CBS was exploited, undervalued, and undercompensated. It demanded an end to the unpaid and affective labors women were asked to perform and insisted on a workplace culture that would no longer demean work conducted by women. Since these concerns were particularly applicable to secretaries, WAC focused much of its occupationally specific reform on those workers. It devised training and advancement schemes for secretaries that challenged beliefs that the "explicit labor" of these positions fully satisfied women's occupational goals and utilized their professional competencies. When CBS offered training for the executive career path and reimbursement for college courses to all employees, WAC argued that these opportunities should be earmarked for secretaries. As for the "shadow labor" of secretarial jobs, this was no longer to be expected. WAC stipulated that job descriptions for secretaries be clearly defined and adhered to by supervisors and that male supervisors be retrained about their sexist behaviors toward support staff.

Secretarial work was a particular priority for WAC's reform efforts, so much so that WAC dedicated an entire subsection to "Secretarial Problems" in the presentation its leaders made to Taylor in 1973. WAC's recommendations for improving work conditions for secretaries included formal policies and training as well as experiential aspects of power differentials in the workplace. The group advised CBS to revise the company manual for secretaries to "make it acceptable to intelligent, professional" women and to restore the once-clear function of a secretarial position as a "training ground for management."[91] Noting in its 1974 presentation that there were "some places in CBS where a woman must notify her supervisor when she goes to the ladies' room," WAC rebuked CBS for infantilizing its female workforce and overstepping professional boundaries with them.[92] WAC argued that when "secretaries are treated more like 'office wives' than employees," the relationship was not cooperative but based on exploitation and an abuse of power.[93]

Given patriarchal assumptions that women were responsible for men's comfort and ease in the workplace, WAC had good reason to be concerned. While particularly egregious in the treatment of secretaries, these dynamics permeated every rank of women workers who had contact with men in positions of authority. Even after being promoted to vice president at CBS, Ethel Winant, the only woman in any given room where executive decisions were made, was charged with feminized tasks typically associated with secretarial work. Winant recalls that William S. Paley would go through his mail and then "always turn to" her and instruct her to convey the mail to his secretary Rather than agree, Winant "would take a deep breath and think, no, I'm not going to do that," and would instead instruct Paley to ask the CBS butler in the room to carry out such work.[94]

Attitudes such as Paley's were ingrained in the culture of CBS, which WAC needed to confront if women were ever to be seen as colleagues and coworkers rather than work-wives. Men's learned helplessness forced women, regardless of position, to take on the work of dealing with paperwork, mail, and phone calls and arranging and packing for business travel. Winant's refusals of work for which she was not compensated testify to the types of labor that women at CBS—even executive women—were assumed by men to perform. "It was just automatic," Winant recalled. "If there was a woman in the room, you were the one who took the mail, and you were the one who made the phone call. And the truth was, nobody in that room knew how to make a long-distance call. They didn't know how to get an outside line."[95] When traveling with other senior vice presidents, all men, Winant realized that she was the only one among them who knew how to buy an airline ticket since this had always been the responsibility of their secretaries or wives.

CONTENDING WITH RACE

Given the relatively high rate of employment of women of color in support staff jobs, by prioritizing the needs of secretaries and other employees who labored at the peripheries of media production, WAC implicitly addressed intersectional issues of race and gender at CBS. As a group that focused explicitly and solely on women's issues, WAC acknowledged its difficulties in addressing issues of race and successfully recruiting women of color for the group. CBS contributed to these problems, as it identified "minority" concerns as separate from those of women's issues in its policies; employment programs; and other efforts for recruitment, hiring, training, and advancement. In defining concerns of racial equity as distinctive from those of gender equity, CBS reinforced cultural scripts that led to what WAC member Priscilla Toumey described as the "hesitancy" of Black women in joining WAC. According to Toumey, these women were afraid that, in supporting workplace improvements for women, they were depriving people of color similar opportunities. With perceptions of CBS support as finite and competitive—particularly in issues of racial versus gender equity—women of color were concerned that CBS's efforts to improve racial inequalities "may be compromised in this rush to do things for women."[96]

It is difficult to determine the racial composition of WAC's membership. Information about individual members, when available at all, is generally restricted to a short list of names for women who attended a meeting, issued a memo, earned a promotion, or sat for a radio interview. If women occupied higher-visibility, higher-prestige jobs, they were pictured in industry publications, which provides some evidence of their racial identity. Unsurprisingly, an overwhelming majority of these women were white. Sheila Clark proves a notable exception. She was listed among the twenty-nine women from the WAC Steering Committee who met with CBS management on July 11, 1974.[97] By 1978, Clark was working as the director of minority programs at CBS; her position meant that she served as the public face of the company's diversity initiatives. In 1981, *Billboard* published a photo of a luncheon where students who aspired to careers in music met with CBS executives.[98] Clark was identified in the photo caption as one of those executives. This photograph provides visual confirmation of Clark's identity as a Black woman and indicates at least a small degree of racial diversity within WAC's leadership.

Most of the women involved in the CBS group whose racial identities are ascertainable occupied executive ranks or higher-level creative work at the time of their group membership or later ascended to these positions. This leaves out of the picture WAC members who worked in secretarial, clerical, and support staff positions and likely included large numbers of women who were not white. The impact and involvement of women of color in WAC and the other network women's groups are, for these reasons, unquantifiable. Nevertheless, women of color were part of the groups and contributed to their functioning and agenda-setting, even if the long-standing racism of the television industry meant that they made up a less visible part of the workforce than their white counterparts.

The difficulties of quantifying the role women of color played in WAC, even in the most basic of measurements, illustrate a larger research problem in assessing women's contributions to and presence in media workplaces. In their research on women's employment in the British film industry, Natalie Wreyford and Shelley Cobb needed qualitative data to demonstrate the scale and consistency of gender inequality's operation in the system. Although this data was indispensable to their project, employment figures available to them were "imperfect and unstable." According to the traditions of ostensibly objective research, this evidential deficiency compromised the validity of the project. But rather than let it sideline scholarship of value for women production workers and feminist scholars alike, Cobb and Wreyford reassessed the impact of flawed data and proceeded with their project. By doing so, their research facilitates new understandings of the issue of women's employment in British filmmaking specifically and more broadly illustrated the illusory nature of comprehensive datasets by underscoring the "ellipsis" that underlies the "presentation of academic writing in a neat and ordered way."[99]

In the absence of statistical data on the employment of women of color at CBS and their participation in WAC, contextual labor trends offer one way to identify their presence. Following the civil rights movement, Black women and men moved from farmwork and private service work to white-collar jobs. The US Department of Labor reported that, out of all of the Black women employed in wage-earning labor, 22.7 percent worked in clerical jobs in 1972; by 1980, that figure had risen to 29.3 percent.[100] Employment in the television industry followed a similar pattern, with a significant number of women of color working in clerical positions. In their 1977 publication *Window Dressing on the Set: Women and Minorities in Television*, the US Commission on Civil Rights reported that "minority" women constituted 28.7 percent of clerical workers at the television stations involved in their study and that 58.9 percent of "minority" women employed at the stations were office and clerical staff.[101] Given these figures, it is statistically probable that women of color were employed in considerable numbers as clerical, support, and secretarial staff at the networks. Dorothy Sue Cobble's labor history indicates as much. Cobble's research finds that "African-American women did not enter clerical work in any appreciable numbers before

World War Two, but by the 1970s almost as large a percent of African-American women were in clerical jobs as held jobs in the overall labor market."[102] Since there is clear evidence that WAC prioritized outreach to secretarial and clerical staff and developed policies aimed to improve the existence of these workers, it is reasonable to surmise that women of color were participants in WAC and beneficiaries of the group's actions.

From the start, WAC took steps meant to address racial disparities in employment. In 1974, its first year of existence, the group pushed CBS to implement required "conscientious" searches for women and "minorities" for all job vacancies. On WAC's suggestion, the network also instituted training programs for women and people of color in the same year. These training programs were intended for employees who wanted to work in more prestigious positions but had not profited from "the advantages of training and experience needed to successfully move into these highly qualified areas."[103] Training comprised three components: "attachment," a position that paired employees with a supervisor to learn more about a department; "internship," in which the employee "learns by doing rather than by observing;" and "on-the-job," which placed employees in a job, "permanent in nature," that provided advancement in a current area or entrance to a different area of the company in which the employee wished to specialize.[104] By the spring of 1976, the program was still intact. At that time, *Columbine* reported over one hundred enactments of the training program in the company's New York City–area holdings, thirty to forty more to come in the upcoming months, and forty-three promotions that resulted from the program.[105]

In its report on their "women/minority training programs," published in a 1976 issue of *Columbine*, CBS did not differentiate between the numbers of women and men who participated in the training programs, nor did it specify the racial identities of the women involved.[106] The company newsletter, however, suggested that women of color were central in the program's outreach and a measurement of its success. An illustration that accompanies the *Columbine* article features a Black woman sitting at a small desk in front of a typewriter, flanked by an overflowing trash can and file cabinet. With her hand resting on her chin, she looks at her imagined future, which floats near her head in a thought bubble. In this future, she is sitting at an organized, spacious desk with a phone and appointment book at her elbow. Behind her, a reel-to-reel tape player, a record player, and a speaker fill a credenza and shelves. The article opens with direct address to a "secretary in radio sales"—presumably the figure featured in the article's illustration—who aspires to an executive position, an assistant to an editor in publishing who longs to become an editor themselves, and an assistant in the personnel office who wants to work in the newsroom.

If the ideal outcome of woman/minority training programs was a Black woman's promotion from secretary to executive, as the article suggests, it required long-term investments. CBS demonstrated its commitment to the program by extending it for at least three years beyond its inception. It also continued to

FIGURE 4.
Illustration for a
June 1976 article
in *Columbine*, the
CBS company
newsletter, detailing
information on the
company's Women/
Minority Training
Programs provided
to employees. (CBS
News Reference
Library)

earmark the program as one designed to explicitly correct inequalities of race and gender. Joan Showalter, director of the training program and WAC member, noted that there had been "a few complaints of discrimination from white males" about the programs but that the company would continue its focused efforts on career training until there were "more women and minorities distributed throughout all areas of the Company."[107] Yet even with their intentions to correct disparities in workplace opportunities for women and people of color, CBS continued to specify redress for racial inequities as separate from gender disadvantages, which, in turn, fostered a lack of coalition building among workers. Although WAC's goals of inclusivity were hampered by this situation, the group operated under the assumption that it represented all women. From this position, WAC addressed intersectional issues of gender identity that included race, economic status, and age, with a primary aim, according to Priscilla Toumey, "to equalize the system to bring it where it should be so that everyone has an equal chance."[108]

HOLDING THE CORPORATION RESPONSIBLE: HEALTH CARE AND REPRODUCTIVE RIGHTS

Impediments to coalition building are among many examples of corporate culture's negative impact on WAC's reform agenda. Yet for all of the restrictions that CBS's corporate logistics, ethos, and design imposed on WAC, the group challenged fundamental philosophies that underpinned the corporation. Nowhere is this more evident than in the reproductive health care and childcare provisions WAC secured for workers. This success repudiated fundamental aspects of what Joan Acker identifies as the "non-responsibility" of modern corporations. According to this capitalistic model, corporations seek to restrict their obligations to workers' well-being, whether in terms of environmental protections, childcare and health care, or protections of a limited workweek and child labor laws. Policies developed within such organizations therefore reinforce "everyday inattention to the non-work lives of participants" and "render peripheral and usually invisible the essential social activities of birthing, caring, and even surviving."[109] Nonresponsibility holds serious consequences for women workers. They not only are charged disproportionately with the unacknowledged labor in the "nonwork" lives but also are jeopardized by the very conceptualization of a worker under corporate nonresponsibility. As Acker argues, "Non-responsibility consigns caring needs to areas outside the organization's interests, and, thus, helps to maintain the image of the ideal, even adequate, employee as someone without those obligations."[110]

WAC's proposal for comprehensive maternity benefits promised, in its words, to "put CBS in the vanguard of social responsibility."[111] By framing its plan for health care this way, WAC offered the corporation a means to distinguish itself from competitors through its socially responsible policies, a goal clearly expressed by Taylor and other CBS executives. Thus WAC recentered gendered concerns that had been eroded in corporate philosophies of nonresponsibility.

Given the broader sociopolitical context of 1974—the year in which WAC secured reproductive protections for employees—WAC's success in this area is particularly impressive. Various "right-of-conscience" bills and acts were proposed immediately following the January 1973 *Roe v. Wade* ruling. Of these, the one with the most impact was the "Church Amendment" to the 1944 Public Health Service Act. Adopted in 1973, this refusal law protected any health care professional involved in federally funded research from performing abortions or other reproductive health procedures that "would be contrary to his [sic] religious beliefs or moral convictions."[112] By August 1973, a total of twelve states had passed legislation aimed to "skirt or subvert" *Roe v. Wade*.[113] From May through October 1974, the Senate Subcommittee on Constitutional Amendments held a series of hearings to consider "possible Supreme Court negligence" in its decision to legalize abortion.[114]

It was within this reactionary political climate that the CBS Women's Joint Steering Committee, a subdivision of WAC, designed a plan to redefine abortion as a medical need. In July 1974, CBS accepted significant elements of the Committee's proposals. In doing so, CBS expanded coverage for women's medical needs that ranged from improved maternity leave to free, on-site breast cancer exams and mammograms.[115] The Committee's proposal also pushed CBS to normalize abortion as part of medical treatment and health care when it successfully argued that maternity policies should include not only "pregnancy-related disabilities" and illness but also abortion and miscarriage as grounds for sick leave for "the purpose of recuperation."[116] CBS agreed that all illnesses and medical procedures related to pregnancy, including abortion, would be treated "as any other illness" and would be afforded sick days.[117]

While unable to shift CBS policy to increase coverage for pregnancy-related hospitalization, something CBS deemed too expensive, the Women's Joint Steering Committee succeeded in redefining the most conservative and paternalistic aspects of reproductive rights and parenting roles in company policy. CBS agreed to strike the "dependent coverage" women had previously been required to take out while pregnant in order to "protect themselves financially against the possibility of abortion or miscarriage."[118] The Committee argued that this was an unacceptable policy based on an inaccurate definition of a fetus as a dependent, a reflection of antichoice ideologies. CBS agreed to this redefinition of personhood and dependency and struck down the related policy. This decision was particularly momentous, considering that the fifth session of the Senate Subcommittee on Constitutional Amendments, held just two months earlier, on May 1974, had debated whether a fetus was a human being with the same attendant rights and deliberated "at what time in the reproductive cycle life actually commences."[119]

Under the influence of the Women's Joint Steering Committee, CBS also reimagined caregiving for children. The company's revised policy assumed that fathers as well as, or instead of, mothers would be involved in the labor of child-rearing. Extended leave had previously been available only to women and for a four-month period. In 1974, this became available to both men and women for the care of children "natural or adoptive" and was extended to six months.[120] This policy was a clear victory for the CBS women, and one won through persistence. When they first proposed this policy revision in 1973, they were denied and were told that CBS did not grant "non-medical leave, maternal or paternal, for the purpose of child-rearing."[121] A year later, CBS not only agreed to a more generous timeframe for parental leave and more expansive definitions of parenting roles requested of them by the Committee but actually improved upon the Committee's original plan by no longer requiring that this leave be taken "directly following childbirth."[122]

ASSESSING WAC

By 1975, WAC's efforts had measurable effects, which an article published in *Columbine*, "What Progress Women at CBS?," conveyed to employees. This article provides an unusual assessment of work conditions for women in television. Reports on the status of women in television generated at the time typically tended to the industry's obligation to the public interest (to protect FCC licensing) and adherence to legislated employment practices (to ward off lawsuits). As a result, most evidence was numerically driven and focused on employment, hiring, and promotion of women at television stations. In 1974, the *Milwaukee Journal* expressed frustration at the limited means of evaluating women's progress in the television industry. While conducting research for their article "On or Off Camera, Women Move Up in TV Jobs," it found that "the only comprehensive survey deals with local stations, not networks," and was restricted to the "number of women holding important jobs."[123] These figures not only lacked breadth but also were subject to manipulation. In the same year that the *Milwaukee Journal* expressed its concerns about the scarcity of available data, the United Church of Christ (UCC), who were centrally involved in FCC licensing challenges and media advocacy work in the late 1960s and early 1970s, questioned the validity of employment statistics stations submitted to the FCC. While numbers indicated improved employment for women, the UCC charged that stations likely manipulated job categories to reclassify positions without corresponding increases in prestige or salary.[124] The *Columbine* article on CBS women, by comparison, provided an unusual and information-rich rubric by which to gauge women's status in the industry. It focused on employees at CBS headquarters rather than stations, offered a mix of quantitative and qualitative assessments of women's progress, and addressed company insiders rather than the public and/or the FCC. As a publication internal to CBS, *Columbine* was not designed for public relations or designed to ward off broadcasting licensing challenges; therefore it assumed a less protective position and, presumably, provided a more reliable perspective.

To offer a "fresh set of eyes to the assessment of our programs to date," CBS "turned to an outside writer," Judith Hennessee, who was charged with evaluating the progress women had made at CBS.[125] By hiring Hennessee, who was a member of NOW and was deeply involved in its media reform campaigns and whose journalism appeared in feminist publications such as *Ms.*, CBS announced its investment in feminist assessment and outsider evaluation. After interviewing employees, compiling statistics, and narrativizing her findings, Hennessee found that "several hundred of CBS's working women seem to have already benefited directly" from changes in management practices.[126] Promotions and raises clearly demonstrate these benefits. In 1971, women constituted 13.2 percent of promotions within salaried positions; by the third quarter of 1974, this figure had increased to 36.2 percent.[127]

In Hennessee's evaluation, women's progress at CBS was not confined to economic indicators. Hennessee also gauged experiential evidence and found, overall, that interpersonal and cultural aspects of women's work lives had improved. The "substantial changes in basic intangibles of attitudes," something that WAC deemed necessary for true workplace reform, manifested in interpersonal, affective ways.[128] Kathryn Pelgrift, Arthur Taylor's assistant who had been promoted to a vice presidential position, noted that it was "'no longer fashionable to put women down around here.'"[129] Even a bureaucratic detail, such as the revision of the title of a training manual from "CBS Secretarial Manual" to "CBS Office Practices," helped transform the tone of vocational instruction from one of condescension to professionalism. Whereas the earlier iteration of the manual indicated that secretarial duties included making coffee and "playing the gracious hostess," the revised version "[stuck] strictly to business."[130] As a result of such changes, women who worked various "lower-level" jobs noted a decline in various on-the-job "indignities."[131]

Despite the many workplace improvements Hennessee identified, not all employees had been helped by CBS's new policies, nor were they convinced that they would be. Although some women felt the effects of the revisions to policies, "many more thousands of CBS women (and men) [were] watchfully waiting to see if the company's 18-month-old push to change policies and attitudes toward women [would], in any direct way, affect them."[132] Hennessee interpreted this skepticism not as an indictment of WAC's reform efforts but as a persistent effect of the corporation's organization and the subcultures it fostered. Depending on the CBS division in which she worked, equality employment measures affected an employee differently. News and radio divisions, which reported on "women's issues in the outside world," adapted quickly, while CBS Records suffered from a legacy of "'macho' and 'groupie' mentality" and was therefore slow to change.[133] The hierarchical organization of CBS also had an effect, and trickle-down adoption of policy was not ensured. One woman interviewed by Hennessee attested to the problem, saying, "'If it doesn't filter down to my boss, then it doesn't matter how good Arthur Taylor's intentions are.'"[134]

In her 1975 report, Hennessee was careful to acknowledge the uneven implementation of policies within CBS along with the positive impact of WAC's efforts, but she did not predict the looming challenges to women's workplace reform and to WAC's efficacy. As the 1970s continued, WAC became less active and less powerful, not least because of the larger sociopolitical environment of the US in the 1980s. Arthur Taylor's departure as CBS president in 1976 was also a loss given his concern about the advancement of women in the workplace. And, as with so many activists, some group women experienced burnout, while others missed the energizing effects of grassroots activism. Once WAC and the women's groups gained official status within their companies and formal recognition by their employers, "a lot of the thrill of the original underground feeling [had] gone."[135] Finally, and perhaps surprisingly, the success of all network women's groups contributed to their decline. Women throughout the corporation came to depend upon group women to the point that they grew complacent and "believed that the activist women would take care of things."[136] More generally, given the significant improvements for women in the broadcasting industry under their watch, group members felt that the "movement had paid off" and that women's "problems were over."[137]

THE LEGACY OF THE WOMEN'S GROUPS

By 1983, television journalist Marlene Sanders witnessed "backsliding" on gender equity issues at ABC, her previous employer, and "dissatisfaction" at CBS, her current employer, but "no organized effort of any significance" to address these problems.[138] As a response to deteriorating conditions, women formed new women's groups. Sanders recalled that the "most shocking revelation" about a women's group that was forming anew at ABC at this time was that the new group was unaware of the women's groups that had come before just ten years ear-lier.[139] Unfortunately, a lack of institutional memory among generations of women media workers is not unique to this time period, the broadcasting industry, or US media workplaces.[140] Fortunately, feminist scholarship on histories of labor move-ments and media activism can help bridge generational disconnections. Such work, as modeled by Frances Galt's recent project on women's unionization efforts in British film and television industries, "seeks to build a body of evidence which could support current stakeholders to effect change."[141]

Given WAC's brief life span, its reform focus and actions internal to the corpo-rate workplace, and the difficulties of accessing evidence of the group's activities, it is unsurprising that media workers and scholars alike are unaware of WAC's exis-tence and impact on CBS. The group's legacy, however, like that of so many other women's media workplace collectives, is worth recalling for its place in feminist media histories and for its applicability to contemporary labor conditions facing women. WAC's strategies for changing a media workplace, its ability to harness its members' collective skills and energies, and its adaptable ways of articulating feminist ideas bore significant outcomes. WAC improved the bureaucratic func-tioning of the corporation and operated as a conduit by which women could voice their grievances to executives. It educated men who held positions of power to not abuse that power and to attain heightened awareness of gender issues. It rede-fined traditionally feminized and undervalued work so that the terms of that work were formally defined, recognized, and respected. It instituted services and pro-grams that trained women in professionalizing and educational measures, which helped them achieve greater status and economic compensation. And, finally, it demystified the processes behind instituted corporate policies so that women workers could effectively intervene in and shape those policies. For all of WAC's many accomplishments, the most remarkable aspect of its story, perhaps, is that, at a time when activist groups faced outright refusals from network television, a women's group operated inside the industry's corporate stronghold to affect feminist change.

2

From "Jockocratic Endeavors" to Feminist Expression

Billie Jean King, Eleanor Sanger Riger, and Women's Sports on Television

"Women have real problems that cannot be solved by *I Love Lucy* and *The Dating Game* and some sports event or some other jockocratic endeavor." So said Florynce "Flo" Kennedy when she appeared on *Yes, We Can* in early 1974. When expressed by the cofounder of the National Women's Political Caucus and the National Black Feminist Organization, founder of the Feminist Party, and creator of the Media Workshop on a daylong program dedicated to women, this assessment of television's shortcomings carried particular weight. As discussed in chapter 4, *Yes, We Can* was an unprecedented break with commercial television traditions. Rather than programming that typically involved "six hours of sports" on a given day, which was, in Kennedy's estimation, "hardly of interest to any woman," Boston station WBZ produced and aired a different kind of special event broadcast. *Yes, We Can* addressed women viewers for sixteen hours with content presumed to be of interest to them, including career counseling, health care, Black feminist activism, and nonsexist childrearing, as well as highlights from state government hearings about the status of women.

Kennedy's criticism represented prevailing attitudes of feminist leadership of the time. The assumption that television sports addressed men only and accomplished nothing on behalf of women reflected a commonplace outlook within the women's movement. But as important as programs like *Yes, We Can* were, and in spite of negative feminist response, sports television became a vital arena in which feminist politics were articulated and proven viable. When it began showcasing women's athletic events, profiling women's athletes, and hiring women athletes as commentators in the early to mid-1970s, television proved invaluable to the popularization of women's sports. It also provided opportunities for women to express the feminist potential of sports.

This chapter explores the growth of women's sports on television throughout the 1970s and, despite feminist misgivings, its potential to promote equality, occupational and personal satisfaction, and empowerment for women. Two women in particular, professional tennis player Billie Jean King and ABC Sports producer Eleanor Sanger Riger, played a vital role in shaping how television would come to envision women's sports during this critical period. Jointly and individually, they made inroads into employment for women on sports television behind and in front of the camera; they explicitly articulated feminist ideas through television coverage of sports; and they understood and exploited television's abilities to serve the interests of female athletes while framing women's sports in ways that appealed to viewers. Yet despite these many victories, King's and Riger's careers also illustrate the many difficulties women faced while working in sports television during the 1970s. Perhaps more than any other sector of commercial television, sports television operated as a masculinist enclave. In seeking a place there, women provoked patriarchal anxieties about female assertiveness, competence, and occupational prestige.

SPORTS AND THE WOMEN'S MOVEMENT

Even though the world of professional and amateur athletics operated as a convergent site for a number of feminist concerns, there was little visible conversation within the women's movement about the need to focus activist energies on sports. Feminist historian Susan Ware hypothesizes that some of the reasons for this low level of interest were ideological. To many feminists, sports stood for masculinist values of competition and aggression and exemplified "crass commercialism," all of which were antithetical to core tenets of Marxist and radical feminism.[1] A 1974 article in *off our backs* exemplified this position when it cautioned feminists about the co-optation of the movement by capitalist forces. The article singled out Billie Jean King's celebrity as evidence of the all-encompassing commercialization of feminist politics. When Lincoln Bank of Philadelphia announced new nonsexist lending and employment practices, the bank appointed King to its board to oversee the project. The hiring of King, to the radical feminists of *off our backs*, was nothing more than another tactic by the "patriarchal banking system so that they can get more of women's money."[2] King operated as a front for capitalist interests intent on neutralizing the revolutionary threat of feminism and profiting from consumerist markets invented for "liberated" women. From this perspective, King's visibility did not register as a political gain for feminists but instead meant that businesses could "sell all the stuff you buy little boys to little girls."[3] King's media presence did not help matters. Since "the Media State has never shown the women of America a real radical feminist and it never will," readers were advised to "beware of men bearing gifts even if they look like Billie Jean King."[4]

Fears about capitalist co-optation were not the only reason for the disconnection between feminists and sports. Concerns about the objectification of women and specious biological arguments about women's inferiority complicated feminist celebrations of women's bodies. Issues of embodiment were not only theoretical but also practical and born from lived experiences. Many early leaders of feminist organizations, according to Ware, were "physically inactive and/or had no exposure to or interest in sports" and therefore did not have firsthand experiences of empowerment that came through sports. The geographical realities of the women's movement also had a part to play in the matter. With the origins of the movement centered in New York City, an urban environment that was "hardly a hotbed of athleticism for women," prominent feminists acted in accordance with the prevailing culture of their location and failed to connect to athletics as a meaningful experience.[5]

It was not just feminists who accounted for the lack of sports activism in the women's movement. Women athletes were also responsible for the separate interests of organized feminism and organized sports. Since the majority of female athletes succeeded "on their own by distancing themselves from traditional definitions of female behavior," they did not easily adapt to or see the need for feminist collectivity. In addition to behaviors produced through the culture of competition, distancing oneself from feminism was a pragmatic survival strategy for some women in the world of athletics. A clear and obvious relationship to feminism invited homophobic judgement and gender policing; leaders in women's physical education shielded themselves from scrutiny with various adaptive behaviors and appearances. Feminist identification put their hard-won gains and their relationships with "important male allies" at risk and made them vulnerable to being perceived as "strident, unfeminine, or worse (i.e. lesbians)."[6]

Despite the obstacles to merging feminist organizations and athletics, sports did play an important role in publicizing key feminist events and in raising feminist awareness. Nowhere was this more evident than in the 2,600-mile torch relay conducted in conjunction with the National Women's Conference in 1977. The relay started in Seneca Falls, New York, home of the first women's rights convention in 1848, and ended at the conference location in Houston, Texas. As Ware argues, the relay provided visibility for the conference and made for effective public relations that "captured the public imagination."[7] Regardless of the popularity of this event, the issue of "athletic equity" was not "deemed important enough to be a major focus of the Houston plan of action, although a small band of sports activists tried to push the issue."[8] The question of sports as a feminist concern, as exemplified in the 1977 National Women's Conference, was characterized by both its promise for and its marginalization by the women's movement.

While feminist organizations were ambivalent about embracing sports, television was relatively quick to see the positive potential of the female—even feminist—sports star as an asset. As Leslie Heywood and Shari L. Dworkin argue, the viability of female athletes as celebrities reached new heights in 1996, when they reached "full iconic status."[9] It was at this moment that female sports provided "solutions" to women's problems, a valuable quality in an era of intensified consumerist ideas promulgated by "media culture" in "late global capitalism."[10] While contemporary sports celebrity is informed by an economic climate that emerged in the late twentieth century, there is a longer-standing connection between mass media and the development of athletes as stars. Sports sociologist Jennifer Hargreaves traces the popularization of sports to coverage in American and British print journalism in the 1920s and the 1930s. The introduction and widespread adoption of radio added to the popularity of sports by introducing coverage of sporting events into the home with an immediacy and excitement that came with the sounds of live action and commentary. While radio was the medium in which "achievements were celebrated, and the making and breaking of records dramatized," television intensified this effect and advanced the process of transforming sportsmen and sportswomen alike into celebrities.[11] Hargreaves makes the case that while men in sports "predominated as well-known personalities," women achieved international fame in the 1920s, as exemplified by swimmer Gertrude Ederle, the first woman to swim the English Channel in 1926, tennis prodigy Helen Wills, and skater Sonja Henie.[12]

The 1970s marked a transitional stage in media relationships with women athletes. Commercial television in the US built upon radio's earlier interest while anticipating female sports icons that would emerge in the mid-1990s. By amplifying the celebrity status of women athletes and by associating feminist ideals with female athleticism, the television industry reinvigorated sports television. Women athletes provided television with new events to televise, gendered narratives to develop, and opportunities to experiment with aesthetics and formats. During the seventies, women athletes clearly made for good business, and their profitability presaged the full-blown commodification that was to come. But they were not yet inextricably linked to consumerist solutions for women's issues. As a result, they introduced to sports television issues of equitable pay, career opportunities, and workplace respect for women while providing women athletes with a forum in which to articulate issues of sexism in their sport.

BILLIE JEAN KING AND TELEVISION'S BATTLE OF THE SEXES

Of all of the athletes who defined a new type of female sports celebrity in the 1970s, none was more famous or more connected to television than Billie Jean King. King also figured prominently in the world of feminist politics. She was also one of fifty-three high-profile women who signed their names to the famous "We Have Had Abortions" statement. Published in July 1972 in the first issue of *Ms.*, this document listed women who had abortions or who supported legalized abortion. This was but one public statement King made in support of women's reproductive rights. In a 1972 *Washington Post* interview that preceded the *Ms.* statement by several months, King made her position on the subject clear by declaring, "'I feel strongly about abortion.'" Her feminist ethos was founded on the principles of women "having equal choice," a perspective that linked reproductive rights with career success and equal pay. Her personal story testified to the cause-and-effect relationship, which headlines such as "Abortion Made Possible Mrs. King's Top Year" made abundantly clear.[13] In 1971, after she underwent her abortion early in the year, King went on to win nineteen tournaments and earned more than $100,000 in prize money, a first for a female athlete.

Economic inequality was a key point of reform for King. Her awareness of differential pay for women and men came in 1968 in relation to her status as a professional tennis player. After her win at Wimbledon in Women's Singles that year, King was shocked to find out that her male counterpart, Rod Laver, had received £2,000 to her £750 prize money. When she recalled this moment in a 2013 interview, she noted that she "didn't have any idea we were going to get different prize money" and "thought it was totally unfair." After 1968, the disparity between men's and women's professional earning potential in tennis was increasingly obvious, with "horrendous" ratios of prize money at "10, 11, 12 to 1." This inequity, along with the lack of women's events at professional tournaments, further motivated King's activism.[14]

King's arguments for equitable economic compensation centered on women's worth in the public sphere. Although rooted in a key tenet of liberal feminism, they exceeded a strict political framework. Rather than identifying financial success and income equity as a sole mark of feminist achievement, King understood exclusionary traditions in sports as intertwined forms of racism, classism, and sexism. In a press conference following her victory at the 1973 Battle of the Sexes match with Bobby Riggs, King told a seemingly simple story about her political awakening: "I love tennis very much. I wanted it to change ever since I started in this sport. *I thought it was just for the rich and just for the white* and ever since that day when I was 11 years old and I wasn't allowed in a photo because I wasn't in a tennis skirt, I knew then that I wanted to change the sport" (emphasis added). While King's comments have circulated widely since this press conference—on her own Twitter account, in interviews, and in inspirational quotes scattered across the internet and other media—they have assumed a revised or truncated form that emphasizes gender politics and excises issues of race and class.[15] Her remarks at the 1973 postmatch press conference afford a more nuanced perspective on the exclusionary nature of sports and suggest King's awareness of oppression beyond a single issue of gender. Her comments also suggest that experiential as well as material aspects of exclusion are significant, a notion that has been overshadowed by issues of fair financial compensation for which King is now known.

Equal pay for female athletes was an issue that King tied to celebrity culture and its affective impact. In an interview with Dinah Shore on *Colgate's Women's Sports Special* (ABC, 1974), King articulated the connection between the amorphous qualities of fame, glamour, and celebrity with clear-cut monetary worth for women athletes. Shore first observed that women's sports had "come such a long way" in both spectatorship and women's participation. She then asked King, "What do you feel is the biggest step forward that women's sports have made?" King responded by identifying "two significant steps: the money as well as appreciation from the public." As a result of gains in both areas, female athletes, in King's estimation, felt like "stars and entertainers for the first time in their lives and have a lot more self-respect because of it."

Increased public interest in women athletes helped King argue for their worth. Differences between the games women and men played, which were based on assumptions about women's inferior physical stamina, justified unequal prize money. Wins in women's pro tennis matches depended on winning two out of three sets versus wins in men's matches, in which three out of five sets constituted a win. Shorter matches rationalized paying women players less than their male counterparts. King countered this formula for assessing players' worth through women players' star quality and entertainment value. In a 1972 *Sports Illustrated* interview, King justified demands for significant pay for women by identifying the "big business" of sports and the ways that athletes were increasingly part of an "entertainment industry." King concluded that "if we can get the money, we deserve it."[16] To illustrate this point, King consistently emphasized in the press and in media appearances her growing fan base and resulting ticket sales. King's celebrity was clear by the mid-1970s. In comparison to her earliest match, which drew two spectators, her matches now drew crowds that numbered in the thousands.

King's media savvy made her, as Ware succinctly describes it, the "right feminist in the right sport at the right time."[17] King famously beat Bobby Riggs in the "Battle of the Sexes," a televised tennis match that aired on ABC on September 30, 1973. The event was a highly anticipated, well-publicized one that demonstrated the might of female athletes, made a compelling case for the viability of women playing sports on television, and proved the correctness of Title IX. ABC publicized it as a feminist battling an egotistical misogynist. This concept sensationalized the match and hyped its entertainment value while, at the same time, it expressed ideas about gender and women's legal rights that were at the forefront of contemporary cultural conversations. ABC's approach, which hybridized spectacle with cultural relevance, both tested the viability of women's sports on television and set a new precedent for how television would present sports.

The King-Riggs match happened only a year after the passage of Title IX, the "early days" of the law when "public awareness of the law in general and its impact on women's sports in particular" was not clear or widespread.[18] Title IX served as a remedy to the Civil Rights Act of 1964 and addressed discrimination in education.

It was broadly conceptualized through "admissions, counseling, course offerings, financial aid and scholarships, facilities and housing, health and insurance benefits, and discrimination based on marital or parental status."[19] The sheer scale of Title IX and strategic efforts to downplay certain elements of the legislation so as not to draw undue attention and counterattacks meant that "discrimination in sports was simply not on the radar" in its first few years of existence.[20] Title IX's impact on sports only became clear and well publicized in early 1974. At this time, the National Collegiate Athletic Association (NCAA), the regulatory body for college athletics, began intensively lobbying against Title IX to defend the primacy of men's football in college sports. These efforts resulted in the Tower Amendment, a legislative proposal that would restrict Title IX's influence on college athletics.[21]

This timeline meant that, at the time of the Battle of the Sexes match in 1973, Title IX gains were not yet part of the general public's consciousness.[22] According to Ware, no publicity for the event made mention of Title IX. While the King-Riggs match predated common awareness of Title IX's relationship to sports, it increased visibility for women's sports and for the value of women athletes, which bolstered positive public opinion about Title IX in the years to come. Once Title IX's impact on women's and girls' sports was recognized, King served as a public and persuasive figure in the successful fight against the repressive Tower Amendment. In 1973, she used her newly minted status as a sports celebrity to testify in support of the Women's Educational Equity Act (WEEA), legislation that provided financial grants to secure the aims of Title IX.[23]

Amid legislative battles over Title IX and the growing participation of girls and women in sports, television reassessed the viability of broadcasting women's sports, the value of female viewers for televised sports events, and the benefits of employing female sports talent as stars and commentators. Nowhere were these shifts in the industry more apparent than in the Battle of the Sexes match. The game unsettled traditions of sports television with new types of gameplay, storylines, and audience appeals as well as unconventional means of producing, selling, and marketing the event.

With the King-Riggs match, Tandem Productions, the independent television company cofounded by Norman Lear and Bud Yorkin, entered the world of sports television. While best known for socially relevant situation comedies, Tandem applied its unconventional approach to business to this special event program. It bought the rights to the match from Hollywood promoter Jackie Barnett for $75,000. In a stance similar to one it would later use to get *Mary Hartman, Mary Hartman* to air in 1976 (discussed in chapter 3), Tandem was prepared to bypass the networks, if necessary, to procure the best possible deal. If a network would not pay its asking price, Tandem planned to "arrange either an independent network or a closed-circuit presentation of the match."[24] ABC made a deal with Tandem, paying $700,000 for the two-hour, live television broadcast; the deal proved profitable to both the production company and the network. Tandem

FIGURES 5 & 6. Graphics reflect the "Battle of the Sexes" theme: the score board header and a split screen of Billie Jean King and Bobby Riggs at match point. ABC, September 20, 1973.

reached a $1,000,000 payday with an additional $300,000 guarantee from the Houston Astrodome, and ABC recovered what it had paid to air the match by moving ad time in a "fast sale," with advertisers paying $80,000 per minute.[25]

While figures indicate both the anticipated and proven success of the event, critics were unhappy with the production quality of the program. In wondering, "Where Was the ABC of Yesteryear?," *Variety* compared the match negatively to ABC's previous broadcasts. In the 1960s, ABC established itself as an innovator in televised sports by utilizing new technologies to cover major events. The network's handling of the Olympics, in particular, established their reputation. ABC broadcast the first televised coverage of the Games in the US in 1960. In 1964, they flew back footage from events in time to put them on the air the same day. Their coverage of the 1968 Summer Olympics produced several firsts: record-breaking remote coverage with the greatest "number of hours, personnel and pieces of equipment," color broadcast, and satellite transmission that made live viewing of events possible.[26]

Variety may have lamented a decline in quality associated with ABC Sports, but King and Riggs provided an entertainment event in keeping with the network's established style. When Roone Arledge became president of ABC Sports in 1968, he ushered in a new era of sports television that "privileged building stories over displaying events and assumed viewers might watch the tales it packaged no matter their interest in sports. It humanized competitions by presenting them through familiar narratives (rivalries, records about to be broken, battles against the elements) and by making their participants relatable."[27] The production of the King-Riggs match prioritized drama and spectacle rather than the technical intricacies of tennis play. In doing so, it drew spectators, both in person and at home, who were not tennis fans or even sports fans.

Although by this point outsized narratives and exciting visuals had become the cornerstones of ABC Sports programs under Arledge's guidance, the Battle of the Sexes drew particularly pointed criticism. *Variety* attributed what it considered substandard production values to the celebrity-driven aspects of the event and complained that ABC "certainly weren't shy about using their ground level camera to show us the celebs in the $100 seats."[28] By privileging the celebrity element of the match, ABC minimized attention to the on-court action. Other criticisms of ABC's coverage focused on fundamental technical elements, including poor camera placement that failed to highlight the finesse and athleticism of the match, Howard Cosell's "ineptitude" in announcing plays, and the infrequency of score information.[29]

Whatever the flaws in the broadcast, viewers were not deterred. With an average audience of forty-eight million viewers and at least seventy-two million viewing the broadcast for some part of the coverage, the "wildly promoted event," set in the "carnival atmosphere of the Houston Astrodome," "dominated TV viewing."[30] Trendex reported a 34.2 rating and a 52.4 share for the match. NBC and CBS programs that aired at the same time lagged in ratings, with CBS's *The Waltons* earning 14.4 and 22.0 and NBC's *The Flip Wilson Show* earning 12.0 and 18.4.[31] ABC's ratings win proved women's sports to be a sound investment and female sports fans a new audience to be considered. As Travis Vogan argues in his history of ABC Sports, if dramatic and spectacularized formulas "quickly became clichés" and were therefore "easy to discount as commercialized pandering," they also "function[ed] through engaging the cultural codes that make TV so important."[32] Regardless of its commercialized aspects, the King-Riggs match captured the changing gender politics of the day and had tremendous viewer impact. It signaled a new stage of development for ABC's sports broadcasting, which would require that resources be allocated to women on the playing field, in television production, and in the audience.

A "LIBBER-LOBBER" AND TELEVISION CELEBRITY

King emerged from the Battle of the Sexes a celebrity. More than that, she attained "sex symbol" status, something she acknowledged, though as an "advocate of women's liberation" she did not "know what to do about it." A 1974 *Boston Globe* profile on King describes how, since the match with Riggs, King had been the recipient of "mash notes, sexy suggestions and passes thrown by amorous makes [*sic*]."[33] Although not an out lesbian by this point—something that would not happen until her personal assistant Marilyn Barnett filed a palimony suit against her in 1981—King implicitly presented an unconventional gender identity and incompatibility with heteronormativity, something that coverage about her sex symbol status both suggested and managed. The *Globe* article described King's "fetching" appearance when she wore a pink sweater, printed flowered blouse, and gold jewelry as something that made her look, "well, feminine." In this assessment, King's feminine allure proved a surprising counterpoint to her athleticism rather than confirmation of queer identity. King "looked like anything but one of the great athletes of our times." The *Globe* reporter indicated that, despite her feminine appearance, King had not been to the hairdresser or "wor[n] a speck of makeup" and that "clearly, she thinks little about" her sex appeal.[34]

Characterizations of King's "sex symbol" status affirmed her athleticism and her feminism. King countered media constructions of feminists as unlikable, unattractive activists who aggressively worked to destroy long-standing social institutions. She instead operated "out on the firing line, commanding respect on the tennis court and in the competitive field of commerce."[35] Her athleticism, discipline, and striving made her a feminist celebrity who meshed easily with all-American notions of accomplishment and individual endeavor and reframed negative associations with feminism.

When ABC hired King at the end of December 1975, her celebrity feminist credentials played an important role. In the publicity surrounding the hire, King was described as a "libber-lobber," a new type of hybridized feminist-sports celebrity that sports television eagerly embraced.[36] Immediately following the Battle of the Sexes, King was hired as a commentator on ABC's *Wide World of Sports* (1961–98) and various sports specials, and as host for *Women's Sports Special* (1976). At this same time, King also developed a syndicated show, *The Billie Jean King Show* (1974–78), with ABC Sports' Jim Packer as executive producer.[37]

King's success in television indicates the acceptability of feminist celebrity when it underscored capitalistic terms of success. King parlayed the interest in her contract negotiations and lucrative television contracts, as evinced by articles like "How Green Was Her Volley" and "Billie Jean Courts Fat TV Contract."[38] But despite the conservative fashioning of King's celebrity and publicity that used King's accomplishments to tout television's progressiveness, King brought critical attention to gendered inequalities under capitalism and sexist employment practices in television. When she negotiated her contract with ABC, King underscored the issue of income parity for women in television, just as she had with professional sports. Rather than responding to media speculation about the exact dollar amount of her "fat TV contract" with ABC, King sidestepped the sensationalized aspects of her salary. She instead repeated the simple mantra that she used in her demands for equal prize money in tennis: "I won't take less than the guys."[39]

ELEANOR SANGER RIGER AND THE DEVELOPMENT OF WOMEN'S SPORTS AT ABC

Producer Eleanor Sanger Riger was a driving force behind the decision to hire Billie Jean King. Throughout her career, Riger helped introduce women's sports to television and agitated for increased roles for women in its production. Riger worked at ABC from 1965 to 1969, moving up the ladder from manager of client relations to producer of promotional films to writer and producer. In 1973 she was hired at ABC Sports, the first woman "to hold full producership and executive position in network television sports."[40] In this position, Riger produced numerous

FIGURE 7. Eleanor Sanger Riger behind the camera (date unknown). (Eleanor Sanger Papers, Sophia Smith Collection SSC-MS-00286).

segments for *Wide World of Sports*, including the US–East Germany Swimming and Dual Diving Event from East Berlin, World Weightlifting Championships, the National Figure Skating Championships, Women's World Cup Skiing, European Women's Gymnastics, and the Pro Bowler Tour. She produced and wrote "two landmark prime-time specials on women's sports;" the *Colgate's Women's Sports Special* (ABC, 1974), hosted by Dinah Shore; and the second edition of the Colgate Special, *The Lady Is a Champ* (ABC, 1975), hosted by Billie Jean King. Riger also produced and coproduced segments for the 1976 Summer and Winter Olympic Games, for which she won two Emmys.[41] Throughout the 1970s, Riger would play a pivotal role in asserting the viability of women's sports at ABC Sports and identifying actions the network needed to take to compete in the increasingly profitable area of televised women's sports.

With the express purpose of guiding the network in its "development of sports programming for women," Riger was hired in response to NOW's FCC license renewal challenge to WABC-TV in 1972.[42] With a career so deeply enmeshed in liberal feminist activism, Riger worked toward equal employment of women and increased representations of women in sports television. While these approaches made inroads, they were not without limitations. By focusing on inclusion of women in existing systems, as Jennifer Hargreaves argues, liberal feminist approaches fail "to examine the extent and nature of male power in sports in the specific context of capitalism" and "to incorporate the ideological and symbolic dimensions of gender oppression."[43] Riger, however, did not only depend on the admission of greater numbers of women to the ranks of sports television as a corrective to its sexism. She also worked to reformulate what women's sports on television looked like, to change production standards to accommodate women's athletes as television workers, and to alter the ways that women's sports were presented to audiences.

Riger's unaired project on Olympic figure skater and US national champion Maribel Vinson Owen illustrates her investment in elevating women's achievements in sports and her methods for articulating women's athleticism on-screen. In 1976, Riger coauthored a biographical teleplay on Owen. It was under consideration at 20th Century-Fox television but was never produced. Riger's script told a dramatic story of Owen's struggles to gain recognition as an athlete, her disastrous marriage and years of abuse at the hands of her alcoholic husband, her attempts to sustain her professional aspirations alongside domestic obligations and child-rearing, and her untimely death in a plane crash. In the midst of this compelling melodramatic narrative, Riger stressed the structural issues of patriarchal power that had shaped Owen's life and balanced uplifting, pioneering story elements with sobering reminders of what Owen and other female figure skaters of her time experienced. These athletes were deprived of access to facilities and coaching, mistreated by fathers and coaches (often the same person), and forced to relinquish their careers far too early when they married (often to abusive husbands).

As she would in other programs she produced, in relaying Owen's story Riger maximized televisual techniques to balance emotional storytelling with athletic accomplishments and skilled athleticism. One scene features Owen in a practice session in which dramatic music plays under the voices and sound effects and then moves to multiple moments of training. At this point, Riger offers detailed instructions on camerawork in a script that, until then, was largely composed of narrative content rather than staging and shooting directions. She directs the camera to focus on the "intricate twists and turns of the skate; the intense concentration of skater and coach; the beauty of the precise and fascinating movements which are the basis of all skating."[44] The technical aspects of production included in Riger's script involved relatively complex camerawork, sound design, and editing. They underscore her priorities in representing athletic performances: to pair emotionally rich storytelling qualities of an athlete's struggle to succeed with the intensive physicality of the sport and the spectacle of athletic achievement.

PIONEERING WOMEN'S SPORTS IN FRONT OF AND BEHIND THE CAMERAS

While women were making gains in television production, they still lagged behind in sports television. Riger's concerns for women's advancements in sports television were as much about the workplace as they were about programming. In 1973, when ABC Sports hired Riger as a producer, network news had already hired "hundreds" of women as writers, producers, and reporters but sports television had none in similar positions. "Why was I the first? Why was it such a rare thing— a news item—when I got the appointment?," wondered Riger. Her questions were rhetorical ones, as she understood full well the fictions that kept women from this job: only male sports were "salable" on television, women lacked interest in and had no "feeling" for sports, women lacked the "intelligence or dedication or stamina required for the admittedly demanding routine" in television sports, and women could not cope with the grueling travel schedule required for the job.[45] Riger worked to counter these myths and to close the gap between women working in sports television production and other areas of television production. To accomplish this, Riger linked the pioneering accomplishments of women athletes with the capabilities of women for sports television work. Through this connection, she argued for the suitability of women for sports television on both sides of the camera.

To Riger, the success and talent of women as athletes, on-air talent, and behind-the-scenes production staff were all related. She saw the increase in collegiate athletic programs for women—556 colleges with athletic programs for women in 1974–75 and 806 in 1976—as a reason for ABC to pay more attention to women's sports. The growth of athletic programs, set in motion by Title IX, provided evidence for a steady supply of interest in women's sports and made programming women's sports a low-risk proposition. Television sports and college athletics, to Riger, were inextricably linked. She argued that "the most important factor for the future involvements of women in sports on television is the accelerating worth of college sports for women," since men's college sports served as the "backbone" of participation in the Olympics and in "major" professional sports, which, together, made up "99 percent of the sports television programming."[46] Riger also capitalized on the growing celebrity of women in professional sports to pitch women's involvements in television sports. She repeatedly made the case to ABC that the very qualities that made these athletes interesting to viewers would translate to their work on television as commentators and hosts. Their personalities would draw audiences to the broadcast just as they had to their sports matches.

Unsurprisingly, given both her public support for Title IX and her celebrity status, Billie Jean King was a crucial figure in Riger's plans. King's celebrity and her authority as an athlete-activist broadened her appeals beyond tennis and garnered viewer interest across multiple sports events, making her a credible television personality. This was particularly so after the Battle of the Sexes, a time when Riger urged ABC to make the most of the success of the King-Riggs match. In a November 13, 1973, memo to Roone Arledge, president of ABC Sports, Riger expressed the need to move quickly. The "quite urgent" circumstances, according to Riger, involved increased competition among networks to hire King and an unprecedented opportunity to address growing demand for women's sports on television.[47]

Riger equated King's unprecedented athletic accomplishments with her own groundbreaking status as a woman producer hired to help shepherd ABC into the untested arena of women's sports. In advising Arledge to hire King, Riger emphasized the investments ABC had already made, the role women would play in ABC's future success, and the benefit of continued investments in women:

> After all you have done in trying to get more recognition for women's sports by hiring me and [producing] that kind of programming, that we should lose the biggest attraction of all would be terrible. You really built Billie Jean up with the telecast of the King-Riggs match. You took a gamble on the price and it paid off. . . . I am sure you wouldn't want to see all the momentum ABC Sports has built up dissipated by an NBC coup with Billie Jean King. Certainly with women's Olympic Sports like gymnastics, skating, skiing, track and field, swimming and diving, volleyball and rowing becoming more and more popular because of our television exposure, we would be at a disadvantage in this area too.[48]

Given Riger's logic, it was not enough for women in sports to occupy more programming time: it was also necessary to train and cultivate the expertise of women working in production if ABC was to remain competitive.

By 1974, Riger felt that, with the growing number of female athletes, the financial security of major advertisers sponsoring programs, and the ready-made audience of "sports-conscious women" and men who would watch women's sports on television, ABC needed to invest in production via female employees. With key elements in place for ratings, profit, and content, the only "real challenge" facing ABC was its need to "develop female commentators" who could announce women's sports "both on action coverage shows and more feature-oriented programs."[49]

After sponsoring a Women's Sports Special in 1974, produced by Riger, Colgate conducted a study that found that women were increasingly inclined to watch women's sports. This information was somewhat surprising to them, since they "didn't know if women would really want to watch a show about women athletes" and had commissioned the special with some reservations. The study, surveying attitudes before and after watching the show, found that "the special generated definite increases in interest among women in watching TV programs dealing with women's sports" and that all of the sports featured in the special "showed attitude gains." Although Colgate tracked women's interest in sports television for the purpose of corporate profits, the proven impact of Riger's special also helped create change that benefited women, albeit in capitalistic terms. The special demonstrated the viability of women's sports to a major company who could sponsor and fund future programming; it also made the company rethink its conceptualization of women consumers. Sally O'Brien, director of market research at Colgate, reported that the company could no longer depict women in "some never-never land, or where she's in that tacky old role some marketers still think women are playing, or where a product is positioned as some kind of father figure." Instead, ads would need to acknowledge that "housework isn't fun and games" and to recognize the interests of women had outside domestic work.[50]

Riger leveraged corporations' changing perceptions of women into increased and improved programming of women's sports. When companies wanted to capture a new market of women viewers, as Sears, Palmolive, and Fabergé did when they sponsored women's golf, tennis, gymnastics, and amateur athletics, Riger transformed their interest in women as consumers into opportunities for women to work at ABC. She used corporate sponsorship to persuade the network to "develop a whole new slant on its sports programming, both expanding the coverage of women's events and bringing women into the behind-the-scenes production and on-air talent areas."[51]

THE *COLGATE WOMEN'S SPORTS SPECIAL*: RIGER'S PLANS IN ACTION

Broadcast on January 10, 1974, on ABC, the *Colgate Women's Sports Special* realized Riger's goals for women's sports television. The special employed female celebrity sports figures as on-air talent, displayed women's athleticism through high-impact production values, and invited audience identification with inspirational moments of women's athletic triumphs. In the buildup to the special, Riger emphasized the program's ratings potential to promote the program and to

FIGURE 8. Billie Jean King and host Dinah Shore appear in a promotional photograph for the *Colgate Women's Sports Special*. (Photofest)

encourage ABC to increase their investments in women's sports. She argued that the prominent female sports figures featured in the program would inspire women and girls to participate in sports, which would then create an ever-increasing audience, thereby ensuring a payoff for ABC Sports in the years to come. In the byliner to the program, Riger explained these benefits: "Television exposure will generate interest in women participating in sports themselves and in watching their sport on television. Star building in the media has enhanced the popularity of men's sports—it has to do the same for women's sports—for both sexes."[52]

In the special, host Dinah Shore emphasized the unique power television had to create sports celebrity. In an interview with Billie Jean King, Shore described television's ability, through compelling technical and emotional production elements, to personalize sports and demonstrate the achievement of the individual athlete. The "enormous close-ups" showed the experience of the "tension and pressure" of the athletic event and made the viewer "realize here's a human being battling for victory but also battling for a large amount of money and for a little niche in history." This presentation meant that a sports event "really takes on tremendous significance it never had before," with enhanced "star quality," which "television has been able to do beautifully." Riger's approach to producing the Colgate

Special was coordinated with what Travis Vogan describes as ABC's investment in moving "sports television's previously narrow aesthetics scope into the realm of cinematic storytelling."[53] In order to differentiate itself from its competitors, ABC Sports privileged production elements that created narratives of triumph over obstacles and cultivated the celebrity status of athletes.

The *Colgate Women's Sports Special* opens with a voice-over by Billie Jean King, in which she advises the viewer to "be sure to stay tuned for this exciting women's sports special," a teaser that offers the anticipatory pleasure of King's presence. Dinah Shore, in direct address to camera, promises viewers a perspective on "great women athletes" and invites them into "a world of exhilaration, excitement, and beauty." This invitation is followed by a montage featuring Princess Anne, King, and gymnast Olga Korbut, along with female athletes racing horses, golfing, bowling, high diving, ice skating, and running relay races. "I Wish I Knew How It Would Feel to Be Free" accompanies the montage. This lengthy introduction emphasizes select dramatic and emotional moments across a range of sports events. An element of Korbut's routine on the uneven bars is captured in slow motion and plays with the lyrics that describe flying "like a bird in the sky," followed by a shot of women in the audience clapping and cheering. The final image of the montage is a freeze-frame on an Olympic hopeful track and field athlete crossing the finish line of a race. This montage establishes women's triumphs across sporting events, highlights women's sports fandom, creates identification for the at-home viewer, and signifies the emotion of iconic moments in women's sports.

After this affective opening sequence, Shore voices over a still shot of King holding aloft the trophy she won at the Battle of the Sexes. With a soundtrack of a cheering crowd playing under her voice-over, Shore describes the match as a "great triumph for women in sports." Shore emphasizes the importance of the event through audience enthusiasm, which she describes as "the cheers of thirty-five thousand spectators in the Astrodome," and the "decisive" nature of King's "victory" over Riggs. During this description, camerawork animates the still shot of King. It starts on a close-up of the trophy and then pans down and widens out to include King's face. These aesthetics memorialize a landmark moment in the still shot and create a dynamic, exciting feeling through camera movement.

The next scene features footage of King's entrance into the Astrodome and underscores the spectacle and gender politics that defined the match. As a rebuttal to Riggs's male chauvinist pig persona, King is carried into the Astrodome on a jeweled and feathered litter carried by shirtless men. Shore introduces the segment as one that highlights King's own experience. "Here's how she remembers it," Shore says. A series of dissolves follows, with images of King's presentation of a pig to Riggs overlapping with one of King's serves. Melding the publicity circus surrounding the match with gameplay reminds viewers of the athleticism King brought to the event. This strategy helps counter criticism that identified the match with, as *Variety* put it, the "Dawning Era of TV's Gimmick Sports."[54] According to detractors, the King-Riggs match reinforced the idea that only a "certain kind of match," rather than the sport of tennis itself, was worthy of television's time and money.[55] By briefly acknowledging the publicity-friendly moments but framing retrospective game analysis through King's experience and images of her performance, Riger's special downplayed the "gimmick" qualities of the match. It underscored the significance of King's win and the value of women's tennis instead. It did so by emphasizing the feminist stakes of the match, the high level of King's investment, and the strategic plays King made to win.

After an introduction to gameplay on the court, King takes over the voice-over and, in keeping with Riger's approach, stresses the emotional stakes of sports and the identification between television viewer and on-screen athlete. King provides a play-by-play of key moments in the match and describes her approach to the match, which depended on fatiguing Riggs quickly and playing a short game. "I have to get this first game. That's all I kept thinking. I have to get this first game," recounts King in voice-over. She adds to this assessment a first-person rejoinder, "Come on, make him move. Make him move." This voice-over provides viewers a subjective experience of the match and access to the athlete's emotional and psychological state. During one volley with Riggs, King talks to herself, much as she would have during the match: "Oh, I'm so nervous. Come on. Get the ball up. Get to the net. Get in there. Hustle. Get in. Get your racket up." Later, King describes Riggs as an opponent in terms of emotion and strategy that matches King's self-assessment. According to King, Riggs was "a little nervous," as evinced by his "really white" face King saw when they changed sides. King's evaluation of Riggs's gameplay draws attention to his strategy for defeating women: "This is the serve he thinks gets every woman. It's a nothin' serve."

The segment on King exemplifies a "perceptive analyses of motivations," a quality that is central to Riger's producing. This technique lets viewers experience sports events they have already seen on television in a different way; this second viewing emphasizes the subjective, emotional, and tactical elements of the athlete's experiences. King's voice-over, for example, gives additional insight into a well-known sports event. It underscores the physical and psychological challenges of the match, punctuates Riggs's sexism, and heightens tensions both players felt as they took this so-called gimmick match very seriously.

By privileging athletes' perspectives, Riger made room for analysis of the structural and cultural aspects of gender discrimination in sports. During a segment on horse racing, jockey Robin Smith acknowledges that female jockeys are typically weaker than male, a physical difference that was used to bar women from the profession. She also asserts that the qualities that make for a good jockey are gender-neutral ones. Once she gets on the horse, she feels both "light" and "strong." Smith's physicality is transformed into a positive asset, a source of personal empowerment and pleasure, and is redefined as a nonissue for her professional capabilities. Rather than physical strength, which carries gendered differences, "it's finesse, it's communication, it's using your head" that wins races. Smith also reconfigures feminized emotional states that mark women as unable to cope in a world dominated by men or physical risk. Smith describes fear, a "spontaneous reaction," as something she experiences when she sees an opportunity to take the lead in a race. She then acts on that emotion to compete. Smith presents herself as an able competitor not through special accommodation or the dilution of the sport but through an instinctive response that could be attributed to either women or men.

The special's segment on marathon running dealt with the exclusion of women in two ways. First, it refuted the importance of women's physical differences from men. Second, it validated feminized cultural norms around competition and training. Until Roberta Gibb ran the Boston Marathon without registering in 1966, major marathons in the US barred women from participating. In 1972, women were finally allowed to participate in the Boston Marathon. When Nina Kuscisk, one of the thirteen women who participated in the New York City Marathon in 1973, appeared on the Colgate Special, she described her motivation to run long distances as "natural," as a challenge to "see how far you could go on your own two feet." Boston marathoner Kathy Switzer also attested to the individual achievement of running and the "satisfaction" of self-sufficiency. Women and men both, in spite of any physical differences, ran against a "universal foe" of distance, weather, and their own limitations.

The only significant differences Kuscisk and Switzer acknowledged between women and men were cultural rather than physical, which sidelined key arguments used to discriminate against women marathoners. In calling attention to women's behaviors, Kuscisk validated them according to a cultural feminist model that, according to Rosemarie Putnam Tong, celebrated the "values and virtues culturally associated with women ('interdependence, community, connection, sharing, emotion, body, trust . . .')."[56] As she trained in Central Park, Kuscisk noted that women ran in groups, "running together and really enjoying it," and checking in with each other on progress and the day's experience. This communal behavior helped transform the masculinist qualities of competition and individualism traditionally associated with sports into a positively feminized experience that defined women as different from but not inferior to men.

STRATEGICALLY SELLING WOMEN'S SPORTS

In a 1968 profile published in Smith College's alumnae newsletter, Riger expressed her preference for certain sports. "Perhaps as women we don't have the feeling for sports men have," she said, "though for some sports I rather think I do. I don't know that I would like to produce a football game, but I find horse racing and tennis just as attractive."[57] Riger's "feeling" for horse racing and tennis rather than football potentially reinforced sexist assumptions about her professional capabilities. Neil Admur, the *New York Times* sports writer who wrote the profile, offset Riger's career success, something that "most men would envy," with conventional notions of her femininity.[58] Admur described Riger as a "vibrant, attractive blonde" and discussed her marriage and children before listing her awards and other career achievements.[59] Situated within this framework, Riger's comment about her preference for certain sports threatened to underscore a polarized world of gender in which a female sports producer would be disinclined or unable to take on a thoroughly masculinized sport such as football. But Riger's positive attitude about horse racing and tennis and uncertainty about football were calculated. By the time she was interviewed by Admur for the *Smith Alumnae Quarterly*, Riger had, in fact, already worked in football. She had produced NFL segments on the *Today Show* in 1961 and served as associate producer for *The Pros*, a "pilot for halftime on NFL Pro Football" on CBS in 1962.[60] After that she would become increasingly involved in football. She worked as a writer-producer-director for ABC's *1968 NCAA Football Highlights*, a fifteen-minute special aired in 1969, and produced regional and national football games on ABC into the late 1970s, thus belying her purported lack of interest in the sport.

Riger clearly did have the capability and inclination to produce football broadcasts, so the "feeling" she had for some other sports expressed genuine personal interest and served as part of a strategic plan for elevating women's sports. Having already worked on productions that garnered a Peabody and two Emmys at the time of the alumnae magazine interview, Riger was a proven authority on what made for good sports television. From this position, she championed horse racing and tennis for their "attractive" qualities, particularly their inclusion of women.[61] According to Riger, the 1972 Summer Olympics in Munich demonstrated that "growing interest in sports participation by women is being reflected in the numbers of women who are sports spectators as well."[62] ABC Research supported this assertion; it found that more than half of the viewers for ABC's prime-time coverage of the 1972 Olympics were women. With this information, Riger focused on Olympic events that "attracted particularly high numbers of women viewers"—gymnastics, volleyball, track and field, canoeing, crew, and equestrian disciplines—as the basis for her Colgate Special.[63]

Equestrian competition proved particularly interesting to Riger, primarily because of its rare lack of gendered handicaps for women athletes. As Riger wrote in her proposal for a prime-time Colgate-Palmolive sponsored special, it was "one of the few sports where men and women can compete with each other on an equal basis."[64] Because of this unique value, Riger fought for increased budgets and high-impact productions for it. In planning for the World Show Jumping Championship on August 16–20, 1978, held in Aachen, West Germany, Riger presented Dennis Lewin, coordinating producer for *Wide World of Sports*, with a plan for a "meaningful film supplement" for the event.[65] With "electronic coverage" that was "all pretty much high and wide," Riger proposed that ABC provide her with a film crew to "supplement" this unimaginative existing footage.[66] Riger emphasized the importance of the Championship to help justify her request. Aachen was not only the "most prestigious and most famous show in the world" but an unprecedented moment for gender neutrality in sports. As Riger emphatically wrote in her treatment of the championship for ABC, "THIS IS THE FIRST TIME THAT MEN AND WOMEN HAVE JUMPED TOGETHER. PREVIOUSLY THERE WERE SEPARATE CHAMPIONSHIPS."[67]

For all her ambitious plans, Riger was also a pragmatist who suggested economical solutions to achieve her vision. She acknowledged that ABC would want to keep costs down and attempted to assuage their concerns about the expense of the supplemental material she suggested for Aachen coverage. Rather than shooting sync, Riger planned to record voice-overs from the riders with a Nagra recorder. She also budgeted for the sound equipment as a rental to avoid customs and transportation fees involved in using an ABC-owned recording device. With the goal of giving the coverage "more meaning" and with the likelihood of the American team and individual riders winning gold medals, Riger argued for the need to produce a nuanced and carefully considered segment on the event, or "added dimension" rather than "run-of-the-mill supplementation." Riger's proposal for this "high speed signature piece" reflected the approach she would repeatedly call on to advance women's televised sports. Through carefully considered aesthetics, Riger created "spectacular pieces" that highlighted women's athleticism and the excitement of their sport.[68]

WORKPLACE SEXISM IN SPORTS TV

From the very start of her career as a production assistant in 1957, Riger recognized that the television industry valued women for their willingness to work hard. Riger was hired for her first television job at *The Open Mind* (PBS, 1956–) because of her high grades. In Riger's opinion her academic achievements were not a mark of her intelligence but instead an indication of "a reputation for hard work." The demands of that first job prepared Riger for gendered double standards of television production work. Riger learned that when working in "any job above the secretarial level women have had to prove themselves in a way a young male college graduate entering business has never had to do." Although keenly aware of the unfair burden placed on women in the workplace, Riger used women's compensatory work ethic to promote their superior value. She noted that she personally preferred employing women to work with her because they "worked much harder and with greater conscientiousness and initiative than the average man."[69] While potentially exploitative of women's insecure position in a sexist workplace, Riger's attitude also helped demonstrate women's capabilities and made visible unjust workplace conditions for women.

The difficulties Riger encountered in television production were magnified by working in sports. As the formation of a Women's Action Committee at ABC in 1972 demonstrates, the network was not inclined to acknowledge the needs of its female employees or to reform sexist practices without a watchdog group. As discussed in chapter 1, NBC women formed the first of three women's groups that sprang up at each network's headquarters in the early 1970s. The Women's Action Committee comprised women employees who represented women's concerns to management and instituted an affirmative action program, sensitivity training, and a Grievance Committee. They also programmed lectures that addressed "interests of interest to all ABC women," such as the ERA, gender discrimination in language, assertiveness training, and legal advice on workplace discrimination. In its January 1976 newsletter, the Committee awarded the sports department one of its "brickbats" for its "continued locker room morality" and called out an unnamed ABC executive who "expect[ed] his secretary to take care of his dirty squash clothes."[70] Whether manifesting in the working environment of the department or the leisure activities of powerful male employees, sports television contributed to a hostile and belittling workplace for women at ABC. Perhaps no one working in television knew the propensity for sexism in television sports better than Riger. According to Riger, "Television was mostly a man's business," and the "locker room rationale" (the argument that all-male enclaves were unsuitable for women) made careers in sports television particularly difficult for women.[71]

While Riger achieved success at ABC Sports, as evinced by the numerous Emmy wins for her work as producer there, she encountered obstacles to career advancement. She experienced behaviors on the part of her bosses and network executives that she regarded as workplace discrimination. By 1976, she sought legal representation in anticipation of negotiating a new contract with ABC. She supplied her legal counsel with documentation of her "constant struggle to get more assignments and more live assignments."[72] She tracked decisions and kept records of various moments in training and job assignments denied her. In a file she labeled "ABC Sports—Historic Discrimination," Riger kept dozens of memos she had written to executives at various levels in the sports department— including John Martin, vice president, Roone Arledge, president, and Chuck Howard, vice president of production—asking for more producing experience that would expand her skill set. These requests started as early as 1975 and carried through into the 1980s and the end of Riger's career in television.

Riger made the sexist practices of television public in 1977 when she recounted her experiences at ABC in Judy Fireman's *TV Book: The Ultimate Television Book*. In "Women in TV Sports," Riger's contribution to the edited collection, Riger contrasted the experience she had in films and pretaped shows with the relative lack of experience she had in other forms of production. ABC's reluctance to assign her live broadcasts made Riger "suspect that uncertainty about whether a woman is up to the pressures of the live telecast" motivated decisions to prevent her from

FIGURE 9. Eleanor Sanger Riger's file folder that held evidence of discrimination she faced in her job as producer at ABC Sports (Eleanor Sanger Papers, Sophia Smith Collection of Women's History, Smith College, SSC-MS-00286)

producing such events.[73] This prejudicial assessment kept Riger from developing women's sports as she wished and prevented her from highly valued opportunities to produce live events.

Riger's frustrations centered on a general unwillingness of ABC Sports executives to grant her on-the-job experience that would position her to take on increased, improved, and varied assignments. In addition to assumptions about a woman's capabilities to deal with high-pressure broadcasts, ABC cited Riger's inexperience when rejecting her requests to produce particular events. This alleged inexperience was something that ABC created, perpetuated, and used to justify denying Riger opportunities and experience, thereby creating a self-perpetuating cycle. Riger kept logs of her producing credits versus those of other producers and retained handwritten notes made on memos from her bosses at ABC that indicated stalling tactics and outright rejection of her requests for work. These documents corroborated Riger's claims about the disparity between her opportunities and those afforded her male coworkers and the network's consistent practice of confining her to lesser productions.

In one of the earliest memos kept on file, written in November 1975, Riger asked Chuck Howard, VP of programming for ABC Sports, for the opportunity to build her proficiency in live broadcasts in anticipation of the 1976 World Series of Women's Tennis. Riger had already been passed over as a producer of the US Women's Open golf tournament in July 1975. Given that women's sports were the "logical place" where she should work, Riger was troubled that she had missed out on such a high-profile event and felt it had cost her an opportunity for professional growth. Women's golf tournaments in the mid-1970s were scarce and, as "the most difficult of live shows to produce," would have been an invaluable experience for Riger as a producer. Riger presented the upcoming tennis series as compensation for missing this earlier opportunity and pitched her involvement as vital, since tennis was "the most likely women's sport to get increased production." Well aware of ABC's prioritization of women's sports at this time, Riger called upon her mandate as the woman who was hired to help ABC expand and improve its coverage of women's sports. She assured Howard that if she were given the chance to produce the World Series of Women's Tennis, then when ABC Sports covered "more women's events live," Riger would "be prepared to work on them."[74]

In early 1976, Riger continued to push for inclusion in live event production through her proficiency in women's sports coverage. Fresh from an Emmy win for her role in ABC's coverage of the Winter Olympics in Innsbruck, Riger wrote to request that she be just as involved in the 1976 Montreal Summer Olympics. But this time she would focus on women's rowing, basketball, volleyball, equestrian, gymnastics, swimming, and track. Riger felt she could bring "a certain amount of expertise to the women's events" and that her "talents would be better utilized" in these live events than "in the film unit exclusively."[75] In August of the same year, Riger again utilized a strategy of calling upon a recent triumph to ask for a better assignment. She reminded Roone Arledge, president of ABC Sports, about the significance of the Colgate Special, which was "good to do and made a necessary contribution."[76] With Colgate "having done their bit on that," Riger hypothesized that "the future lies in live reportage of events."[77] She wanted to produce segments on women's sports, but major coverage would not happen "until 1984," presumably in conjunction with the Olympics. In the meantime, Riger asked to be assigned to regional college football games and track and swim meets. She reinforced this request in another memo a few days later to Howard, in which she expressed her interest in producing live football broadcasts and mentioned multiple attempts to broach the topic with Arledge and others.

By November 8, 1976, Riger had renewed requests to work on live football events. When asking to produce the Harvard-Yale game, Riger called on personal connections to Harvard. The retiring athletic director was a friend of hers, her son was applying to Harvard in the next year, and her family had long-standing ties to the school. In a memo to Chuck Howard, Riger explained that the experience "would be sort of a nice relationship since my father was class of '15, and four great-grandfathers etc. going back to Zedichiah Sanger, Class of 1771," had attended Harvard.[78] Validating her interest in and abilities to produce the Harvard-Yale game through patriarchal lineage was a necessity. Riger had not attended Harvard and did not personally possess insider knowledge that would enrich the production. She did, however, strategically deploy this disadvantage. She reminded Howard that if she had wanted to attend school in her hometown of Cambridge, Massachusetts, Radcliffe would have been her only option. Harvard did not admit women at that time. By calling on her past experiences with institutionalized sexism and loss of opportunity, Riger implicitly, but none-too-subtly, called out the same problems she faced at ABC.

Despite Riger's persistence and multiple rhetorical strategies, her requests to work on live production were repeatedly rejected. In a December 1976 petition to produce the Colgate Triple Crown, Riger again called upon her previous association with Colgate as her qualification to continue working on their sponsored events. Howard wrote back to inform Riger that he was planning to produce it. For the 1977 *Women's Superstars*, a special rematch from an earlier *Battle of the Network Stars* program, Riger asked to be involved in order to "improve."[79] Dennis Lewin, coordinating producer, responded by informing Riger that, after discussing "various possibilities," Roone Arledge "wanted to see [producer/director] Doug Wilson do it."[80] Rather than being deterred by these rejections, Riger continued to ask to work on live broadcasts as well as on tape in 1977. Throughout the year she wrote memos that asked her bosses to assign her to a number of live events, including the Kentucky Derby and Preakness, baseball regionals, NCAA Football, and the Pro Bowler's Tour.[81]

By March 28, 1978, the situation had not improved, and Riger expressed her frustration to Arledge about the upcoming production schedule. With no live shows assigned to her for three months, she was concerned that the quality of some of her recent producing efforts was being used against her. Riger challenged perceptions about her shortcomings as a producer; she described a lack of support provided to her by others (namely men) on the production team and rushed production timelines. A recent National Figure Skating Show, which Arledge had found "choppy without enough transition," was compromised by flawed supervision of the project: she had received "little guidance" from Lewin and had been erroneously told that she could fix problems in postproduction with a larger window of time than she was granted. The production values of the show were further compromised by the "experimental direction" of director Terry Jastro.[82]

This correspondence marked a turning point in Riger's career and her attitude toward her job. Rather than accept blame, Riger pointed out the disappointing efforts of others working on the production and the challenging circumstances of producing over which she had no control. She asked for better support staff that would allow her to "do as good a job" on live events as "any of the Associate Producers who have been given the chance."[83] She also asked "to be brought along with a reasonable amount of help to develop a strength in doing live shows," a request that marked a new approach in Riger's appeals to management. Whereas Riger had previously called upon her own strength and successes in previous productions, in this communication with Arledge she began to identify external forces that impeded the type and quality of work she wanted to undertake.

Riger took a proactive stance to address her lack of experience. In early 1978, she offered to take on bowling and other lower-prestige programming in preparation for higher-level productions but was informed by John Martin, vice president of ABC Sports, that she "was too 'good'" for such assignments. When she was kept off the production schedule, she cited Martin's objection and sardonically commented, "I guess I'm too good to work for three months."[84] Riger also bypassed her usual channels of communication at the producer level and voiced her concerns to higher-level members of the executive ranks. In January of 1978, Riger wrote directly to Martin to provide him with evidence of being refused production experience. She enclosed with her correspondence the memos she had previously written to Arledge, Howard, and others about her "interest in becoming a more productive and valuable producer at ABC sports." While she felt "fortunate" to be assigned to three football regionals in fall of 1978, this opportunity was the exception to the rule. She recounted the "discouraging" responses she had to other requests and the lack of response to other memos. She also expressed how "anxious" she was to talk to Martin, along with the management at ABC Sports, "about the chance to do more live shows and more responsible *Wide World* [*of Sports*] shows."[85]

Involving Martin seemed to improve Riger's opportunities in producing live and electronic productions, yet when Riger continued to campaign for opportunities she was met with rejection at best and hostility at most. In a memo to Martin on August 6, 1979, Riger voiced her appreciation for being assigned to produce the Women's and Men's Gymnastics Trial, the Prescott Rodeo, and the Lumberjacks and Firemen's competitions and asked to do the same for surfing shows based in Hawaii. Riger used what had become by this time her strategy: approaching multiple executives at different levels of power within the sports department. She informed Martin that she had asked Howard and others if she could produce the surfing shows and asked for Martin's "consideration and help in this matter as well." Martin wrote in response, "Don't get greedy now!"[86]

CULTIVATING WOMEN ATHLETES AS SPORTS COMMENTATORS

Although many of Riger's career ambitions were thwarted, she tirelessly championed other women and created a mentoring workplace, particularly for on-air talent. She saw her training and support of commentators as a major contribution to ABC and emphasized it as one of her "assets" when she communicated her worth to her bosses at the network. When writing to Martin in 1978 in an exchange of memos concerning the stagnation of her career, Riger argued that she "work[ed] well with talent and [took] great pains and effort to help color people and announcers." She backed up these assertions with a long list of color commentators—including high-profile talent Al Michaels and Frank Gifford, female commentators Cathy Rigby and Andrea Kirby, and male athletes-turned-commentators Ron Johnson, Mark Spitz, and Verne Lundquist—who would attest to her skill and dedication to talent development.[87]

If ABC understood the value of "expanded programming" because of viewer interest and commercial investments, Riger argued, they should regard the development of women in production as equally important. Women athletes should be hired and trained as play-by-play announcers and color commentators, as their expertise and "point of view" would "add to the excitement of the telecast."[88] Play-by-play announcers "describe the pertinent action" of the game "without delving too far into minutiae," while color commentators offer analysis based on their own experience in sports and create narrative arcs, often with emotional elements, for gameplay.[89] In supplementing the technical aspects of play-by-play announcing, color commentators help attract viewership, elevate viewer enjoyment, and provide a sense of "quality" and "enhanced entertainment value."[90] Both are vital to the success of televised sports, and Riger felt women could fulfill both roles.

When proposing retrospective highlights of the Olympics to be aired in December 1975, Riger approached both Bruce Jenner (Caitlyn Jenner, who was then known as Bruce and publicly presented as male) and Dorothy Hamill as on-air talent who would speak to the Olympic experience even before she approached ABC with the details of her production plans. When she did propose commentating teams to the network, she suggested that if Hamill was not available speed skating champion Sheila Young could be the next person to consider for the job. Thus Riger built into her proposal a (presumed) male and female pairing of the commentators and alternate plans for the female (but not male) commentator. This extra care preserved the gender balance in on-air talent and testifies to Riger's priorities: creating space for women in sports broadcasting and naturalizing their presence there. When Riger promoted women for commentator jobs, she was not just providing them with important career opportunities, she was also shaping representations of women athletes. The language of commentary on televised sports is steeped in ideological assumptions about gender and race and "tends to weave a taken-for granted superordinate, adult masculine status around male athletes. Typically women are "linguistically infantilized and framed ambivalently" according to physicality and traits (e.g., aggression that makes them good athletes but atypically gendered women) and fall at the bottom of the "hierarchy of naming" (e.g., are called by their first rather than last names and are referred to as "girls" rather than women).[91] More women commentators, even when paired with men, promised to correct those issues.

Riger converted the profitability of women's sports into opportunities for women to work in television in positions previously considered unsuitable for them. She fought for Olympic gymnast Cathy Rigby as a color commentator and argued for Rigby's potential in spite of criticism about her on-camera persona and delivery. As she did in many cases of athletes who were working on television for the first time, Riger volunteered to undertake Rigby's training. She had briefly assumed responsibility for the task when Rigby worked as a commentator on a gymnastics event in Moscow. Riger felt that Rigby did "very well on her on-camera pieces" and was careful to explain any flaws in Rigby's performance. The production context was a challenging one: a "horrendous editing fiasco" caused an eight-hour delay in the voice-over, which started at 11:30 p.m. and ended at 3:00 a.m.[92] Considering the circumstances, Riger felt Rigby had performed well.

Riger also addressed the volume and pitch of Rigby's voice. She noted the differences in male and female voices but minimized concerns about the "difficult contrast" created "with a male announcer off camera." When Rigby appeared with a male cohost on camera, Riger told Chuck Howard that "the softness of her voice is not so jarring in contrast with the male voice."[93] Riger's assurances about the quality of women's voices for broadcasting address long-standing anxieties about women and sound technologies. As numerous feminist media scholars demonstrate, women's voices have been scrutinized and deemed unsuitable for various sound technologies, from phonographs, radio, and telephones to film and television.[94] Amy Lawrence's historical overview of sound-based media notes that "woman's place has been an issue argued in marketing reports, hiring practices, advertising strategies, in sound studios and in programming. And her 'place' in sound media is measured by the presence of her voice."[95] In a 1975 *LA Times* article that focused on the growing numbers of women in sports radio and television, Roone Arledge acknowledged that the "sound of women's voices" was one of the many "prejudices" facing them in sportscasting.[96] Under Arledge's leadership, ABC had invested in Billie Jean King with the hopes that she would make an "excellent" commentator. According to Arledge's criteria, King possessed knowledge that enriched play-by-play analysis as well as "a certain kind of voice, a heavy voice" that would "cut through crowd noise" and overcome "technical problems" of live broadcasting.[97]

When advocating for women to join the ranks of ABC Sports, Riger called upon known signifiers of "excellent" production work while identifying additional qualities that were specific to her own experience and priorities as a woman in a male-dominated industry. In her first year as producer at ABC, Riger pushed to hire swimmer Donna de Varona as the "first woman commentator under contract to a TV Network for regular work on television sports." Her memo to Arledge underscored the value in the forward-thinking hire, with a subject line "ABC's First Staff Woman Commentator" and language that reinforced the payoff for ABC. Riger used her own hire as a "first" and the subsequent publicity it brought to the network as incentive for them to hire the "FIRST regular [female] commentator." Just as she had done with King's hire, Riger called on future demand and the possible loss ABC would experience if they were not the frontrunners in all areas of women's sports. She emphatically predicted the "expansion of programming in women's sports," which she saw evidence for in "clients' interest, magazine coverage, public response." With this guaranteed future in women's sports, Riger painted a troubled future for the network if it lost a vital worker who could assist in their success in a competitive marketplace: "WE MUST STAY AHEAD! CBS is trying to make up ground and they already used Donna and are making noises about more work for her. We should really put her under exclusive contract or we will lose her."[98]

Riger's comment positioned de Varona as a symbol of ABC's progressiveness and as a sought-after worker with strong qualifications for the job, all of which challenged assumptions of women's unsuitability for sports announcing. Riger took care to stress de Varona's professional capabilities. Her "talent and experience," evinced in local broadcasts and talk show interviews, and her knowledge of sports, including and beyond swimming, made her capable of commentating on a variety of events. Riger also credited de Varona with affective and interpersonal skills that were less typical qualifications for the job and instead were used to disqualify women from commentating. As someone who "knows and is liked by her athlete peers," de Varona possessed qualities typically associated with women and femininity—likability and cooperation—which Riger identified as assets for the job.[99]

RIGER'S LEGACY, OR DOES IT MATTER IF A WOMAN WORKS IN SPORTS TELEVISION?

Unlike the legacy of her on-air contemporary Billie Jean King, Riger's contribution to women's sports on television is not an obvious one, in part because of the relative invisibility of production staff versus a sports celebrity and in part because of the lack of opportunities Riger experienced at ABC Sports. Even as Riger advocated for women in sports television, she met obstacles in her own career aspirations to the point that, in the late 1970s, she publicly aired ABC's discriminatory practices and took legal action. After that, she continued to produce for ABC, most notably segments for the 1980 and 1984 Olympics. In 1985, Riger shifted to part-time employment at the network, where she continued to produce high-profile events like the 1988 Summer Olympics but increasingly focused on lower-budget productions in cable television.

As her producing career shifted to cable, Riger continued to champion female talent in sports television. While she had worked in prestigious network programming, Riger felt that women's programming in cable offered an opportunity "for entertaining as well as enlightening women."[100] She worked on *Basic Fitness with Diana Nyad*, a ten-minute exercise segment for *Daytime* (1982–84), a four-hour programming block for women on cable television that, through a series of mergers, would become Lifetime Television Network in 1984. Riger was committed to the value of cable television for women and proposed, in 1982, "future programming" featuring Nyad.[101] In 1985, Riger continued to work in exercise programs with women at the center, producing *ABC Funfit* (1985–86), hosted by Olympic gymnast host Mary Lou Retton. She suggested ABC-Hearst hire Kaoru Nakamuru, the "Barbara Walters of Japan," as someone who should become part of *Daytime* and arranged for videotapes of Nakamuru's show in Japan to be viewed by the head of programming.[102] In 1983 she wrote to James Spence, the senior vice president of sports at ABC, to express how "impressed" she was in his interest in "developing female talent" and his "perceptive way of going about it" and recommended a "serious training program for new and also most current talent" that she would supervise.[103] In 1984, Riger also put herself forward as someone who could develop European programming for ESPN.[104] While few of her plans came to fruition, Riger continued, to the end of her career, to identify areas of growth for women's sports on television and paired her own ambitions with those of other women who wanted to break into sports television.

In addition to her influence on sports television, Riger's legacy was one of making visible the gender-specific circumstances women had to deal with across professions. In 1981, Riger joined the board of directors for the Wonder Woman Foundation, an organization that awarded grants to women over the age of forty so they could pursue their occupational goals. The organization's recognition that women's careers were frequently delayed because of marriage and child-rearing resonated with Riger's own experiences. She knew that her time away from production in the late 1960s had put her behind her male contemporaries when she was hired as a producer by ABC in 1973. In a 1977 letter to Roone Arledge, Riger described the disadvantages she faced with the gap in her career at ABC: "Unfortunately the years I missed were those years of training in live production which production assistants and associate producers received at ABC Sports. I have observed how associate producers like Terry O'Neil, Terry Jastrow, Bob Goodrich, etc. have been brought along by this route. I hope I can still be allowed to catch up."[105] By 1979, Riger negotiated for better pay, realizing that she did not have "that many more maximum earning years."[106] In addition to the professional development she had less time to experience, Riger's shortened wage-earning lifetime was something she felt keenly.

Last, and not least, Riger offers instructive lessons about unprecedented television careers for women. With the sexism endemic to sports television and the feminist activist pressure that brought about her position, Riger was often treated as a token hire at ABC. Despite this constraint, Riger influenced the aesthetics of sports programs, proved an important advocate for female talent, and served as a meaningful mentor to women working in sports television. Riger did not just pressure ABC to make room for women within the traditions of sports television, she sought to alter the terms of these traditions. She challenged what defined a viable worker, a marketable athlete, and a ratings-winning broadcast in sports television. She used ABC's investment, regardless of motivation, in her pioneering role to argue that in order to succeed in a competitive new era of sports television, the network needed to value women as viewers, the subject of programming, and workers in the industry.

3

Working in the Lear Factory

Ann Marcus, Virginia Carter, and the Women of Tandem Productions

When television writer Ann Marcus proposed writing a memoir about her time working on *Mary Hartman, Mary Hartman*, she described the project as "the very subjective—but funny (and sometimes painful) story of my experiences as the co-creator and head writer of America's most talked-about television show." To illustrate what she had in mind, Marcus recalled a lengthy description of the pressures she faced in resolving the numerous cliffhangers left at the end of the first season. She set up an appointment with Norman Lear, the show's producer and head of Tandem/TAT Productions, to discuss her concerns about starting the second season. She wrote about her exchange with Lear as follows:

> "Norman," I said, "we're in terrible trouble. The hiatus is almost over. Production is going to start up in two weeks and we haven't decided whether the bullet ricocheted off Merle's belt buckle and shoots Charlie's ball off or not!" "Annie," said Norman, pinching my cheeks, "there are six hundred million Chinamen [*sic*] who have never even heard of MARY HARTMAN." What he was telling me was that the world would survive whether the second season of MARY HARTMAN started or not and that was all well and good, but there were times during the first season of MARY HARTMAN when I damned well didn't think *I* would survive.[1]

Marcus's anecdote underscores the offbeat qualities for which *Mary Hartman* was famous, as well as the intensive demands of managing the program's complex story world. It also reveals that, even though Lear is credited for the innovative output for which Tandem was known, women like Marcus were central in cultivating and sustaining the company's signature style.

While Ann Marcus was working on the second season of *Mary Hartman*, another writer, Paddy Chayefsky, was pondering the state of television. With the release of *Network* in 1976, for which he wrote the screenplay, Chayefsky expressed, both in his script and in publicity for the film, concerns about the growing alienation of the professional and creative classes. Rather than finding satisfaction in work itself, people had "become involved in the product of the work" and gauged the value of their output through its profitability. To Chayefsky, the television industry exemplified the worst of this phenomenon. In its unrelenting drive to create simply "another merchandising situation," television created intense anxiety in its workers and drove them to the place where they would "kill for ratings."[2]

At this point in his career, Chayefsky had a long-standing relationship with television, starting with his work in early live dramas. In 1957, Chayefsky, heralded as "America's leading television playwright," characterized the conditions of television work as fulfilling. "I enjoy writing for television a good deal for personal reasons," said Chayefsky, who praised his employer, *The Philco-Goodyear Playhouse* (NBC, 1951–57), for allowing him to "write as well as I care to." Unlike the stage, which proved "too weighty," and film, which proved "too intense," television was the perfect medium for Chayefsky to deal with "mundane problems and all their obscured ramifications" and to "dispose our new insights into ourselves."[3]

By the 1970s, Chayefsky's estimation of television had changed. In 1973, he tried to sell to NBC a show about the "contemporary thing," of "people whose work is so damned dull, so unrewarding, that it becomes a major trauma in their lives." The network passed on the project. Their decision, in Chayefsky's estimation, signaled how restrictive television had become since its halcyon days. Television's drive for profitability made it a medium that dared not deliver meaningful content to its viewers. Therefore, it was doubly flawed: because of profit motives, it created "damned dull" and "unrewarding" conditions for its own workers, and because of these same motives it would not air content that realistically represented the problems of labor experienced by viewers.[4] When asked who could be an antidote for the industry's problems, Chayefsky named Norman Lear.[5] Yet for all of Lear's visionary creativity and boldness, Chayefsky predicted that Lear would ultimately be corrupted by television once he had to chase ratings. Chayefsky believed that male creatives suffered in their exposure to a corrupted television industry, a notion that informed his failed television project and *Network*, the film it would eventually become.

Marcus's and Chayefsky's differing accounts about television and the conditions of its making illustrate larger issues that emerged in the television industry during the 1970s. Chayefsky hails Lear as the savior of the industry and laments the downfall of male ingenuity and integrity that comes with a new type of television. In contrast, Marcus's involvement in an innovative program challenges ideas about Lear's single-handed influence over television. Marcus also underscores the difficult labor of crafting the complex television that Chayefsky decided was the antidote to mindless, ratings-driven television. Yet this content was unapologetically melodramatic, serialized, and sourced in soap opera conventions, all of which bore marks of the popular, a supposed threat to the integrity of television and male creatives. If indeed television produced at Tandem saved the industry, then women's culture, knowledge, stories, and energies played a crucial part in that salvation. By recentering women who were occluded in the many assessments of Lear's genius, this chapter provides a richer, more precise history of "relevant" television of the 1970s and challenges opinions that hold the influence of women and feminized television genres responsible for television's downfall.

MARY HARTMAN UNSETTLES TELEVISION

Tandem Productions functioned as one of the most politically aware and successful independent production companies in the 1970s. The company challenged fundamental ideas of how the television industry worked, which audiences mattered and what would appeal to them, and who should be responsible for creating television content. Its programs, including *All in the Family* (CBS, 1971–79), *Maude* (CBS, 1972–78), *Sanford and Son* (NBC, 1972–77), and *Good Times* (CBS, 1974–79), "tend toward legendary status," as they ushered in "all manner of controversial subjects to prime-time entertainment television."[6] Airing Tandem's shows helped CBS achieve a desired "turn to relevance," a commonly accepted narrative about television's interest in programming that, in Todd Gitlin's description, skewed "young, urban, and more 'realistic.'"[7]

Tandem was famous for contending with hot-button issues of race articulated through aesthetic and narrative realism. This topic matter and style, as Kirsten Marthe Lentz notes, stood in contrast to the gender concerns and "quality" style of MTM Enterprises, the other leading independent production company of the era, who was responsible for *The Mary Tyler Moore Show* (CBS, 1970–77).[8] Although it was not known for exploring gender in the way that MTM was, Tandem nonetheless was concerned with changing gender norms. Women who worked at Tandem played important roles in expressing those concerns. They used their political awareness, skills developed in genre-specific productions of "women's television," and knowledge of women's experiences to enrich the company's "relevance." They also shaped the company's political awareness and its production cultures according to feminist priorities. Their contributions therefore broaden Tandem's cultural impact beyond questions of race and reorient focus from Lear as an individual, visionary auteur wholly responsible for Tandem's output.

Arguably, no Tandem program demonstrates the centrality of women both in subject matter and in its production more than *Mary Hartman, Mary Hartman*. The show featured Mary Hartman, a housewife who lived in Fernwood, Ohio, amid a bizarre set of sexual, economic, and psychological circumstances. It employed the melodramatic conventions of daytime soap operas but magnified the tone and content of the genre to politicized effect. Mary's obsessive investment in her home and her inability to distinguish between the fictions presented to her on television and the real world around her expressed the psychological state of women who felt trapped in the role of wife, mother, and homemaker. The program not only critiqued the capitalist underpinnings of domesticity—from women's unpaid labor in the home to the unrelenting consumerist address to women—but did so through storylines that were considered taboo by television.

The story of a discontented, disturbed housewife facing problems that ranged from waxy yellow buildup on the kitchen floor to serial killers to her husband's erectile dysfunction made selling the program in conventional ways difficult. Lear's success in getting *Mary Hartman* to air bolstered his reputation as a change-maker and enabled him to challenge network television's core business practices, narrow scope of representation, and unassailable programming power. After failing repeatedly to sell *Mary Hartman* to the networks, Lear invited independent station owners to his house for an evening meal and then passionately pitched the show. As the story goes, one brave station owner stood up, moved by the power of Lear's plea and the promise of the show, and pledged his support by buying a twelve-program contract. The rest of the crowd quickly followed suit. Lear's strategy for launching *Mary Hartman* prompted reports that Lear would deliver a "blow" to the networks and would have a "revolutionary impact on the way the TV industry works."[9] Lear's strategy bypassed the networks, who were cast as a paternalistic force similar to the ones that constrained Mary herself. With their nearly monopolistic control over programming and their "play-it-safe approach," the networks dictated what America "sees—and doesn't see" and kept viewers from experiencing challenging and controversial content.[10] Lear, along with the Writers Guild, Directors Guild, Screen Actors Guild, and other producers and production companies, had already brought a $10 million lawsuit against the networks' "Family Viewing Hour," a 1975 amendment to the National Association of Broadcasters' Television Code that restricted "programming unsuitable for the entire family" from airing between 7:00 and 9:00 p.m.[11]

Once it was on the air, *Mary Hartman* successfully competed with television news. The program offered audiences melodramatic but nonetheless newsworthy material as well as a forthrightness that, to many, conventional newscasting lacked. It ran opposite the eleven o'clock news in many markets and, according to Elizabeth Ewen and Stuart Ewen, encouraged people to relinquish their "well-groomed compulsion for the late news" and its "paternalism" embodied in "authoritative figures" like Walter Cronkite, David Brinkley, and Harry Reasoner. Credited with "doing toe-to-toe combat" with Cronkite, "the father authority of the late-night news," *Mary Hartman* used its hyperbolic news reports to comment on the absurdity of gender norms and sexual mores, the seductions of commercial culture, and television's relationship to capitalism, something that network news failed to deliver to viewers.[12]

Mary Hartman drew viewers away from the late-night news and "occasionally outrate[d] at least one of the competing news shows" in the all-important urban areas of New York, Chicago, and Los Angeles.[13] In an effort to compete, a Los Angeles station developed its own "news spoof" program, *MetroNews MetroNews*, a "bizarre half-hour of soft-core items about nudity, prostitution and vasecto- mies."[14] With such an effect, *Mary Hartman* was cause for concern for the main- stream news establishment. In a *60 Minutes* interview, Mike Wallace told Louise Lasser that the show was "driving news broadcasts off the air," to which Lasser blithely responded, "I know, isn't it wonderful?"[15] In a climate of growing skepti- cism about cultural institutions and detached patriarchal figures, the dramatic and affective expressions of *Mary Hartman* provided an important alternative to the traditions of network television news.

Controversial topics were the hallmark of *Mary Hartman*, which earned it both plaudits and criticism. Although television already dealt in sex and violence, par- ticularly in daytime soaps and local news, *Mary Hartman*'s scheduling and tone differentiated it from these programs. *Vogue* argued that, unlike its daytime coun- terpart, the "hip" nighttime soap was "different" because of its "stylized" reality, which made it "more real than realism, more like life."[16] Others were not as ame- nable to the program's frank sexuality. When a Cleveland station programmed *Mary Hartman* at 7:30 p.m., protests threatened to take the program off the air. The city was positioned in the top-ten Nielsen market, and the station was a CBS affiliate, so Lear took action. He met, via satellite, with a panel constituted of a city council member, a member of the clergy, a television critic from the *Cleveland Plain Dealer*, a member of a citizens' group, and the head of an area PTA. He defended the early evening scheduling of the program by characterizing the objec- tionable content of *Mary Hartman* as relatively tame compared to its competition, the five o'clock and six o'clock news. Lear argued, "If your news is like our news in Los Angeles and other news shows around the country—local news especially—it starts with any homicide that happens to be in the news, any rape, any fire, arson, any kind of violence you can manage." The PTA member responded by saying, "That's not as real as Mary Hartman." Lear recalls his "stunned" reaction to this assessment: "She didn't feel that all that news, as violent as it was, was as real as two women in bed for a moment on Mary Hartman."[17]

In a 1976 issue of *Socialist Revolution*, Barbara Ehrenreich noted the politi- cal impact of *Mary Hartman*'s story structure. "We jolt from Mary musing about death to brisk homemakers competing in a paper towel wet-strength contest," she wrote. "The contradiction is overpowering. Maybe the Waltons can sell gra- nola, or Mary Tyler Moore can sell pantyhose, but how can Mary Hartman sell *anything?*"[18] In its fractured and multiple storylines and characters, *Mary Hart- man* deployed the narrative strategies of soap operas that enculturated women as domestic consumer-laborers in order to comment on these conditions.[19] As it moved serialized melodrama from a daytime schedule and the associated view- ership of those who labored inside the home, *Mary Hartman* attracted an audi- ence that included women who worked outside the home. *Ms.* writer Stephanie

FIGURE 10. *Ms.* authorizes feminist identification with *Mary Hartman, Mary Hartman* on its May 1976 cover. (Photofest)

Harrington argued that the melodramatic terms of the soap opera always held appeal to a broader audience and were "not peculiar to an innately feminine sentimentality."[20] Rather, *Mary Hartman* viewers may have always been attracted to soap operas but "all weren't home at the right time for the daily sudsing."[21] *Mary Hartman* challenged prevailing ideas about television audiences and dayparting, or the organization of programs according to the time of day in a broadcaster's schedule. The show's success revealed that the television industry's assumptions about who watched what and why formulated and constrained, rather than reflected, audience identification and pleasures.

The long-dismissed genre of the soap opera, rearticulated in *Mary Hartman*, appealed to sought-after viewers across gender, regional, and class demographics. The show assured stations of a "rabid cult following among the trendy" across the nation and, in particular, the most desirable from "Manhattan high-rises to the Hollywood hills."[22] *Ms.* reported that, "on the authority of an international representative of the United Auto Workers," when *Mary Hartman* began airing, "the hottest topics of conversation among the men on the assembly line were Daniel Patrick Moynihan and 'Mary Hartman.'"[23] San Francisco's Commission on the Status and Rights of Women adjourned its meetings by 10:30 p.m. so as not to conflict with the program's 11:00 p.m. airtime. Viewer mail to local stations confirmed the show's outreach to women who were alienated from television's conventional representations of gender. "I've never been able to sit through a soap opera before," asserted one woman, "and I've never written to any TV station, but your show is the BEST show of any kind I've seen made for TV in years! Keep up the great scripts."[24] "This is my first letter to a t.v. station," wrote another, "but I had to write to let you know how much I enjoy Mary Hartman. I'm an Oakland school teacher, a 33-year-old single woman and I spend every evening watching MH MH before I go to sleep. My friends all do the same. It's a great show. I am involved in the women's movement and theater and from that point of view I want to say 'right on!'"[25] A woman who watched every night with her husband declared, "I don't follow any of the daytime serials, but I have become addicted to Mary Hartman."[26] "I have never watched daytime TV from 9:00 a.m. to 6:30 even though I am home all day," another woman wrote. "I can't stand either soap operas or games shows. Then last week I found Mary Hartman, Mary Hartman. *I* think it is a soap opera spoof and the funniest thing I've ever seen."[27]

WOMEN AS THE "DRUNKEN LENS MAKERS" OF *MARY HARTMAN, MARY HARTMAN*

Mary Hartman, Mary Hartman pushed the boundaries of television's conventions to such a degree that it disturbed even Lear's own employees. In a 1976 profile of Lear on *60 Minutes*, Mike Wallace described *Mary Hartman*, the "sleeper hit of the television season," as "slow-moving, some say soporific," and listed the topics the show "deals with, satirically we are assured": "mass murder, exhibitionism,

FIGURE 11.
Norman Lear looks
on while Sally
Struthers saves
Carroll O'Connor
from an uncomfort-
able discussion
about *Mary
Hartman, Mary
Hartman*.
60 Minutes, CBS,
April 11, 1976.

impotence, venereal disease, and the yellow waxy buildup on Mary's kitchen floors." When Wallace asked Carroll O'Connor, who played Archie Bunker, "What do you think of *Mary Hartman*?" O'Connor talked over the question, ignored it, and continued his thoughts on his ongoing salary negotiations for his work on *All in the Family*. When Wallace came back to the question later, a visibly uncomfortable O'Connor struggled to respond. "Uh, I haven't seen . . . well, I, uh, enjoy it," he stammered. He then asked Wallace, "You're not asking for uh, a, uh, a kind of a, uh, of critical thing . . . ?" Wallace pointedly countered, "I'm asking for a television criticism." At that moment, costar Sally Struthers came to O'Connor's rescue. She instructed Wallace to "ask [O'Connor] again what he thinks of *Mary Hartman*" and then held a "Do Not Disturb" sign up to the camera.[28]

The hesitancy, equivocation, and stonewalling of the *All in the Family* cast responses indicated wider unease with *Mary Hartman*. Although the pilot was initially scripted for CBS, the network did not pick up the series. CBS's reaction seems surprising, considering that Tandem supplied the network with socially responsive content that was both highly rated and critically acclaimed. By the 1972–73 television season, the network had revamped its image and positioned itself as a formidable ratings winner by using "three sitcom anchors" (*All in the Family*, *The Mary Tyler Moore Show*, and *M*A*S*H* [1972-83]) to contend with "overtly with social issues of the day."[29] By the time of *Mary Hartman*'s airing in January 1976, CBS had aired Tandem programs that addressed a host of "controversial" concerns (*All in the Family*, *Good Times*, and *The Jeffersons* [1975-85]) and centered female protagonists who represented changing gender roles and the influence of women's liberation (*Maude* and *One Day at a Time* [1975-84]).

Seemingly, *Mary Hartman* would have complemented CBS's evolving relationship to relevance and, more particularly, would have worked with what Elana Levine describes as the "politicized brand of sexual humor" of its comedies. In the early 1970s, CBS led the way into "new sex-themed territory," and the other networks soon followed.[30] NBC relaxed its standards and practices, and dramas at ABC and NBC featured content involving sexual issues and identities. With depictions of and discussions about sexual dysfunction, exhibitionism, bisexuality, a relationship between two men, gay marriage, and group sex, *Mary Hartman* effectively merged the soap opera with comedy and social commentary that fit in with television's new sexual frankness and experimentation.

Despite what seemed like an ideal product for television at the time, all three networks passed on *Mary Hartman*, and Lear turned to Rhodes Productions—a company that specialized in syndicated programs, including game shows and animation—for distribution.[31] Publicity generated by Tandem redefined rejection by the networks into a positive value. The press kit for *Mary Hartman* uses the networks' reactions to underscore the program's unprecedented unconventionality: "Regardless of the impressive credentials of Lear (*All in the Family, Maude, Good Times*) and his superlative writers and cast, all three networks rejected the series on the grounds that it was 'too far out' for their viewers."[32] Lear amplified the oddity of the program by describing *Mary Hartman* as "simply taking a look at our life and times through another kind of prism" and followed this innocuous description with a more unsettling one: "Of course the prism may appear to have been fashioned by a drunken lens maker in a darkly wooded German forest."[33] This promotional framework positions Lear, the only named figure involved in the production, as responsible for shepherding a perversely innovative show past the unimaginative gatekeepers of the television industry.

Crediting Lear as the central agent of *Mary Hartman*'s success is tempting and perhaps inevitable. Erin Lee Mock's scholarship on *Mary Hartman* identifies the problems of focusing on individualized creation mythologies, given the collaborative dimensions of television production. Yet Lear is a difficult figure to decenter. Mock maintains that "*Mary Hartman* could only have existed due to the stewardship of Lear, whose prominence and history of genre play prepared him to create this unique program and prepared viewers to accept it."[34] Journalistic coverage at the time of *Mary Hartman*'s airing supports this assessment. A *Newsweek* article decreed, "Only Norman Lear has the power—and the chutzpah—to bring such a mind-blowing mélange to television."[35] Lear's creative abilities were matched by his talent to generate publicity through his dynamic and self-assured personality, all of which made him a central character in the story not just in *Mary Hartman* but in all of Tandem's productions. In his 2014 autobiography, Lear looms large in his retrospective history of the company's ingenuity and popularity:

> The way I experienced the wonder we were caught up in was on a number of red-eye flights from L.A. to New York. I would look down anywhere over America and think it just possible that wherever I saw a light there could be someone, maybe an entire family, I'd helped to make laugh. In my dissociated fashion I marveled at this, but it was nothing compared to what I understand now, that I was the architect of all that.[36]

Despite the mystification of collective labor through the exceptional individual, other workers—the drunken lens makers who skewed conventional storytelling to tell unsettling truths about contemporary culture—very clearly played critical roles in Tandem's products.

At the height of his and his company's success, Lear took care to acknowledge the collective force of workers and to minimize his centrality in Tandem's operations. Although, given the ways that Lear's auteur status was advantageous to the company and his career, this move seemed counterintuitive, it was crucial in challenging the reputation of Tandem as "the Lear Factory." This moniker was used by Wallace in his *60 Minutes* profile of Lear to sum up the company's intensive productivity and method of content creation. When, in the interview, Lear claimed that television's commercialism and concerns of retaining advertisers made getting Tandem's shows to air difficult, Wallace countered by claiming that Lear's interests were very similar to those of the forces he criticized. With seven shows running concurrently at the time of the interview, Wallace asserted, "the Lear Factory is in the business of improving last year's profits." In Wallace's assessment, the organization of the company mimicked an assembly line workflow, with Lear functioning as "a foreman" who "spots problems and solves them fast, because time is money."[37] While Lear evaded the issue of his drive for profitability, the physical organization of Tandem confirmed a goal of maximizing efficiency. The production of all programs at the time of the *60 Minutes* interview, with the exception of *Mary Hartman*, took place in a single building. This arrangement afforded Lear efficient access to the company's shows and reinforced the factory concept.

A factory model positions Lear as the central figure who drives the output of the company; all other workers are rendered invisible or envisioned as cogs in the machinery run by Lear as overseer. Lear rejected this conceptualization of his company, and Wallace noted that Lear "hated" to hear Tandem called the Lear Factory. In a rejoinder to Wallace's characterization, Lear argued, "Each show, as you well observed, is staffed by the best writers, the best producers, the best directors, the best actors, the best in this town."[38] Regardless of Lear's true feelings about profitability, in order to maintain Tandem's brand Lear needed to foreground the creativity, individual perspectives, and exceptional skills of each of the company's workers. With such qualities, the company's workforce positioned Tandem as a unique entity within the commercial television industry.

Lear's investment in Tandem's image as artisanal and collectively driven was doubtless strategic as well as ideological. Lear championed progressive movements through his own celebrity and the programming his company produced, and his sense of self and public persona were clearly grounded in "liberal" politics. Therefore, his valuation of workers aligned with his political sensibilities and commitment to innovative television production. But it also made good business sense. Relying on its workers for their unique insights and talents helped Tandem respond to changing cultural norms and enriched the company. This was particularly true of women workers at Tandem. They brought with them important points of view about gender, professional capabilities and work practices atypical for prime-time television production, and personal commitments to projects about women that shaped the company, enriched its product, and fostered its standing as a maverick force in the industry.

Mary Hartman was notable for the number of women involved in its production. In its first season alone, the show employed women as producer (Viva Knight), two out of four directors (Joan Darling and Harlene Kim Friedman), three out of seven writers (Ann Marcus, Peggy Goldman, and Lynn Phillips), one out of two program consultants (Elizabeth Haley), two out of four creators (Gail Parent and Ann Marcus), both of the costume designers (Rita Riggs and Sandra Baker), the casting director (Jane Murray), the production assistant (Susan Harris), and the director of publicity (Barbara Brogliatti). With a cast that featured Louise Lasser as protagonist Mary Hartman, the "project was further enhanced" with Joan Darling as a director.[39]

When publicity was not focused on lauding Lear as the guiding force of the production, it highlighted the accomplishments of these women and, in doing so, touted Tandem as a company that offered women remarkable opportunities for advancement. The press kit for *Mary Hartman* included biographical information on producer Viva Knight that traced her journey from North Texas University to California. Along the way, she had worked as a secretary while taking courses in television production, and then had taken jobs as a student talent coordinator for a local television show, an assistant to the producer for a local public affairs program, and a script secretary for a network series. Her success "prove[d] that a woman's place is anywhere she has the desire and initiative for it to be."[40]

The story of Knight's career at Tandem countered concerns that the hiring boom for women in television in the early to mid-seventies was merely, as the 1977 Report of the United States Commission on Civil Rights described it, "window dressing on the set."[41] When Knight came to the company in 1973, she rose rapidly through its ranks, and her talents were recognized even when she was working in a traditionally feminized and undervalued position. Knight started out at Tandem as a secretary for *Good Times* producer Allan Manings and was promoted to associate producer of the show within six months.[42] When the show went on hiatus, she served as the associate producer for Lear's pilots, one of which was *Mary Hartman*. Knight's impressive "performance" on the job, along with a producer's unexpected leave, prompted Lear to "break precedence" and make Knight—who was not a writer, as would be expected background for such a promotion—a producer for the show. Her entire trajectory from secretary to producer at Tandem took "some two years and two months."[43]

In an interview with *Ms.*, Ann Marcus confirmed how her personal background shaped her vision for Mary; it was based in her own "sense of the everyday absurd, based on years of housewifely domesticity."[44] Although Marcus shepherded the program through its complex development across two seasons and 195 episodes and is named as one of the show's creators, she credited other women with bringing the titular character and her gender complaints to life. She acknowledged Gail Parent as the originator of the characterizations of Mary and her family, initial ideas that Marcus used to build a fully formulated story. Lear wanted to make a "funny soap opera," and from that guidance alone Parent worked "solo for a long time" as a "first creator" to produce a show bible that, in her description, was "more than a treatment." Whereas a treatment would typically run ten pages and cover what a show was "going to be about," the bible, in comparison, "actually took you a little more into a season" and was "about what could happen."[45] Although Parent was not directly involved in Marcus's work on the show—she was working on another project by the time the show moved into production—and was "not there on a day-to-day basis," Marcus honored Parent's contribution to the development of *Mary Hartman*'s story world.[46] Parent also inspired Lear to cast Louise Lasser as Mary Hartman, as both women had a "very slow way of talking" and Lear wanted to bring that aspect to screen.[47] Marcus also credited Louise Lasser as the other primary influence on the character. Lasser "became Mary Hartman" and, in this transformation, "created that crazy little girl look . . . puffy little housedress and slow way of talking."[48]

Lear himself recognized the influence women had on *Mary Hartman*. The show "became an amalgam of what [he] wished to do and of the great gifts that Louise Lasser as an actress brought to it and that Joan Darling brought to it." Lear went on to argue that one could not "separate" the contributions these women made: "'Mary Hartman' would not have been the same 'Mary Hartman' had another actress played the character, and it probably would not have been the same if another director had directed it. All of those components were important."[49]

Acknowledging the collaborative nature of a television show's creation answers back to the rise of auteurism that was taking hold of Hollywood and film criticism, both academic and journalistic, during the 1970s. Television was following a similar path, searching for the singular authoring figure that would redeem it from the commercial morass of the industry. In 1977, Horace Newcomb named Lear as the "most prominent of the 'self-conscious' producers, a type of television worker that brought added value to productions."[50] Their personal vision, Newcomb argued, made it possible to "suddenly cut through the massive anonymity of television."[51] In centering women in American film of the 1970s, Aaron Hunter and Martha Shearer identify the "critical construct" that is New Hollywood and the ways that the "academic cult of the auteurist New Hollywood" "only replicates and reinforces the industry's own exclusions."[52] Centering women in television places similar pressure on notions of authorship and how texts identified as key to the era of "relevant" television in the 1970s were produced. The women involved in making *Mary Hartman* merged their individual creative visions and acknowledged as much, thereby accurately and ethically reflecting the shared labor of television. Their testimony about their communal creativity also calls into question Lear as the primary creator of *Mary Hartman* and the notion of the "self-conscious producer" as television's analogue to New Hollywood's auteur.

Women including and beyond Parent, Lasser, and Marcus put their talents and labor toward creating a "prototypical" 1970s housewife who, in Marcus's words, "never felt she was living up to her full potential and didn't know what her potential was."[53] The impact these women had on the program surpassed their job titles. Lasser credited both the director and the costume designer as key contributors to the character of Mary Hartman. The actor described Darling as a "director that cast everything, and it was her vision of the show that got shot, and she was the one that was like an acting teacher, so we were very dependent on her."[54] The genesis of Mary's look came with the unusual intervention of costume designer Rita Riggs. After consulting with Lasser about the types of colors she liked, Riggs told Lasser, "I'd like to make a costume for you" —a unique offering at the time because, according to Lasser, "no one in those shows had that kind of a separate costume before."[55] With this "brilliant costume to take through everything," Lasser and the women who worked on her hair "all sort of nursed [Mary] along."[56]

ANN MARCUS AND THE FEMINIST-HELMED WRITERS' ROOM

Ann Marcus's expertise as a soap opera writer allowed her to actualize *Mary Hartman*. The program needed to both satirize the conventions of the soap opera and "have enough of a storyline going for it, so that it would attract people on that level, too." When she interviewed for the job, Marcus was working on *Search for Tomorrow* (CBS, 1951–82; NBC, 1982–86) and understood very well the work demands of soap opera writing. Marcus "didn't have a reputation as a top comedy writer" but won the job as head writer for *Mary Hartman* over "a lot of male top comedy writers at that time" who interviewed for this highly coveted position. None of them could capture the complexity of the storylines and tone of the show. Marcus, however, knew how to "keep the story going" with a storyline, "a lot of characters," and intermingled stories. Such work was not just rarefied but onerous. As Marcus said of the work, "It's difficult. It's hard. It's tricky." Knowing how to keep up the pace of producing a daily program was something Marcus brought to the production. She maintained focus and efficiency in the writers' room and moved conversations to larger-picture issues when others in writing meetings were mired in smaller details. The "chore" of working on a serial and the "hard, hard work turning out five scripts a week" was something, again, that Marcus knew well.[57]

As *Mary Hartman*'s head writer, Marcus took responsibility for story structure in the development of scripts and often reminded the writing staff and Lear about the structural elements that the serial form required. Given her background in soaps, Marcus was able to prioritize story arcs, economy in reaching climatic moments, and believability in the midst of heightened drama. In one meeting, the writers struggled to find a satisfying end to an episode that involved a dramatic death of a character and the ongoing decline of Mary's marriage. They debated the consequences of two choices: a discussion of a funeral or a scene with Mary in her kitchen. The argument for the former was the alleviation of work for Lasser, who already had two full scenes, or half of the episode, in which to act. Anything additional would be "a nightmare to handle." Marcus countered with a bid to end with Mary in the kitchen. "All we're trying to do is to give it a kind of flow," Marcus reasoned, "and to remind [viewers] to tune in tomorrow so they'll tune in."[58] In other meetings, Marcus guided writers on what and how much content would successfully constitute an act, what would help move storylines along, and what would help remind viewers of multiple storylines and conflicts.

While Marcus was capable of fostering a culture of productivity, she also pushed back against pressures on output, particularly when they compromised her own needs and the pacing of work she felt necessary to work through a script. Seemingly without exception, these pressures came from male coworkers. *Mary Hartman* writer Daniel Gregory Browne said to Marcus in a writers' meeting, "I just want to throw you ahead to what Norman had said in terms of the end of this week and where we go from there." Marcus replied, "I haven't finished because I'm getting to there," and proceeded to return to the plot concern that was under discussion.[59] At a meeting held in late December, before a vacation break, when someone asked Lear when he wanted an outline for a complex storyline, Lear answered, "They're due. The scripts are due. They should be done right before you hit the slopes." Marcus responded, "You're kidding. You have two weeks of scripts."[60] After this comment, Lear relented and asked for outlines rather than completed scripts before Marcus left for her vacation.

As head writer on *Mary Hartman*, Marcus occupied an authoritative position on the production of the show, something that she worked hard to define and defend. She struggled in the first season of the show to balance "wanting very much to succeed, to be loved and needed and admired," with the difficulties of working in "the midst of all those other people with egos just as big or bigger even than mine." Even as she negotiated her desire for acceptance, Marcus kept sight of the importance of her perspective and held the line on telling stories that reflected women's experiences. When Lear and the show's writers proposed their various storylines, Marcus was "most times the only woman in the meeting."[61] As transcripts for *Mary Hartman*'s writers' meetings demonstrate, Marcus was keen to offer women's perspectives and was able to insist on introducing them to and keeping them in the script.

In a writers' meeting held on December 30, 1975, program consultant Oliver Hayley raised an objection to a storyline involving a pregnancy that ended in a miscarriage. The ensuing conversation reflects the contested efforts to ground a storyline in realistic and meaningful women's experiences. Hayley began the conversation by asking, "May I just say something, and everyone can get offended? I HATE dead babies. I don't think there is anything funny about dead babies." He then pitched "an outrageous idea" from director Joan Darling. Darling suggested that the pregnancy itself could be a false alarm: and that rather than carrying a fetus, the character would have a misdiagnosed fibroid tumor. Marcus responded to this suggestion by saying, "I think it's hysterical" and proceeded to build, with others in the room, a string of humorous scenarios and lines. Writer Jerry Adelman was not convinced by this plan, arguing that "this is a honest-to-God tragedy." After Hayley further defended the comedic possibilities of the scenario, Lear asked, "How big a mistake is that for a doctor to make?" Someone else in the room argued, "It's a ridiculous mistake." Hayley replied, "It is not. There are a great many women who think that they are pregnant and turn out to have a fibroid tumor."[62] The fibroid storyline that originated with Darling made it to air on the twenty-fifth episode of season 1 with very few changes made to the idea generated in the writers' meeting. The successful corrective to the original storyline revised a potentially unfunny storyline about "dead babies" to one that highlighted women's experiences with reproductive health care; it also indicates how the writers' room, under Marcus's guidance and with collaborative efforts, protected an idea that originated with another woman on the production team.

The very notion that *Mary Hartman* should explore a woman's dissatisfaction, something that defined the series, was a concept that had to be defended in its early stages of development. In a writers' meeting that took place on January 20, 1976, just two weeks after the inaugural episode aired, Lear outlined the terms of Mary Hartman's unhappiness as a working-class wife and mother. The complications of her situation stemmed from her desire to be something more, which conflicted with other messages women like her received from powerful anti-feminist, anti-ERA forces and television's consumerist address to women. Lear reminded the writers of the class-based dynamics of the character: "We forget all of these commercials that are interrupting our shows are about oven cleaners, etc. and it's because the bulk of America is still wrapped up in those problems and we forget about all those products if we can afford to have somebody do this for us, we forget how much time is spent cleaning ovens, etc." Lear wanted to develop the complexity of Mary's awakening as someone who "lives where she lives, has only as much knowledge as she has," and is therefore "trying to break out and denying at the same time that that's what she's trying to do." Marcus supported this characterization for the efficient way it determined the story world. "Giving her this whole inner thing that you're talking about," she argued, "defines the other characters immediately" because Mary gauged her sense of self through the women in her life who presented various options for emancipation.[63]

Not everyone in the room was supportive of this framework. Writer Daniel Gregory Browne responded negatively to characterizing Mary's struggle with empowerment. He described the central conflict as "very boring and not very comedic because it's been done to death all over the country." Browne elaborated his misgivings by asserting, "I think it's done on television a great deal. I think that everyone is somewhat into it—I think we're very deep in the women's movement now." After some back-and-forth with others in the room, Browne noted that *Alice* (CBS, 1976–85) was forthcoming and "we don't want to ace Alice out on this." Someone else felt that the frustration of a woman was not unique and that it "doesn't manifest into terribly exciting or funny scenes because it's where every woman is at."[64] The objections raised in the writers' room suggest the fragility of launching a project that expressed women's disillusionment and connected to themes of the women's movement. Resistance to such a project was based on assumptions that there was a finite capacity for stories about women on television, that they were abundant, and that women's concerns had been more than adequately expressed.

Here Marcus intervened and clarified that those who objected to the idea were mistakenly "taking what Norman is saying as a story line, this is only a subject." When the discussion continued along the same lines, Marcus broke in to move the discussion forward to more productive outcomes. "I don't think we should spend any more time on the philosophical underpinning of Mary Hartman," maintained Marcus. "I think we are in agreement on that. We need strong stories that aren't just 3 or 4 scenes. But based on this kind of character we have to build a strong story that has all kinds of things—we have to do wonderful inventive things. I haven't come up with these things yet because we haven't talked about them yet and I hope we can talk about this."[65] Marcus pushed the meeting past its sticking point. She prioritized her agenda—the development of "inventive" ideas—while asserting consensus on women's liberation as a central issue in the program. This small but effective gesture put an end to the momentum that was gathering against telling the story of a female protagonist's complex relationship to the women's movement.

In writing to Gloria Steinem, whom she credited, along with Simone de Beauvoir, with her feminist consciousness, Marcus described her staunch allegiance to feminism. "I have been in the Movement, spiritually, ever since I was a kid," Marcus informed Steinem.[66] Marcus's feminism played an important role in shaping *Mary Hartman*, particularly because, from her perspective, "Norman was a chauvinist in 1975."[67] Although Marcus credits Lear with being a "modern," "open-minded liberal" with an "incredibly inquisitive kind of mind," the timeline of his conversion to feminism is unclear.[68] Sometime in the 1970s, during his marriage to Frances Lear, whom their daughter Kate Lear described as a "feminist who changed the lives of many women," Norman Lear began to identify as a feminist.[69] "Frances was very much engaged in the women's movement," Lear recalled, "and I, as the father of three daughters at that time, was also. So we all became feminists."[70] Regardless of when, precisely, Lear identified as a feminist, his gender politics were not fully evolved at the start of his professional relationship with Marcus. If Lear's chauvinism was intact and on display in the year prior to the premiere of *Mary Hartman* in January 1976, then it follows that Marcus, rather than Lear, was a central agent in articulating feminist sentiment and progressive gender perspectives in the planning of the show.

Marcus's feminist consciousness helped move script ideas in development away from offensive and regressive content. When one of Mary Hartman's neighbors, who was a closeted gay man, was outed to Mary by another character, a writer suggested that the line read, "By the way, your neighbor is a fag [*sic*]." Someone else at the meeting suggested that the "best euphemism you can find," along the lines of "They weren't really brothers after all, you know," should be used instead of the homophobic slur. Another writer questioned how anyone would know someone's secret sexual identity: it was "awfully convenient that a total stranger drops in" and, after a brief encounter, knows that Mary Hartman's neighbor is "a fag [*sic*]," repeating the slur introduced earlier in the conversation. The writer then suggested that, rather than an uneventful, off-screen encounter that results in the revelation of the neighbor's sexuality, "there has to be something there to build it up. I think if it's made funny, it will work." Without hearing further details, Marcus shut down this potential storyline by saying, "That isn't funny."[71] Given the offensive language used in the pitch, it was likely that anything else that would make a gay man's sexuality signify clearly enough for a stranger to identify it would be equally offensive.

HYSTERIA, MONSTROSITY, AND OTHER GENDERED ANXIETIES ABOUT THE STATE OF TELEVISION

Among its many accomplishments, Tandem introduced feminized genres into prime-time and late-night programming, appealed to women viewers, and acknowledged and accommodated activist concerns. Because of this, the company was credited with ushering in a new era of television that would reverse the industry's worst offenses. In other contexts, however, these very same changes were ones that alarmed the most vocal of television's critics at the time. In bemoaning the fate of television, even as they praised Lear, these critics identified women and minorities as the forces that were diluting and perverting television and its artistic potential. Most notably, as discussed at the opening of this chapter, self-professed Lear fan Paddy Chayefsky worried about feminizing forces corrupting even the most visionary creative who worked in the industry in the 1970s.

When he predicted Lear's corruption by the "monstrous test pattern," Chayefsky described how "hysterical" Lear would become once he encountered problems with ratings.[72] In calling on hysteria, or "the symptom, to put it crudely, of being a woman," to describe the downfall of a fellow television innovator, Chayefsky signaled anxiety about the state of television in gendered terms.[73] Lest it seem that notions of monstrosity and hysteria are casual linguistic formulations, those responsible for the problems with the television industry and its labor demands are writ large in *Network*. As Chayefsky made clear in interviews, television had become a crushing, traumatizing industry that consumed and alienated both its workforce and its audience. To register that trauma, Chayefsky's script for *Network* indicts television's feminized and feminizing forces and lays much of the responsibility for television's degradation at the feet of women. Women in the television workplace humiliate men and dehumanize relationships both professional and personal. Their appetite for ratings introduces sensationalized news and coverage of political fringe organizations formed of, not coincidentally, Black and women radicals.

Network tells the story of Howard Beale, "a mandarin of television, the grand old man of news," in the style of Walter Cronkite; Max Shumacher, the head of the news division and a friend to Howard; and Diana Christensen, a woman who replaces Max and ushers in a new type of television news that displaces both men. When Howard learns that he is going to lose his job because of poor ratings, he tells viewers that he is going to commit suicide on-air. The next night, when he appears on what is to be his final broadcast, he admits that his suicide threat was "madness" and that his thirty-year marriage to a "shill, shrieking fraud" exhausted his capacity for disingenuity. His unhappy personal life and the end of his professional one, both determined by women, meant he "ran out of bullshit." With his newfound maverick reporting style to sustain him, Howard channels "the Truth" from a godlike voice he begins to hear, which results in increased ratings and saves his career. In the ensuing drama, Max is seduced and then discarded by Diana, and Howard becomes capable of heroically "articulating the rage" of Americans.

Christine Chubbuck, a twenty-nine-year-old television news reporter who shot and killed herself during an on-air broadcast on July 15, 1974, serves as a clear referent for Howard Beale.[74] Journalistic accounts of Chubbuck's death framed it in terms of her despair about her failed heteronormativity and femaleness. *Washington Post* coverage included a bullet-pointed list that ticked off Chubbuck's problems so numerous and obvious that they seemingly did not require elaboration. This list related Chubbuck's "sexual status" as a "spinster" and explained Chubbuck's distress, which ultimately led to her suicide, as caused by her self-identified virginity, her failure at dating, the removal of one of her ovaries, and a coworker's rejection of her romantic overture.[75]

Chubbuck's suicidality, however, may have had less to do with despair over her gender transgressions and failures than with a workplace in which her self-assurance and success on the job threatened her male coworkers. One of these coworkers described Chubbuck as "a liberated woman, a pain in the ass, not very attractive, almost manly," and conflated her capabilities as a news anchor with perceived gender failures. Chubbuck "was doing a man's job, only doing it better than

FIGURE 12. Diana Christensen (Faye Dunaway) as "television incarnate" welcomes Black militancy—in the form of Lauren Hobbs (Marlene Warfield)—to UBS. Christensen's growing influence as the network's head of programming signifies the problems of television in the 1970s, according to *Network* (1976).

a man. She was precise and efficient. There was nothing feminine about her.'"[76] Chubbuck's skill as a news anchor, doing a "man's job," functioned as both a professional and personal liability, and her colleagues judged her harshly for it.

In choosing to tell Chubbuck's story through the figure of an older white man, Chayefsky revises the tragedy of a woman who was beleaguered by misogynistic forces and occludes the realities of sexism and racism in the television workplace. Chayefsky's retelling of Chubbuck's story fundamentally alters its ideological framework and expresses anxiety about the growing influence of women and racial minorities over television. Unlike the real-life story of Chubbuck, who faced intense pressure as a woman struggling to succeed in a hostile work environment, *Network*'s male newscaster and male news division president are victimized by a power-hungry female executive, who is identified as "television incarnate." By the film's end, a newswoman's on-air suicide becomes a newsman's tragic assassination engineered by a career-obsessed female TV executive and carried out by a Black militant group.

In the world Chayefsky creates, men no longer exert influence over the television industry, much to its detriment. Unlike Howard Beale and his commitment to authenticity, Diana Christensen corrupts truthfulness and chooses spectacle over authenticity. Unlike Max Schumacher and his upholding of news traditions, Diana transforms television news into an outlet for sensationalism. She understands that "TV is show biz and even the news has to have a little showmanship." This awareness ushers in a new era in television news that conflates entertainment with reality. Newsroom staff pitch stories about Manson cult member and murderer Squeaky Fromme; guerilla fighters in Chad's Civil War; and kidnapped heiress and member of the Symbionese Liberation

Army (SLA) Patty Hearst. Such a lineup indicates a sea change in what count as newsworthy figures and issues and replaces the traditions of television journalism with stories of racial, ethnic, and gender unrest. The political uprising of African and Middle Eastern peoples and the social disturbance and violence propagated by white women have, with the aid of news media, victimized the "grand old men" of television.

Indicative of her drive to deliver increasingly sensationalized news and her corrupting influence on the industry, Diana produces *The Mao Tse-Tung Hour*, a program based on the Ecumenical Liberation Army (ELA), a group of Black militants who kidnap a rich white female heiress. Diana sees their criminal actions, clearly patterned after the SLA's kidnapping of Hearst, as "something really sensational." She hires the ELA to film real footage of their crimes and creates a fictional show based on the footage. The group is eventually hired to assassinate Beale on-air to boost ratings. The series and Diana's revamped news show reverse the news division's losing profits and propel the network from a last-place to first-place finisher in ratings. Diana's success leads her to dream of even-greater perversions of television standards, with plans for a soap opera called *The Dykes*, a "tragic story about a woman who's in love with her husband's mistress." Diana's projects push the limits of television programming, excise white men from the industry, and hasten television's focus on marginalized political and cultural groups.

Network was not alone in raising the alarm about the state of television and the terms of its demise. Chayefsky's anxieties link him to other contemporaneous critics who identified the corruption of television with feminized and racialized forces. In state-of-television assessments that emerged in the mid- to late 1970s, the dehumanizing, degrading, and dangerous forces within television were linked to unwelcomed newcomers who challenged the traditions established by white men. *USA Today* published Robert Balon's sci-fi article "Prelude to Big Brother? Measuring Broadcast Audiences in the Year 2000," which expressed fear for the contemporary moment, 1978, through an imagined apocalyptic future. In Balon's scenario, by the year 2000 the value of demographic audience capture that started in the 1970s has driven the industry to near ruination. Television has become a "junkyard of third-rate shows," and programming looks like "verbatim reruns of *Police Woman*." A dystopian culture, decreased human freedoms, and loss of creativity and innovation in television all function as by-products of television's interest in women viewers and responsiveness to female empowerment, as symbolized by the woman cop drama. "Prelude" predicts that television will utilize extreme technologies to gauge audience responses to its product, going as far as to surgically implant Internal Audio-Visual Meters into viewers' ears. The meter "instantly and continuously translate[s] all visual and auditory stimuli" to a computer center that compiles audience data made available to the highest bidder.[77] The viewer's body, already rendered passive and feminized through its acceptance of television's stock fare of the policewoman genre, is further objectified and commodified through this new surveillant technology.

Nonfiction accounts of the television industry also raised concerns about the influence of activist groups. A 1975 *Newsweek* article, "Do Minorities Rule?," profiled advocacy groups and the complaints they lodged against offensive television content. By leading off with the question "Who owns TV?," along with its title choice, the article implicitly sounds an alarm about encroachments of "pressure groups from virtually all of America's minorities: blacks, feminists, homosexuals, the elderly, youngsters, ethnics and religious sects of all stripes" on the industry's autonomy and self-governance. Although US television had always belonged to the public, only in the 1970s were people aware of the ramifications of this ownership, according to the article's author, Harry Waters. As a result, "Scores of citizen-protest groups [were] demanding—and often achieving—a pronounced say in what viewers see."[78]

The growing influence of "pressure groups" troubled Waters. He cited how the National Organization for Women (NOW) had won "concessions from Detroit's ABC affiliate to increase women's programing" as a landmark moment that was met with a response by the antifeminist group Happiness of Womanhood, who "promptly filed a license challenge against the station for allegedly surrendering its programming prerogatives under duress." The back-and-forth between activist groups, Waters reported, threatened the creative control and innovation of television creatives. NBC refused to air an episode of *Police Woman*— ironically the very program that signaled the banal, dystopian future in Balon's year 2000 predictions—when "homosexual activists" complained about a storyline that featured murderous lesbians. David Gerber, the show's producer, "fume[d]" at the situation and issued a warning about the perils of activist influence: "We're going to end up with sterilized pap. By trying to please everybody, the networks will please nobody."[79]

As imagined in journalism and film during the 1970s, the influence of women over television, whether as viewers, an influential demographic group, on-screen characters, or industry workers, threatened the well-being of the industry. The anxious defensiveness about television's patriarchal traditions and the influence of activist forces rendered women's expanding roles in television incompatible with fruitful, creative innovation. Vilifying them and perpetuating notions that they were destructive to television was one way to nullify their value. The other was to render them and their contributions invisible and instead elevate men as rarefied individuals who operated beyond the constraints of industry. Ironically, while Lear was credited with refusing and resisting the worst impulses of television— the predominance of least objectionable programming, the need to placate networks, and the privileging of ratings over creativity—in reality, he welcomed and depended upon women and feminized television traditions, the forces that critics identified as the corruption of the industry. Exploring the importance of women

to Tandem and tracing their impact on the company's experimentation and creativity therefore counter the erasure of their contributions and help rectify the
disparagement of women's influence over television.

WOMEN WHO WORK: CONTEXTUALIZING
EQUAL EMPLOYMENT

Women's employment at Tandem came at a time when the television industry faced
new legislation and Federal Communications Commission (FCC) policies meant
to correct gender discrimination in the workplace. In December 1971, pressured by
advocacy groups, including NOW, the FCC revised its equal opportunity employment forms, which indicated the employment of members of minority groups, to
include women.[80] In 1973, the first Equal Employment Opportunity Commission
(EEOC) complaints and suits were filed against stations WREC-TV in Memphis
and WRC-TV in Washington, D.C.[81] In 1974, the protections created by the Equal
Employment Opportunity Act (EEOA) became federal law. While these actions
promised to open the television industry to women and minorities, the resulting protections often fell short of their intended effects. The television industry
often tried to skirt or minimize equal opportunity employment measures while
appearing to comply with them by manipulating statistics and job categories. And
even when data accurately reflected increased numbers of women employed in
television, television workplaces often continued to perpetuate inequities and differential treatment for women.

As a group composed of industry women, American Women in Radio and
Television (AWRT) was aware of the differences between official EEOA reports
and actual workplace realities. In 1972, it launched a large-scale, multiyear survey
of women's employment. The study was designed to correct FCC findings based
on television stations' self-reporting of employment figures, which were often
manipulated to protect against FCC interventions. For example, secretarial positions were folded in with male-dominated, higher-level managerial positions in
order to suggest changes in women's employment, which, in reality, was static.
To "overturn some conceptualizations based on purely numerical quantification,"
AWRT surveyed individual workers to better account for where women fell in the
hierarchy of responsibilities, decision-making processes, and management.[82] In
asking for information directly from the organization's members and others working in the industry, AWRT's approach circumvented statistical adjustments that
stations made to mask inequalities in employment practices. These surveys also
offered women the opportunity to articulate what it meant to carry out their jobs
and to meet the demands of the television workplace as they experienced it.

The issue of equal employment in the 1970s helped bring about significant
changes in the relatively conservative AWRT. AWRT had been founded in 1951,
when the National Association of Broadcasters disbanded its women's division,

the Association of Women Broadcasters. From the start, AWRT strove to challenge preconceived notions about what a women's organization looked like and how it could best take the concerns of its members seriously. A form letter used to recruit prospective members described the AWRT as "NOT a social organization, or a union, or a bunch of rattle-brained party-going women" but instead as a "very large group of women," "from heads of networks to agency girls," "who have joined together to work to make our industry better."[83] This document reflects the basic, defining goals of the organization: to position women as serious-minded professionals, to acknowledge a range of occupational influence and power in the industry, and to reassure women that the organization would advance their professional status and improve the industry.

Historically, the organization was averse to anything they regarded as overt politicization and instead positioned themselves as an educational outlet for professional women.[84] In its 1967 report to members, AWRT identified its primary value as "the professional knowledge made available" to members.[85] Although the organization acknowledged that women's professional lives were distinctively defined by gender, it did nothing at this time to acknowledge the presence or usefulness of feminism, even as the women's movement was taking hold in the US. It instead addressed the gendering of work through the work-life balance facing its members. The typical member, according to the AWRT's 1967 report, held "in common with all modern career women" the need to "combine careers with homemaking."[86] This arguably factual statement was followed by more affective and subjective reassurances that women could retain their domestic roles: "Whether married or single . . . 89.6% maintain a full professional schedule and still find time to run their homes" and "only 6.2% have a full-time household assistant."[87]

The emergence of the EEOA and its uneven enforcement helped motivate AWRT to adopt a more active and more critical role in understandings of gender inequalities and obstacles to women in the workplace. In 1975, Lionel J. Monagas, head of the FCC's Equal Employment Office, maintained that "the former impression of AWRT as complacent, quiet and conservative [was] no longer true."[88] Once the organization began to focus on how media industries perpetuated gender inequities, their annual reports on members reflected their critical perspectives. By 1978, AWRT was continuing its practice of publishing statistics about the work-life balance of its members but had modified the ways it framed the issue. Its presentation no longer seemed motivated by a need to reassure women that having both was possible and that they would still assume responsibilities over the home. Statistics that reinforced the need and ability to remain a housewife as well as career woman, such as those included in the 1967 annual report, were replaced by different types of statistical findings. Members who operated as the "sole support of a household" constituted over 50 percent of the organization, and, while "many women combine[d] a professional career with managing a household," there was no longer an emphasis on their abilities to manage the household without assistance.[89]

By the late 1970s, AWRT had been charting incidents of discrimination in the workplace long enough that it could track changes in those areas. In 1978 it noted that while the "typical" AWRT member reported to a man on the job, 40 percent of the women polled supervised the work of at least one man, which marked an increase of 10 percent over 1974 findings. In addition to numerical data about women's place in hierarchical structures, the 1978 report included information about women's workplace experiences in its "Women on the Job" section. AWRT's 1973 survey found that 23.6 percent of members "cited sex discrimination as the major obstacle" in the workplace, but between that survey and the 1978 report, 75.8 percent of members had "personally witnessed or experienced an improvement in attitude toward women in their field of work." By 1978, the "majority" of survey respondents indicated that they had "experienced neither sex favoritism nor sex discrimination on the job, and only 12.2% considered their sex a major deterrent to job advancement." AWRT believed these findings demonstrated "a change in attitude" within the industry and signaled meaningful improvements Although hopeful about the progress women were making, the report was careful to identify new challenges for women in the workplace, primarily in the "lack of opportunity" that "impede[d] their progress."[90]

In her work on equal employment practices during the 1970s, Miranda Banks corrects assumptions about workplace opportunities for women and minorities when these are gauged by statistics alone. She dissects numerical figures and supplements them with experiential evidence from women as they worked on productions. Even when women were employed on television shows that were "comparatively progressive about racial or gender inclusivity (few were both), the experience of women working on the series often involved playing educator to male colleagues about sexism." When women were not in positions of authority on a production or in a company, their efforts at education generally had no measurable effect. For instance, when writer Treva Silverman worked on *Mary Tyler Moore* and called attention to sexism in a script, "the head writers were unresponsive." Even in "best case scenarios," Banks argues, "producers responded well to criticism and made adjustments—but with virtually all series run by white men, the parameters of inclusivity were still determined by white men."[91]

VIRGINIA CARTER AND FEMINIST OVERSIGHT AT TANDEM

When FCC chair Robert E. Lee addressed the AWRT at their 1975 meeting, he advised them on how best to make real gains in their professions.[92] Characterized as a "champion" of equal employment, Lee identified the "divide and conquer" strategy the television industry used to "pit women against minorities for jobs" and advocated for "united action" among all marginalized workers.[93] Lee especially urged "women in minorities" to seek out high-level jobs as "news directors, program directors, producers, directors and editorial writers," where "the real power" in broadcasting was located.[94] Finally, Lee called out the entire film and television industry, including institutions that operated beyond FCC jurisdiction, to account for racist and sexist employment practices. Television networks, film studios, and production companies alike were responsible for improving the number of women and minorities they employed within and beyond creative jobs, particularly in executive positions that held considerable authority and influence.

In 1973, two years before Lee's speech, Virginia Carter was hired as an assistant to Norman Lear and as a consultant for feminist guidance and oversight within Tandem. Concerns about women's role in television motivated Lear to hire Carter. Lear understood that his own production company was not immune from gender inequalities, particularly at its most powerful levels. In a planning meeting for *All That Glitters* (1977), a gender-role reversal satire in which women dominate the executive ranks of multinational corporations, Lear reflected on the persistence of sexism in business, including television. "This company is perhaps as open in that respect as any company I know," observed Lear, "and yet look around. True, Virginia [Carter] and I have talked about this. . . . The doors have not been opened enough." Lear speculated that a woman would not ascend to his job "until the doors have been opened long enough, enough women have been able to write long enough, produce long enough, direct long enough. Women are only beginning to direct. They've never had the opportunities."[95] Lear's assessment reflects his awareness of structural barriers and sexist traditions that restricted women's full participation in the industry. In spite of Tandem's shortcomings, women did possess the all-too-rare ability to control and counsel on certain productions and in specific roles in the company.

Carter was an unlikely hire, in terms of both her job description and her professional background. Her primary purpose at Tandem, according to Lear, was to "establish and maintain equity in our hiring and in our scripts."[96] At the time Lear hired her, Carter was a trained physicist working at the Aerospace Corporation. Lear acknowledged the unorthodox decision of hiring a research scientist for a job in the entertainment industry but explained Carter's worth through her feminist credentials. Lear valued Carter because of "'what she could teach [him] and [his] company about the fledgling women's movement and, in fact, about being a decent human being.'"[97] Given Tandem's status as an independent production company, which operated outside of FCC regulations, Carter's hiring, influence, and ascent in the executive ranks there indicates the company's investment in the types of equal opportunity practices endorsed by Robert E. Lee.

Carter came to Lear's attention through her relationship with Frances Lear, Norman's then-wife and the "resident EEOC" in "the Lear household."[98] After hearing Carter speak in her capacity as the president of the Los Angeles chapter of NOW, Frances championed Carter as a feminist activist whose credentials and experience would benefit Tandem and urged Carter to meet with her husband.[99] Carter

FIGURE 13. Frances Lear and Norman Lear in the early 1980s. (Photofest)

agreed to the meeting only as a favor to Frances, who "was a friend at that point because she was so supportive as I went about my business in NOW."[100] Otherwise, Carter "couldn't imagine why" she would take the meeting.[101] "I was embarrassed about it," she recalled. "It was a waste of my time."[102] Carter had no experience in the television industry, to the extent of being unaware of who Norman Lear was. It was only when Carter's partner, Judith Osmer, told her that Frances's husband was on the cover of *Time* magazine the week she planned to meet with him that Carter understood the magnitude of the meeting.

Although Carter initially was uninterested in a career in television, the benefits of working at Tandem quickly became clear to her. From her first meeting with Lear, Carter was impressed with Lear's sensitivity, which suggested a similarly enlightened workplace and a welcome reprieve from the masculinized world of science to which Carter was accustomed. Since Lear knew nothing about physics, and Carter "didn't know anything about show business whatsoever," they "fell back on one issue we had in common," their past encounters with cancer. Carter, a breast cancer survivor, and Lear, who had had a precancerous growth on his face, bonded over their health concerns. "And we sat there, with facing death as our common ground," Carter remembers, "and we both wept a little. And I had only known men in engineering and physics-type subjects. I had not known this kind of a man who would cry." Lear's emotional intelligence was one of the reasons Carter took the job at Tandem, and the immediate interpersonal, affective bond between Lear and Carter defined their working relationship from that point on. When, in 2019, Carter looked back on her initial impressions of Lear, she stressed how much she valued Lear's personality. "I never met anybody like Norman," she said. "I've never met anyone like Norman since. Just the most amazing man. A gentle, caring man."[103]

Carter had faced considerable sexism and pay inequities in her job as a research physicist, and the prospect of appropriate compensation and respect for her labor was another key factor that led her to accept Lear's job offer. The position granted her several advantages over her previous job. The first was "the kind of decision-making power and respect she had been denied in her scientific work."[104] The sexism of the scientific community meant that Carter was unlikely to advance in her career there. "I felt discrimination every time I turned around," Carter recalled. She did not get paid as much as her male colleagues did, and although she followed the same paths they used to get promoted, this "had no impact on [her] position in the company whatsoever."[105] In comparison, Lear acknowledged the worth of Carter's labor and expertise in financial terms. When Lear offered her a job, Carter requested around $25,000, which significantly surpassed the $18,000 she earned at the Aerospace Corporation. Unfazed, Lear granted her request immediately.

The economic benefits at Tandem continued for Carter after initial salary negotiations. After she had been working at the company for only a few months, Carter received her first end-of-the-year bonus. Unlike her previous employer, which gave employees a turkey, Tandem gave Carter a $5,000 bonus. The unusual compensation and continued pay raises Carter earned at Tandem signaled the company's respect for her abilities and demonstrated their commitment to minimizing sexist pay differentials. Carter's financial security had the added benefit of allowing her freedom and autonomy at work. Once she had accrued enough savings and felt secure enough in her position, Carter realized, "I didn't have to worry about what I said," and acted accordingly.[106]

What Carter had to say was deeply informed by her feminist activism, which was what had attracted Lear to her in the first place. With no previous experience in the television industry, the former president of the Los Angeles chapter of NOW and high-profile ERA advocate explained her unorthodox skills as a worker in this way: "I understood that the only reason possible to explain my presence in television was my expertise in Women's Liberation. I knew I could be very productive with this focus, supplying this deficiency." Carter's activism proved a pragmatic asset as much as an ideological one. Her work within the women's movement lent her translatable skills for her new job. Carter felt that "the way things work in show business is exactly the way they work if you are the president of a local chapter of the National Organization for Women and you're trying to run the Board. The financial stakes are just a whole lot higher. Being president of NOW, I learned a whole lot of stuff, especially about group dynamics."[107]

Famed for representing topics previously considered taboo in the industry, Tandem attracted considerable attention from political groups. Rather than skirt controversial topics to avoid protest, Tandem used "clashes" with groups to reflect more "realistic" concerns in their programming.[108] Described as the person Lear hired to do "nothing but negotiate with the pressure groups," Carter understood input from activists as advantageous for the production process: "We do better story lines when we hear what people are caring about."[109] Tandem provided "advance screenings of his more sensitive episodes" for activists, whose feedback was "discussed in consciousness-raising sessions among the show's writers."[110] Carter's abilities to bridge the needs of the public and the demands of production reflected well on Tandem and resulted in praise from activists who sought to reform television. For example, unhappy with depictions of a same-sex couple on *Hot L Baltimore* (ABC, 1975), the National Gay Task Force met with Carter. The Task Force commended the resulting adjustments, which made the couple "more loving and less given to role-playing," something they attributed to Carter's decision-making authority at Tandem.[111]

It is important to note that not every group was equally pleased, particularly when it came to matters of race. The Congress of Racial Equality (CORE) protested *The Jeffersons* and *Good Times* for "stereotyping black matriarchs and emasculating their husbands."[112] Lear responded by producing three shows written by CORE-approved writers. Even with this concession, certain members of the group remained critical: "Gene Garvin, the chairman of CORE's Los Angeles chapter, still calls Lear 'the father of tokenism,'" and CORE's western regional director, Charles Cook, described Lear's comedic approach as "some white person's idea of how black people live."[113] When Garvin frankly called out Lear as being dishonest—saying that he had "lied"—when making an earlier promise in November 1977 to hire more Black production workers, Carter managed the conflict in the press.[114] She characterized a second, January 1978 meeting between CORE and Lear as "affable" and anticipated that she and Lear and "others in the company will attempt to continue a dialog with these interesting and passionate people."[115]

Carter's job included educating Lear on issues he did not yet understand and people he did not yet know. Using firsthand encounters and interviews, Carter gathered information from members of marginalized groups and created reports for Lear to read or brought people to Lear's office so he could meet and talk with them himself. When he planned for storylines in *All That Glitters*, he asked Carter to assemble members of the LGBTQ communities in the area. Carter brought gay men, lesbians, and a trans man to Lear's office, which resulted in a meeting where Lear knowingly met a transgender person for the first time in his life. In exposing Lear to experiences and perspectives of people he might not otherwise easily come into contact with, Carter helped expand program content to include sexual minorities, presumably—but arguably not always successfully—from an informed perspective. Characters and storylines, which Lear would have had to approve, grew from stand-alone episodes about gay men (*All in the Family*'s "Judging Books by Covers," aired on February 9, 1971) to recurring gay characters (Gordan and George, a couple on *Hot L Baltimore*) and the first recurring transgender character on television (Linda Murkland on *All That Glitters*). Personal interactions were critical in Lear's growing political awareness. Here, too, Carter played an important role. As an out lesbian, Carter was able to "not scare" her interview subjects and acted as an effective conduit between Lear and LGBTQ communities. Lear was "comfortable" with Carter's relationship with her partner, which helped pave the way for their discussions about sexuality. Carter remembers this part of her job as "easy and fun" because of the respect Lear showed her and her experiential authority and the ways that, in turn, that experiential authority played a central role in her job.[116]

When *Hot L Baltimore* featured two gay men as characters, Carter screened the content for twenty-five "major representatives of the gay communities" in Los Angeles and sixty-five in New York City, including press. In spite of the "heated," "intense," and "lengthy" discussion that ensued, Carter reported to the series' writers and to Lear that "it all came to a clear consensus that the show is a major step toward improving the image of gays on television" and that she had been "asked to say thank you to you. . . . For your information, you are appreciated." Carter's understanding of how gay relationships should be depicted on television was based on her earlier interventions on *Mary Hartman*. She conducted research and proposed how the show's writers should consider their treatment of two men who had moved to town, were closeted, but were contemplating coming out and getting married. Her memo outlined three significant concerns: a stereotypical "dominant vs. passive" dynamic between men in a relationship; attempts to explain why a character would be gay, as "there is no real evidence about what made 'gayness'"; and the absence of physical contact between the couple, when "everyone else touched everyone else."[117]

Although a considerable part of her job, Carter's work exceeded meetings with activist groups. She "had involvement in essentially all of the shows" at Tandem. She filled in for Lear when he "had an issue that he wanted to confront, and he couldn't" because of the demands of multiple shows; she sat in on meetings and dealt with network censors. In addition to these bureaucratic tasks, Carter also found herself operating in the creative side of the company. At times, she pitched promising story ideas after they had been initially turned down by Lear. When writers came into Carter's office after Lear had rejected one of their stories to express their disappointment, Carter would sometimes recognize the quality of the story and would facilitate its approval. "Once or twice, I would listen and think it was a hell of a good idea. And I'd wait for them to go," Carter remembers. "And then I'd go into Norman's office and say, I don't get this, why didn't you buy this? And then I'd give him a pitch but use my words, not theirs. And the next thing you know, my office would be filled with flowers" from the grateful writer.[118]

Carter not only acted internally within Tandem to get stories to air but also worked with the networks to overcome their resistance to controversial stories. She remembers "Maude's Dilemma," a two-part episode of *Maude* in which Maude gets an abortion, as the content that created the most objections from Program Practices, the networks' in-house censors. To overcome these objections, Carter constructed pragmatic arguments about the realities of abortion and the economics that made Lear's desires worth heeding. Carter describes her meetings with CBS about the episode as follows:

> My mission was to tell the truth. Abortions are taking place all over the country. I got statistics on that, as well as I could. And then I would go to the network, and say to Program Practices, "Norman has asked me to come." I had to use Norman's name, because they're making a freaking fortune off his shows. They have to pay attention to what he wants. And he wants to do this because it's part of his policy to do things that are real in society.[119]

Carter's efforts paid off. CBS aired the episode in November 1972 and rebroadcast it on August 17, 1973. Merely persuading the network to air the program was reason enough to celebrate, but the real feminist impact of "Maude's Dilemma" made Carter's victory particularly significant. Written during Supreme Court deliberations on the *Roe v. Wade* ruling, the episodes were intentionally crafted to persuade audiences to support legalized abortion. The coauthors of the episodes, Susan Harris and Irma Kalish, turned to newspaper articles about women's abortions to ground the story in the real-world concerns of reproductive rights.[120] The goal of writing such material was, in Harris's perspective, to "have a point of view" and to use television "to raise audience consciousness."[121] According to Kathryn Montgomery, "Maude's Dilemma" played a vital role in making the 1972–73 television season a "critical test year for determining just how far entertainment television could venture into controversial territory."[122]

Carter maintained her political investments throughout her career at Tandem and was named Entertainment Woman of the Year by the American Civil Liberties Union in 1975.[123] She was often frank in her assessment of the industry's and Tandem's shortcomings in employment practices and awareness of marginalized groups. When the Anti-Defamation League (ADL) criticized an episode of *Mary Hartman* for being "libelous to Jews and questionable in taste," Carter arranged for screenings of the objectionable episode and a face-to-face meeting with the organization.[124] Carter represented her actions in the press as an earnest desire to engage and understand the political stakes that drove the protest and to incorporate these concerns into the company's ethos and education. With this motivation, she strove to create immediate and intimate connections with political activists.[125] In response to the ADL, Carter forewent "third party" interventions and arrangements because, as she explained it, "We wanted to hear it in person. We do better shows when we're smarter."[126]

At a 1976 National Association of Broadcasters (NAB) conference panel concerning race and television, Carter's talk was the one that "attracted most of the interest."[127] When challenged as to Tandem's lack of equitable employment practices for Black workers, Carter did little to refute the claim or to defend the rationale behind such practices. She admitted that the television industry was one that had "practiced de facto segregation for a number of years."[128] When asked if she thought the industry was improving, Carter responded, "When I'm not in total despair the answer is different than when I'm tired. It's a subtle blend of yes and no."[129] Carter's forthright appraisal of television's imperfect political evolution did not harm her career at Tandem. Less than a year after her comments at the NAB conference, Carter was promoted from vice president of public affairs to vice president of creative affairs at Tandem.[130] Her promotion, which came on the heels of her critical and public assessment at the conference, supports the notion that Lear genuinely valued Carter's political views and critical awareness and saw them as qualities that enriched his company.

ALL THAT GLITTERS AS MARY HARTMAN, REDUX

Mary Hartman paved the way for greater experimentation at Tandem and offered women who worked there greater opportunities and visibility. *All That Glitters*, the next show Tandem produced after *Mary Hartman*, represented a world where gender roles were inverted: women were the executives at multinational corporations and men were their secretaries; women were wage earners and men were househusbands; and women were confident, driven, and unemotional, while men were sexualized, taken for granted, and unfulfilled. In the initial planning meeting for the program, Lear described it as a "kind of *Executive Suite*, except everything is turned 180-degrees around in terms of male-female, men and women, male-female relationships."[131] Lear based the original sketch for the women characters on men who worked in the television industry: "There's a cool and calculating, utterly brilliant Lew Wasserman-type, and the jokey, rotarian Bob Wood-type, and suave, smooth-talking (these are all women) lothario kind of Grant Tinker-type."[132] The satirical soap opera style and programming strategies for the show promised, much like *Mary Hartman*, to disrupt traditions of "appropriate" content and programming schedules. A *Variety* headline, "Frontloaded with Sexual Titters, 'Glitters' Could Bother Carson,"? emphasizes both the industrial and ideological implications of such disruptions.[133] Additionally, the show helped women solidify or elevate their status at Tandem. From producing *Mary Hartman*, Viva Knight moved to the producer role on *All That Glitters*, and Stephanie Sills was named executive producer.[134] Virginia Carter, whose "special interest and responsibilities" included *Glitters*, rounded out Lear's "top three lieutenants" for the program.[135] Ann Marcus wrote its initial scripts.

The success of *Mary Hartman* and the ways Lear sold it informed Tandem's approach to marketing *Glitters*. A full-page ad in *Variety* signaled Tandem's independence as a production company with "exclusive distribution" of the program.[136] According to this promotion, "Norman Lear and 40 stations made television history" with the premiere of *All That Glitters*. Sold to stations at "big prices," *All That Glitters* benefited from the "success of Lear's 'Mary Hartman, Mary Hartman'" and amplified its formula for bypassing networks.[137] On the heels of *Mary Hartman*, Lear's success was so great that he did not even shoot a pilot, which forced television stations to buy *Glitters* "sight unseen," as many, particularly in top markets, did.[138] The reported asking price for the show was $35,000 a week for five shows a week, a deal that was comparable to the asking price for the then-established hit *Mary Hartman*, which cost $38,000 a week at that time.[139] The novel, controversial content of both *Glitters* and *Mary Hartman* created unprecedented competition for late-night television. Because of family-friendly viewing hours, many stations carried *Mary Hartman* at 11:00 p.m. to avoid viewer complaints.[140] This placed *Mary Hartman* against the late-night news. When these same stations picked up *Glitters*, they frequently scheduled it directly following *Mary Hartman*, which then put it in competition with *The Tonight Show*, which threatened to create "a lot of trouble for Carson."[141]

Glitters promised to build on the success of *Mary Hartman* and cement the challenges it posed to the staid traditions of the networks. Conventional wisdom suggested that the show would thrive. The program registered with elevision insiders and enjoyed a "fast start" in ratings in competitive markets.[142] After an annual meeting of the National Association of Television Program Executives (NATPE), a "five-day sales bazaar conducted by 192 distributors," *All That Glitters* was among the 113 new syndicated shows that "survived" this "first acid test."[143] More than merely surviving, it ranked as one of the twenty-one shows in this pool that were "particularly far along in terms of station and/or sponsor interest."[144] Initial reviews were positive, with predictions that the show would "come on strong" and "could become more controversial than 'MH2.'"[145] Another early review described *Glitters* as "ratings gold," with a target audience of "enthusiastic fans" composed of "young married women who liked the dominant women/inferior men theme."[146] Even in its largely negative assessment, *Time* granted that the show was Lear's attempt to "take on his biggest subject: sexual habits and stereotypes."[147]

Although all signs pointed to the show's potential, *Glitters* was canceled after only thirteen weeks on the air. While Lear's shows had dealt with issues of sexuality and gender before, *Glitters* was the first to place them at the show's center and to use gender role reversal to do so, which likely had much to do with its demise. The show's basic premise involves female executives who run a successful global corporation and men who work as secretaries and serve as women's sexual playthings. Men are sexualized, men are cuckolded, men sit at home worrying that their wives no longer take an interest in them, and men gain weight and worry about it. Virginia Carter remembers that the planning of the show, which was a "whole lot of fun," involved figuring out how to create positions of power for women: "It couldn't be somebody who played football and got all that money, but it had to be something. We had to work out what these women would be in order to have the power positions. And they would pinch their male secretaries' butts and things like that." Lear received hate mail written about *Glitters*, something Carter attributes to the show's "role reversal." "It was just so fascinating to see how the public reacted to that," said Carter. "We couldn't keep it on the air because it was so unpopular."[148]

"Macho male types will be up against the wall," predicted *Variety* in its review of *Glitters*. Regarded as "the tv football wife's revenge," the show's efforts to appeal to a "young female demographic" and "large homosexual following via the male secretaries" did little to appeal to heteronormative male viewers.[149] The New York preview bore out this prediction. Of the male critics present, all but one left after the first two episodes and none was present after the third episode, leaving only women in the audience. At its Washington, D.C., gala premiere held at the Kennedy Center, the show was presented to the audience of "glittery people," where "it became apparent that 90 percent of the laughter came from women."[150] In spite of his argument that the gender politics of the show had nothing to do with its cancellation, *Time* television critic Gerald Clarke spent a significant amount of his column detailing "the wearying jokes" that relied upon gender role reversals and the sexualization of men in the workplace. "The Globatron secretaries are sleek young men," wrote Clarke, "and their female bosses can't take their eyes away from the male derrière, packed into tight pants, as it passes out the door."[151]

The show's overt sexual humor and the novelty of representing objectified men on television dominated reviews of *Glitters* and overshadowed the meaningful gender insights the show offered audiences. At the Washington, D.C., premiere of the show, a male audience member remarked, "I was traumatized" and described how "uncomfortable" he was, to which Lear replied, "That's terrific."[152] The same "traumatized" male viewer also demonstrated signs of conversion from unthinking patriarchal privilege, a hoped-for by-product of the show. He asked his female companion, "Is that the way we really are?," and she responded, "Absolutely."[153] Writer Nora Ephron attended the screening and was "knocked out" at the way that women claimed power for themselves and disregarded others if they impeded their striving for success, particularly in their abilities to "click off" men in the middle of their conversation.[154] While the show was by no means universally received by feminists as an unequivocal good, it did warrant some serious consideration as an effective tool for feminist ends. As Lee Novick, vice-chair of the National Women's Political Caucus, noted, the show, though troubling in its portrayal of women replicating masculinist behaviors once they obtained power, also held potential as a "consciousness-raising vehicle for men."[155]

FIGURE 14. Gender role reversal operates at the heart of *All That Glitters*: executive Christina Stockwood (Lois Nettleton) leaves for work at Globatron Corporation while husband Bert Stockwood (Chuck McCann) keeps house. (Photofest)

Ads placed in industry publications underscored *Glitters'* feminist principles and satirical indictment of sexist workplace culture. These reviews tended to three central themes. The first called upon television's capacity to reformulate the social landscape, with sexism, like other isms, faltering in the face of thought-provoking programming. The *Washington Post* claimed that *Glitters* "could do to sexism what 'Roots' did to racism—show a huge audience the specifics of a whole system of discrimination." Another review anticipated that "*All That Glitters* could do for sexism what *All in the Family* did for bigotry." The second theme attributed distinctively feminist political principles to the show, which then served as a litmus test for sexism. The show promised to "do more to shake up male-female relations than a decade of consciousness-raising." It would "threaten many men, offend some women, and be a breath of refreshing air to the rest," and would serve as "a good test for men and women who are not sure they are emancipated." Finally, a third theme was the claim that the show was "a giant step forward for television" in general and "the most shocking and compelling new show of this up and down television season."[156]

Ann Marcus, who helped create the series, pushed to differentiate the show through unconventional genre depictions of women in the workplace. In a planning meeting, Marcus suggested a dramatic opening scene that featured women in roles typically reserved for action films and their heroic male protagonists. "You could almost start with a sort of catastrophe," she proposed. "I don't mean that this is a formula sort of thing for a Norman Lear serial starting, but like a towering inferno kind of thing. Something where there's danger and you see these women in action, and they are decisive, wonderful and whatever."[157] Marcus's suggestion did not make it to script. Instead, the dramatic opening storyline revolves around an underappreciated man, Michael, who cannot convince his high-powered lover, Andrea, to commit to him or even to say she loves him. In despair, he tries to commit suicide but fails when he faints at the sight of his own blood. The female EMT who arrives on the scene to treat him responds to his condition with little sympathy and instead discusses the best way to get bloodstains out of carpets. The callous nature of women in this inverted gender order carries out the central theme as it was originally conceptualized, but it does not deviate from the "formula" of satirical programs in the tradition of other Lear productions, as Marcus hoped it would.

In her correspondence with Gloria Steinem, to whom she sent copies of her scripts for *Glitters* in 1977, Marcus expressed displeasure in the direction the series took. Although she was "not so sure they're any better than what went on the air," Marcus was clear about her feminist "intentions" in writing the scripts. Marcus describes how, after writing the first two episodes of the series, she "cut out," an action that suggests her awareness that the show was not going to reflect the feminist concerns she had articulated in early meetings. As she told Steinem, "Unfortunately the series got stuck in the bedroom and really never got around to dealing with much more."[158] While *Glitters* ultimately proved a disappointment to Marcus, she persisted in future projects creating television that utilized satire and genre conventions to express feminist ideas.

BEYOND THE FACTORY

When Ann Marcus left Tandem, her work on *Mary Hartman* became a calling card for her abilities to create audacious yet successful programming. She created, with husband Ellis Marcus, *Life and Times of Eddie Roberts* (*L.A.T.E.R.*), which aired as a syndicated show in 1980. At this time, Marcus was regarded as the person who could duplicate the success of *Mary Hartman* and "reopen [the] late-night slot first entered by Hartman." The reputation of *Mary Hartman* and its head writer was so compelling that syndicator Metromedia offered *L.A.T.E.R.* producers a thirteen-week guarantee and sixty-five episodes. Marcus's "association with *Hartman* was not lost on Columbia or Metromedia," where executives at both companies "unabashedly refer to the success" of *Hartman* "when discussing what they expect to come from *L.A.T.E.R.*" Ken Page, vice president for executive sales at Columbia Television Pictures, admitted that, in selling *L.A.T.E.R.*, he had "no particular marketing strategy other than to 'trade off the success of *Mary Hartman*,'" which undoubtedly contributed to the show's cancellation after its first thirteen-week run.[159]

Much as she did *Mary Hartman* and *All That Glitters*, Marcus envisioned *L.A.T.E.R.* as a satirical exploration of gender. Although it "wasn't as outrageous," the show shared "some of those elements" with *Mary Hartman*.[160] Marcus described the show as deeply political, taking on "all of the social problems of the day."[161] *L.A.T.E.R.*'s plot line centered on college professor Roberts, whose "sexual problems" resulted in his wife leaving him. At work, he was an object of interest for a female colleague who wanted to use him as a "guinea pig for [her] new male contraceptive drug."[162] Roberts's chief rival for tenure at his college was a "female, Latina paraplegic," and "had all of those things going for her," but they were nonetheless "good friends," and his wife had aspirations to be the first female professional baseball player in the country.[163] Despite its soap operatic elements, Marcus linked it to the realities of her own aspirations. "It had a lot of me in it," Marcus said in a 2001 interview with the Academy of Television Arts and Sciences Foundation. "I would have loved to have been a baseball player, too."[164]

With disappointing ratings, *L.A.T.E.R.* lasted only one season. Critics were divided as to why viewers were not attracted to the program as they were to *Mary Hartman*. While some identified weaknesses in the show's humor, characterization, and storylines, others suggested that the quality of the show was not to blame. *Variety* critiqued the show for not pushing controversial ideas further but also suggested that television's conservativism, despite the "supposed greater latitude available to producers of latenight programs," was responsible.[165] The fickle and fast-moving genre cycle in television, along with the expectations of fast-developing storylines and immediate audience capture, worked against *L.A.T.E.R.*. According to the

Hollywood Reporter, L.A.T.E.R. was comparable to *Mary Hartman*, but the "exaggerated soap opera approach" had lost the "impact" it had had when it "was a novelty."[166] *New York Times* reviewer John O'Connor suggested, "*L.A.T.E.R.* needs—and probably deserves—time."[167] These sympathetic reviews stress the staid politics of late-night programming and the challenges of sustaining experimental television.

Late-night television ultimately did not foster satirical soaps and their social commentary. Instead, it opted to sustain the paternalism of the eleven o'clock news and talk shows. Marcus, however, continued to find expression for gender politics and associated "taboo" subjects through soap operas in daytime and prime time. Before, during, and after her time at Tandem, Marcus wrote for *General Hospital* and *Days of Our Lives*. Despite her success in daytime soaps, Marcus was reluctant to undertake this type of work after having "been to the heights" by working at Tandem and with the success of *Mary Hartman* Marcus's reluctance to return to soaps was a matter of labor conditions rather than prestige. She was careful not to "put down" soaps in comparison to the other kind of television work she did and acknowledged that some of "best and hardest writing" in television happened on soaps.[168] But Marcus also acknowledged that she could sustain writing for soaps only for short periods, no more than three years at a time.

Programs like *Mary Hartman* and *L.A.T.E.R.* attest to Marcus's influence not just over daytime soaps but over prime-time and late-night programming as well. According to Elana Levine, by the early 1970s soap writers had begun to reshape daytime soaps, with complex storylines, more explicit sexual concerns, and troubled gender identities; these elements "innovated the continuing ensemble drama, crucial to TV storytelling writ large for decades to come."[169] Marcus applied those innovations of daytime soaps directly to prime-time serial dramas when, by the late 1970s, she became the supervising producer for *Knots Landing* (CBS, 1979–93) and *Falcon Crest* (CBS, 1981–90).

Marcus's impact on television extends to the industry's working conditions. She was heavily involved in the Writers Guild of America (WGA) as a six-term member of the board of directors; a secretary-treasurer from 1991 to 1993; and a member of numerous committees that dealt with labor exploitation and unfair labor practices, including one on age discrimination and one supporting an animation strike. In 1999, Marcus received the Morgan Cox award for service to the guild.[170] In addition to the Age Discrimination and Animation Strike Fund Committee, Marcus served on committees on blacklisted writers and on freedom of expression and censorship. With firsthand knowledge of the working conditions facing soap writers, Marcus advocated for better labor protections for them. When she ran for reelection to the WGA board of directors in 1990, Marcus argued that the guild needed to heed the "legitimate grievances of daytime writers who suffer first (and probably most)" from writers' strikes.[171] She urged the guild to "investigate and punish scabs who not only keep the Soaps going during strikes" but also kept their jobs after the strikes ended.[172] Marcus also held the WGA accountable for its lack of respect for daytime TV writers, both in material terms and in orga-nizational culture. Current contract negotiations did not adequately address the conditions those writers faced, and the Guild did not treat daytime writers as "an integral part of the Guild," which made them feel like "second class members."[173]

Although Marcus was one of the most visible and most prolific of the women who worked at Tandem, other women benefited from their involvement in feminist-ori-ented programs at the company. Susan Harris, who wrote for *Maude* and was respon-sible for "Maude's Dilemma," "Maude's Facelift," and "Like Mother, Like Daughter," parlayed her success at Tandem to a considerable career in television, most notably in her work on *The Golden Girls* (NBC, 1985–92), which garnered her multiple Emmy nominations and a win. She maintained creative control over programs when she became a partner in a production company with Paul Junger Witt and Tony Thomas. One of the company's productions, *Fay* (NBC, 1975–76), a short-lived situation com-edy that Harris wrote and created, extended and enhanced the feminist issues Harris had explored in *Maude*. The ripple effect of working on Tandem's woman-centered productions extended to the career of Lee Grant, who played the role of Fay. Grant, along with Nessa Hyams, who wrote for *Mary Hartman*, and Gail Parent, who originated the character of Mary Hartman, were part of the AFI's first Directing Workshop for Women in 1974 and would continue to work in film and television as directors, casting directors, writers, producers, and creative consultants.[174]

Although a "series essentially cancelled by NBC before it aired," *Fay* was tremen-dously important to Harris and to other women who worked on the show and val-ued its expression of feminist ideas.[175] *Fay*'s titular protagonist is a recently divorced forty-year-old woman who returns to work at a law firm, resumes dating, and rees-tablishes her sense of self through personal and professional means. In centering on a newly single, middle-aged woman, the series explored topics of women's sexuality, economic precarity, and refusals of domesticity and femininity in a capitalist-con-sumerist system. Throughout all these concerns, *Fay* explicitly referenced women's liberation. One episode alone, "Not with My Husband You Don't," dealt with work-place misogyny, the passage of the ERA, NOW's political perspective, and the use of "Ms." as a replacement for "Mrs." When asked to describe *Fay* in an interview, Lee Grant, who played the role of Fay, prefaced her response by saying, "It was way ahead of its time."[176] Harris, too, saw *Fay* as a groundbreaking show. She credited Grant with bringing a "different kind of woman" to screen and imbuing Fay with a mode of empowerment that was new to—and ultimately too challenging for—viewing audi-ences: "You could hardly call Lee Grant or the character she played 'sweet.' People were threatened by her acerbity. By contrast, Maude was married, and even though she had a big mouth, Walter, her husband, still prevailed. Maude played so much bigger than life, you didn't relate to her as being anyone real. She didn't pretend to be all that real, whereas Fay was. And I think it was too threatening."[177]

While Harris attributed *Fay*'s failure to viewers' response to the show's bold repre-sentation of women's empowerment, she also held the network accountable for failing to provide time for the show to develop and build an audience. Grant attributed the show's cancellation to its airing during the Family Viewing Hour, the FCC policy that held the networks responsible for programming "family-friendly" viewing from 8 to 9 p.m. This time slot spelled disaster for *Fay*, in Grant's estimation. Grant asserted that the show "would have hit the roof" if it had been scheduled more appropriately.[178]

Fay's cancellation was so abrupt that when Grant showed up to set one day, she found herself "evicted." The set furniture was unceremoniously dumped in the parking lot, and a stagehand was the person who informed Grant of the show's fate. Grant was scheduled to appear on *The Tonight Show* later that same day to promote the show. Despite the cancellation, *The Tonight Show* encouraged Grant to appear, which she did. During her interview with Johnny Carson, Grant literally "gave the finger" to the "guy who canceled the show." When asked about the repercussions of such an action, she denied that there were any and maintained that the act granted her tremendous relief. Grant described the defiant gesture as cathartic, "so much better" than "pulling over to the side of the road and crying . . . so it was over, over in a very healthy, fun way."[179]

Grant's commitment to women's authority and autonomy was evident in her emphatic acknowledgment of Harris's creative control on set. In response to interview questions that suggested a difficult production environment or the influence of male production staff, Grant was careful to correct misperceptions that would detract from Harris's accomplishments. Although Alan Arkin directed the first episode, Lee clearly delineated his contribution only as a director, not as a wide-ranging and influential force in the show. "Susan did all the writing," said Grant. When asked to describe table readings and discuss the level of her input and ability to change content, Grant explained that she was permitted to do anything but did not want or need to because "Susan was a genius. . . . I was just thrilled to have the kind of stuff that she gave me to work with."[180] When asked if scripts were in rewrite until the time they were shot, Grant responded that it never was any problem. By countering assumptions that Harris had failed to create a successful program and a functional workplace, Grant expressed feminist ethics. Most obviously, she supported a female coworker whose reputation was on the line. Grant also emphasized Harris's facilitation of a production environment that fostered cooperation and helped articulate the feminist vision on-screen that both she and Harris shared and collectively built.

DID TANDEM MAKE A DIFFERENCE FOR WOMEN IN TELEVISION?

Norman Lear acknowledges the importance of women workers to Tandem's success. From the start of the company, women were part of the picture. Marian Rees began working with Lear and his partner Bud Yorkin in 1955 as an assistant, advanced to associate producer at the founding of Tandem Productions in 1958 with *An Evening with Fred Astaire* (NBC), and worked as associate producer on pilots for *All in the Family* and *Sanford and Son*. In his 2014 autobiography, Lear describes Rees as the "first of a series of women who provided the glue that held things together in the most hectic of times and situations." In the acknowledgements of the book, Lear asserts, "I've never worked on a production where women weren't 'the glue that held things together'" and names multiple women who worked in creative and executive roles.[181]

While Tandem seemed like a haven for women to express their talents and their feminist politics and Lear a champion of women television workers, the company's investments in progressive gender politics were complicated. Notably, Tandem did not employ women consistently across its productions. In her history of the Screenwriters Guild, Miranda Banks complicates the claims of her interview subjects about their progressive gender politics, Lear included, with statistical data and analysis. According to the WGA's "Women's Committee Statistics Report" of November 7, 1974, for "teleplays" written by women that year, Tandem employed women for 4 out of 69 episodes of *All in the Family*, Fox's *M*A*S*H* employed women to write 1 out of 38 episodes, and CBS/Freeman employed women for .5 (half of a writing team) of 133 episodes of *Hawaii 5-0*.[182] MTM made the strongest showing, employing women to write 50 percent of its *Mary Tyler Moore Show* episodes (25 out of 50).[183] These statistics reflect the realities of underemployment for women writers and indicate that women, when employed, were more likely to write for programs that featured women and/or feminist sentiment centrally. For instance, women at Tandem wrote 11 out of 37 episodes of *Maude* but 0 out of 49 for *Sanford and Son*.[184] While writing afforded women some inroads into television, depending on subject material, other jobs remained out of reach. Even at companies like Tandem where programming brought women into the writers' room and Lear credited women as the "glue" that held a production together, a woman employed on a Tandem show, according to Banks, typically "was not leading it on set or in post-production."[185]

As for television's executive ranks, by the early 1980s the situation for women showed some promising changes. In 1981, *Variety* published "Women Are on the Rise in Television's Executive Suites," which included its own survey findings that women occupied "respectable status in the executive and production ranks in tv." Tandem was one of the companies *Variety* named to support its claim, since, at the time of the survey, the women working at Tandem included Virginia Carter (vice president of creative affairs), Kelly Smith (vice president of business affairs), Pam Fond (assistant treasurer and director of tax), Fern Field (director of development and producer), Frances McConnell (director of public affairs), Molly DeHetre (director of business affairs), and Barbara Bragliatti (vice president of media affairs).[186] The placement of women in the business side of Tandem suggests that the broader company workplace, rather than only its production ranks, afforded a means by which the company addressed employment disparities and utilized women's skills to forward their own business interests. As the case of women working at network headquarters discussed in chapter 1 demonstrates, as impressive as executive job titles are, the conditions of those jobs and the day-to-day functioning of the workplace warrant examination to understand more fully what women's gains in television meant.

To claim that Tandem affected wide-sweeping changes for women working in television or that, by the early 1980s, feminism had converted the entire television industry to enlightened, equitable employment and production practices would be an overstatement. For many women, the realities of working in the television industry in the 1980s and beyond meant continued inequality in pay, occupational status, and employment. Working at Tandem, however, did provide the women who worked there opportunities for feminist expression and for placement in its ranks, even if they did not have conventional credentialing. Their previous employment as secretaries, writers for soap operas, and workers in unrelated industries proved less of a barrier and more of an asset to Tandem, as did their feminist perspectives. More expansively, the state of women's employment in television during the 1970s, as illustrated by the responses of the FCC and AWRT and addressed at Tandem, moved multiple organizations and figures in the industry closer to feminist awareness and action. *Variety*'s hopeful headline of 1981 suggests the not-inconsequential outcomes of these actions.

4

Television's "Serious Sisters"

Experiments in Public and Regional Television
for Women

When WBZ-TV, a local television station in Boston, produced and aired *Yes, We Can* on January 18, 1974, it proved an unprecedented televisual event. The program was dedicated to concerns of area women; was conceptualized and produced by women; and featured an all-woman cast of interviewers, interviewees, and talent. Preceded the previous night by a one-hour prime-time special, the *Yes, We Can Entertainment Special*, which showcased celebrity performances, *Yes, We Can* ran for a total of sixteen hours on a single day. Except for WBZ's *Eyewitness News*, the station aired no other programming that day. The program hybridized live performance with homemaking advice and domestic issues and infused it with feminist debate and government hearings on institutionalized sexism.[1]

Yes, We Can was an experiment meant to address the fundamental shortcomings of television for women. First and most obviously, the sheer number of broadcast hours given over to *Yes, We Can* challenged traditional programming schedules, in which content that explicitly addressed women viewers was restricted to undervalued daytime time slots. Second, producers reimagined issues of interest to women beyond domestic labors and associated consumerist practices. Third, women played key roles in production as show hosts, interviewers, and participants. Fourth, the production drew together multiple and unlikely collaborators in state government, commercial television, civic institutions, businesses, and community groups to support, plan, and execute the program. Finally, the show expanded generic conventions of daytime television for women, which in its inception in the 1950s included "homemaking shows, shopping shows . . . and popular programs the broadcast industry broadly categorized as 'audience participation shows.'"[2]

While *Yes, We Can* was a one-of-a-kind television event, it shared common ground with other feminist-oriented programs designed for women in the 1970s.

These programs challenged prevailing understandings of television for women by reconceptualizing audience, production conventions, scheduling, format, and content. They featured women in front the camera as hosts, interviewees, talent, and expert guests while behind the camera women worked in significant numbers as producers, writers, researchers, editors, and camera operators. *In Her Own Right* (WGBH, 1970), *Everywoman* (WTOP, 1972–78), and *Woman Alive!* (KERA, 1974; WNET, 1975–77) aired in prime-time hours and envisioned women's viewership outside daytime schedules.[3] Women were regarded as active participants by *In Her Own Right* (WGBH, 1970) and *Woman '75* (WBZ, 1975), which solicited and integrated input from at-home viewers. Except for a "sprinkling of men" in the production ranks, *For Women Today* (WBZ, 1970–72), *Everywoman*, *Woman Alive!*, and *Tomorrow's Woman* (unaired pilot, 1972) employed women in the majority of the programs' production team as producers, contributing editors, and directors.[4]

As this sampling of programs suggests, regional and public television productions led the way in revising women's television during the 1970s. In 1972, *Broadcasting* noted that the "serious sisters" of women's television that were emerging early in the decade were "done locally or syndicated."[5] Without network television's inhibiting commercial imperatives and cultural traditions, local, syndicated, and public television enjoyed relative freedom to innovate. *Woman Alive!* producer Joan Shigekawa clarified the importance of alternatives to commercial television and the appeals of public television for feminist workers. She noted that although many of the women who worked on *Woman Alive!* had careers in commercial television, they made a "financial sacrifice" to work for public television.[6] They were motivated to convey stories of "joyful changes" women across the country were creating that were not of interest to commercial television, even as advertisers spent millions of dollars "trying to reach these women."[7] Commercial television's neglect and misunderstanding of women—both as workers who wanted to create different types of television for women and as viewers who would tune into such television—were, to Shigekawa, "their loss, and public television's gain."[8]

As Shigekawa and others like her migrated from commercial television, they brought with them innovative ideas and a hope that television could better meet the needs of women viewers. Their vision for regional and public programs, evinced by this chapter's exploration of *In Her Own Right, Woman Alive!*, and *Yes, We Can*, offered creative and varied solutions for the problems of women's television. All three programs, according to their respective production strategies, addressed long-standing, sexist ideas about television for women by redefining genre formulas, viewers' needs and interests, and the role of women behind and in front of the camera. The interventions of these "serious sisters" prompted an unprecedented period of growth and creativity in what Rachel Moseley, Helen Wheatley, and Helen Wood describe as "television *for* women."[9] In their scholarship on the matter, Moseley, Wheatley, and Wood call for an expansion of the framework of "women's television" and analysis beyond genres assumed to be aimed at women.

The resulting, more expansive scope of television for women, versus women's television, creates a new canon for feminist analysis.

Representative of television's redress to the failings of women's television, the productions included in this chapter—*In Her Own Right, Woman Alive!*, and *Yes, We Can*—expand the boundaries of women's television and engage the concerns of "television for women" identified by Moseley, Wheatley, and Wood. Although they address women viewers, these programs fall outside typical genres, such as soap operas, game shows, and homemaking shows, that have served as the foci for foundational feminist scholarship on women's television.[10] They also reorient analysis from "visible emphasis upon fictional programming over factual programming" in feminist television studies to informational, educational, and news programming.[11] Additionally, these productions foreground and value "feminine competencies" in both production and reception that depart from restrictive conventions and commercialized traditions. Finally, and perhaps most radically, these programs employ feminist production strategies to create progressive content and to address both avowed feminists and viewers who were curious about feminism.

This last point offers a qualification to the "television for women" paradigm. Rather than thinking only of "television *about* or *by* women," Moseley, Wheatley, and Wood argue that women have had investments and found pleasure in texts that were not made by and were not about women. This argument broadens and complicates what texts should count as appropriate objects of study for feminist analyses of women and television. Yet as useful a corrective as the "by *or* for women" paradigm is, it also potentially sidelines programming of value to women that features television productions by *and* for women.

To consider how programs like *In Her Own Right, Woman Alive!*, and *Yes, We Can* deepen and diversify the study of women's television as television for women, this chapter purposefully engages "slippage" between production, content, and audience, with women engaged in all three domains.[12] It does so not out of theoretical carelessness or strict canonical rules, against which Moseley, Wheatley, and Wood rightfully caution, but rather because these programs imagine the women's roles as on-screen authorities, at-home viewers, and behind-the-scenes workers as both central to the production and interdependent within production strategies. To explore the potentials of television for women in an age of US women's liberation, this chapter turns to short-lived, modestly funded, and regional television programs that involved women as subjects, audiences, *and* producers differently and with progressive political intentions.

REDEFINING TELEVISION FOR WOMEN IN THE 1970S

Television that targets women has long been the object of cultural disregard and disdain, yet women viewers figured centrally in profitability for the television industry from its beginnings. As early as 1948, *Variety* reported that daytime television offered networks "their first opportunity to break even."[13] In her work on women viewers and daytime programming of the 1950s, Marsha F. Cassidy finds that, in spite of the "curious assortment of programs calculated to attract the female spectator," "women spectators served as the industry's polestar" during television's early years.[14] Although initially uncertain about how to best appeal to women, the industry quickly cemented a basic formula that privileged commercial viability and cost-effectiveness over quality and innovation. In 1954, NBC's vice president of TV sales reported that advertisers were increasingly aware of the "economy and efficiency of daytime television" and the "unequalled opportunity to demonstrate products to the housewife without having to pay the premium rates of evening time."[15] By the beginning of the year, top-rated daytime programming was confined to soap operas (*Search for Tomorrow* [CBS, 1951–82; NBC, 1982–86] and *Guiding Light* [CBS, 1952–2009]) and game shows with male hosts (*Strike It Rich* [CBS, 1951–58], *The Big Pay-Off* [NBC, 1951–53; CBS, 1953–59], and *On Your Account* [NBC, 1953–54; CBS, 1955–56]), thereby further establishing the links between low-cost programming for women and effective commercialized outreach, a focus on domesticity, and male-helmed productions.[16]

Since television's early days, formulas for women's television were so entrenched that substantive reformulations were nearly impossible, even with evidence that women viewers might not desire what television imagined them to want. This meant that, on the whole, women's programming was mired in traditions of men acting as authorities in feminized television genres intended for women viewers. Much as it did in the 1950s, daytime programming of the 1970s assumed that confident yet non-threatening male talent appealed to women. Even with the visibility of the women's movement, commercial network programs persisted in featuring "charm boys," male hosts who "communicated a commanding but amiable deportment on air."[17] By 1972, the daytime talk show *Dinah's Place* (NBC, 1970–74) was the only network television program on air to feature a woman, Dinah Shore, as host.[18]

Network television's drive for profit defined a successful program by commercial appeals and nationwide outreach, both of which the industry defined in sexist terms. Raysa Bonow, executive producer for WBZ's daytime television show *For Women Today*, commented on this situation in 1972. According to Bonow, the lack of women working in television was a result of conditions in commercial television that "indoctrinated" viewers "into only seeing men in authoritative roles" and were "determined by men who really believe that women are not a saleable item."[19] This want of "salability" meant that, in spite of their desirability as a consumer market and in spite of the profitability of women's television, women were not viable as a part of the product. Instead, the industry's stubborn commitment to the idea that women lacked "salability" limited women's roles in production and held back gender-equitable hiring.

Concerns of salability extended to program content. Profitability depended upon ratings that produced "least objectionable programming," a staple of American commercial television.[20] By the start of the 1970s, the industry was aware of the need to speak to women in different fashion, but it was reluctant to do so with explicitly political content, lest it alienate viewers. As Barbara Walters found in her experience hosting syndicated talk show *Not for Women Only* (1971–76), frank feminist expression could not happen on commercial television because of assumptions that it "'would not draw a national response'" and would therefore compromise the foremost priority of mass audience capture.[21]

Although least objectionable programming impeded significant and fast-acting changes to the traditions of television for women, some progressive movement started to happen by the early 1970s. Television's address to women was shifting, albeit in constricted dayparts and channels. A 1972 *Broadcasting* report noted that despite the continued prominence of "diapers-and-recipes types of programming," daytime game shows, and soap operas, television for women was expanding to include "serious sisters" in regional, syndicated, and public television. These innovative programs sidelined domestic issues of childcare and cooking in favor of "new program forms" with "a greater air of sophistication and intellectuality than their predecessors." *Broadcasting* correlated these improvements in programming for women to the television industry's growing awareness of the "'woman of the 70's'" whose outlook was influenced by feminist politics.[22] While feminist influence on television had measurable effects on television for women, these effects played out primarily—and with few exceptions—in local and public television rather than in commercial television.

While the limitations of network television are obvious, it is important to note that characterizing public, local, and syndicated television productions as an unproblematic feminist haven is inaccurate. The Corporation for Public Broadcasting (CPB) launched an internal investigation in 1975 and found "pervasive underrepresentation of women, both in employment and in program content."[23] According to the CPB report, fewer than 30 percent of public television jobs were filled by women; in children's programs, 69 percent of characters were male; in public affairs, news, and panel programs, 85 percent of participants with speaking roles were men.[24] Local productions failed to deliver on their promise of representing community interests and tried to minimize the impact of advocacy groups on equal air time given to concerns of women and minorities. Faced with threats to FCC license renewals, stations often subverted the system by meeting demands for improved and wider-ranging programming through low-cost programming. Instead of carrying out a thorough overhaul of programming practices, stations often provided underrepresented groups only with "access to cheaply produced public affairs programs scheduled in the late-night and early-morning slots."[25] Even productions helmed by women with feminist aims were not immune from the commercialized and commodifying influence of television, according to some feminist activists. *Yes, We Can*, for example, was disrupted by representatives from thirty-eight organizations who protested WBZ's cultivation of women's liberation "to make a media-thing for commercial uses" and its inclusion of corporations at the women's fair.[26]

Even with the limitations of public and local television, there were genuine opportunities for enlightened change in both arenas. As the 1970s progressed, public television demonstrated measurable improvement in employment. An internal investigation instituted in 1976 and congressional action in 1977 threatened cuts in federal funding to the Center for Public Broadcasting if employment of women and minorities did not improve by 1980; this measure resulted in improved hiring practices. In January 1977, public television reported a 10.1 percent gain in employment for women in public television from the previous year.[27] As for local commercial television, it made improvements throughout the 1970s with regard to women television viewers and workers, "particularly on local schedules."[28] A 1977 *New York Times* article, "Programming for Women—Time for Reevaluation," noted that local programming, in spite of its "relatively low-keyed and unthreatening" tenor, was "often surprisingly successful" in its politically progressive articulation of women's issues.[29]

Despite its marginalization within the larger television landscape and its lack of financial support, the politically conscious, community-oriented local television that emerged in the late 1960s and into the 1970s mattered. It was both innovative in its production and meaningful in its reception. In *Black Power TV*, Devorah Heitner argues for the value of local public affairs programs such as New York's *Inside Bedford-Stuyvesant* (WNEW, 1968–71) and Boston's *Say Brother* (WGBH, 1968–97), which were experimental local television made by Black media workers for Black viewers. Heitner's multifaceted production history involving oral histories of production staff, viewer feedback, reviews in industry publications, and government findings and policies demonstrates that these programs "represented new cultural practices and legitimized activism."[30] Viewers regarded the shows as a "transformative experience" and keenly felt the importance of such programming in a white-dominated medium.[31] Gayle Wald's analysis of the public television program *Soul!* (WNDT, 1968–73) identifies the impact a modestly funded program could have on audiences. Wald argues that "despite competition from the three major networks and technological challenges associated with public television, which tended to broadcast on UHF channels inaccessible to all but state-of-the-art television sets, [Ellis] Haizlip's show attracted a substantial and loyal audience."[32] Wald's focused attention to *Soul!* reveals the significance of production strategies and the ways producers, creative staff, and technicians transformed television for makers and consumers. As the program's producer, Haizlip envisioned unique content and production principles to bring expressions of Black Power to television that "explicitly blurred the boundary between producers and consumers," built collectivity through performance, and "called on embodied memories of past performances while anticipating new feelings and states of being."[33]

Public and regional broadcasting offered unique possibilities to introduce a feminist ethos to television for women. As compromised and short-lived as some of these programs were, each one discussed in this chapter exemplifies indisputably self-aware experiments in television for women. Television's "serious sisters" shared common concerns of revising, according to feminist ideals, content, audience outreach, on-set labor practices, and the composition of production staff and crews. These shows were designed to address women viewers while correcting television's consumerist and—in feminist producers' minds—demeaning conceptualizations of these viewers. They redefined who their viewers were, what they needed from television, and how they would interact and influence on-screen content. They employed majority to exclusively female production teams and, in doing so, challenged the authority and marketability of male-helmed television. Finally, these programs made room for more women at all levels of production and fostered collaborative decision-making that involved all production workers.

IN HER OWN RIGHT: HOW TO MAKE A WOMAN'S SHOW

One of the first feminist interventions in television for women, *In Her Own Right*, was produced by Katharine Kinderman for Boston public television station WGBH-TV. It ran as a series in the summer of 1970 and served as a template for the "serious sisters" that followed, particularly in its public orientation, political-mindedness, and inclusion of women viewers. The station's program order for *In Her Own Right* made clear that television for women should be not only "for women" but "about them as well."[34] From its first episode, "How to Make a Woman's Show," the producers prioritized new ways of reaching women and opening up the processes of television production to viewer intervention and understanding. The entirety of this inaugural episode tended to educating viewers about how a new type of television program for women could be made. Therefore, the program was an exercise in television literacy for audiences and in democratic opportunities for audiences to shape the program through their input. The episode included a panel meant to represent a cross section of viewers—a housewife; a high schooler; an unmarried man; and a member of a radical feminist group, Bread and Roses—who discussed what they would like to see happen on the program.

Kinderman conceptualized *In Her Own Right* as a cooperative effort with the viewing public. The first episode solicited input from audience members about the program's title, its content, and which guests to book. Host Karen Klein assured viewers that the production would continually be "experimenting" with elements of the program "with [their] help." As a result, episodes addressed issues ranging from class dynamics to public and private sphere politics to women's history. Guests included a lobbyist, members of Congress and state governments, psychologists, educators, a childcare worker and nursery school director, and small business owners. An array of women activists frequently appeared on the show: a "radical political activist" on the first episode; suffragette Florence Luscomb on an episode that celebrated the fiftieth anniversary of the women's suffrage movement;

members of Boston-area women's liberation groups, including the Boston Women's Health Collective and creators of *Our Bodies, Ourselves*, for an episode on "Women's Liberation"; and a cab driver who was the sole female board member of the Boston Taxi Drivers Association, along with a factory worker who was the founder of the labor group Boston Women United for an episode entitled "Blue Collar Women."[35]

Although *In Her Own Right* was a formative influence in television for women, its time on the air was short. After just seven episodes, WGBH canceled the show. Michael Rice, WGBH program director, defended the decision by claiming that the show was intentionally transitory. He regarded the program as a "summer test series, which was never intended to continue into the fall."[36] Rice also indicated that the show was dropped to make way for other news and discussion programs designed to meet the station's public broadcasting obligations. The women who worked on the program assumed that the show would have a typical season run, so the cancellation took them by surprise. Feminist newsletter *The Spokeswoman* characterized the cancellation as unjust; it cited the program's "good" ratings that "continue[d] to climb" and argued that WGBH "overlooked" the quality of the program and the work of its women.[37] According to Mary Blau, a production assistant, Rice and the team met after each show, and the shows they "'particularly liked'" were ones that Rice "'liked too.'"[38] Given the show's promise and accounts of Rice's positive reactions, the seemingly abrupt, unexpected cancellation raised suspicions and drew criticism.

Contrary to Rice's public statement as to why *In Her Own Right* was canceled, producers, production assistants, and moderators reported that Rice's personal politics were to blame. *In Her Own Right* was defined by the control these women had over the show's production and the authority they wielded on set. These qualities, in the opinion of the show's production team, disturbed Rice so much that he canceled the program. In an interview with the *Boston Globe*, production staff related details from the meeting during which the show's cancellation was announced. In this meeting, management told them that the show "had been a failure" and "didn't have a warm atmosphere," and Rice criticized them for their "chip-on-the-shoulder attitude."[39] Such comments suggest that the show itself was not at issue but that the workplace and production workers for the program were.

The women who worked on the show countered the implication that they did not meet the needs of the public in ways that the news and discussion programs proposed to replace *In Her Own Right* would. They insisted that they had designed the program for "all women" and "denied any bias" that would alienate viewers.[40] *The Spokeswoman* confirmed the show's audience appeal, describing the show as one that "points up the wide-ranging interests of women at home."[41] Within a week of announcing the cancellation of *In Her Own Right*, Rice promised that the station would develop "a new show devoted to 'contemporary women's concerns,'" something that *In Her Own Right* production staff felt they already had accomplished.[42]

The troubled circumstances surrounding the cancellation of *In Her Own Right*, to some critics, reflected WGBH's ideological trajectory. *Newsweek* voiced concerns that the station, which "by liberal lights" was a "model of admirable aspirations," was dismantling its politically progressive content and equitable employment practices.[43] With *Say, Brother* in 1968, WGBH was the first station in the US to air a show "produced and directed by blacks for blacks," and, in spite of one-third of Black families in Boston watching the program, WGBH canceled the show in July 1970.[44] The cancellation of *In Her Own Right* followed in a month's time. While protests against the station successfully reversed the cancellation of *Say, Brother*, similar actions did not save *In Her Own Right*. Instead of reinstating the show, WGBH promised only to consider future programming about women and to meet with women's groups to guide this decision.

The cancellation of *In Her Own Right* demonstrates the precarity of a television production helmed by women for women. By working in roles typically reserved for men, women challenged the gendered segregation of production and threatened an industry that had long depended on male authority and conventionally gendered behaviors in the workplace. In the case of *In Her Own Right*, these women seemed to provoke anxiety and hostility on the part of male management, and their perceived lack of femininity became justifiable grounds by which to cancel their program. Yet in other instances—as exemplified by programs that followed *In Her Own Right*—women working on innovative television for women challenged gendered standards of behavior in the industry with positive results. They exerted masculinized control over decision-making, technically and creatively, within the production of their programs. But instead of abandoning femininity altogether, they reconstructed their television workplaces as woman-friendly and collaborative and, in doing so, expressed self-determined femininity as an asset in how television could be made.

WOMAN ALIVE!'S REGIONAL FOCUS AND NATIONAL OUTREACH

Described as a program "for, by and about women," public television program *Woman Alive!* began with a one-hour pilot special in 1974, continued in 1975 with a first season consisting of ten half-hour programs, and finished in 1977 with a second season comprising five one-hour specials. The program clearly declared its feminist politics, not just through audience address, production, and content, but also through its funding and institutional backing. Supported by a grant from the Corporation for Public Broadcasting (CPB), the program was coproduced by public television station KERA-TV in Dallas–Fort Worth, Texas, and *Ms.* magazine. The unlikely pairing of an East Coast feminist media institution and a Texas public television station resulted in a unique regional sensibility, a relatively high-quality program meant for a nationwide audience, and strategic outreach to women who felt overlooked by or alienated from well-known feminist organizations and leadership.

In their proposal submitted to the CPB, KERA and *Ms.* announced their goals for the program: to make the subject of feminism a serious and long-standing one, to define the movement through its diversity, and to correct misperceptions about the coastal elitism and white exclusivity of the movement. According to *Woman Alive!* producers, it was time for feminists to take over television's treatment of the women's movement and to emphasize what more there was to be said about it beyond television's existing, shortsighted analysis. By making their own TV show, *Ms.* enacted the next logical step in feminist-controlled media. With their journalistic expertise, they could coproduce a program that effectively circumvented news outlets external to feminist organizations. With public television's help, they would be the ones to relay messages about feminism to viewers.

The direct involvement of feminist organizations in production solved a number of problems, not least of which was accuracy and complexity in coverage of feminist politics. This involvement also helped ensure the women's movement as an ongoing newsworthy presence on television, which was a priority, given the ways that mainstream news coverage treated feminism as yet another fad with a short news cycle. *Woman Alive!*'s producers pitched the show based on the need to provide sustained and serious coverage of a growing, legitimate political movement. With *Ms.* "on sale at the Safeway," the mainstreaming of feminism fostered perceptions that feminist outreach was wholly successful and that nothing more needed to be done to present feminist ideas to the American public.[45] The producers countered these notions by arguing that the movement continued to change and had been neither fairly nor correctly covered.

The question of utility defined *Woman Alive!*[46] The producers wondered, "Now that copies of most of the manifestos are safely in the files of ten metropolitan news dailies; now that every network and local news show has done a five-minute take-out asking, 'Whither women's lib?,' what can a women's show on public television do to make itself useful?"[47] The answer lay in nuanced explorations of feminism and its next stages of development, something the program promised to deliver.[48] Producers argued that, by looking deeper into the issues of the women's movement and reflecting its "more various and more inclusive" aspects, *Woman Alive!* could offer underexplored ideas about feminism to a national audience.[49] In 1976, producers boasted that the show's first season "broke the media stereotype of the women's movement as a small group of radicals defined by narrow perimeters of class and race" and helped its audience see that "their feelings were shared by others throughout the country," thereby achieving its primary goals.[50]

The noncommercial aspects of *Woman Alive!* and their control over production meant that feminists could more accurately represent their movement as they themselves experienced it and wanted others to see it. Producers were particularly invested in foregrounding feminism's diversity and inclusivity, an agenda that

FIGURE 15. The pilot episode of *Woman Alive!* offers multiple visions of feminism, including a consciousness-raising group in Des Moines. (Schlesinger Library, Vt-30)

informed the show from the start and defined it throughout its three-year run. Publicity for the pilot episode emphasized its corrective stand on existing (mis) representation of feminism. Such misrepresentation "ignore[d] black and other third-world women" and the "great changes being made by blue-collar women as well."[51] Media coverage rather than feminism itself, according to this argument, was the force that rendered certain women invisible and defined the movement according to hegemonic categories of gender, race, class, and sexuality.

To counter media representations of feminists as exclusionary, *Woman Alive!* featured profiles on women that highlighted class, race, sexual, and age differences and a variety of women's relationships to feminism. The series' premiere episode included a story about Crystal Lee Jordan, a North Carolina mill worker and union organizer whose life was used as the basis for the 1979 film *Norma Rae*. This same episode reported on feminist organizations and included a consciousness-raising group in Des Moines, Iowa, and the National Black Feminist Organization. Other episodes further diversified depictions of feminists and women's relationships to feminism. They included Elaine Noble, elected to the Massachusetts House of Representatives in 1974, who "freely admitted" her lesbian identity during her campaign, the first elected representative to do so, and the first female roustabout at the Atlantic Richfield Company, who, "like other black women across the country," was fighting for "personal economic independence," even though she "[didn't] think of herself as a feminist by definition." Gloria Steinem was interviewed about her own experiences with feminism, with the same episode covering the "feminist realization of an eight year old girl."[52]

Woman Alive! offered feminist identification to viewers across disparate spaces, populations, and political practices. In offering its audience encounters with previously unknown sights, the program delivered on television's promise of what Ernest Pascucci identifies as an "intimate relationship, a visual relationship, moreover a televisual relationship" with such locations and corresponding identities. Pascucci's theory comes from his own queer engagement with television, about which he writes, "Intimate (tele)visions were not inhibiting of proper interpersonal relations, but *enabling* of a subjectivity that I could barely recognize, a subjectivity that had no recognizable place in the 'spaces of appearance' available to me."[53] Pascucci's perspective acknowledges television's political potential and challenges alarmist assessments of television as addictive, detrimental to the public sphere, and harmful to viewers' abilities to take action and to connect with others.

To many involved in the women's movement, representations mattered a great deal, and with good reason. Images "function politically," according to Bonnie J. Dow, because they "offer visions of what feminism 'means'" and indicate different phases of feminism operating in the culture, which are then reflected by televisual worlds.[54] Given the ubiquity and influence of television in American culture, some feminist activists sought to reform televisual images. Once appropriately revised according to feminist standards or placed under feminist control, television could then serve the needs of feminist politics. This idea took hold in several feminist organizations. In 1972, the radical feminist news journal *off our backs* enjoined readers to "turn on, tune in, and take over."[55] Liberal feminist group NOW also regarded itself as an agent active in shaping on-screen images and using them to further their political goals. With the establishment of a committee for media relations and the publication of its first Communications Kit in 1970, the organization advised members to evaluate each political action for its "*visual interest*" and to think strategically about how to produce images that could withstand postproduction manipulations beyond their control.[56]

Despite the power of representation, television did not always prove as effective in reaching women as feminists may have hoped. Even though televised images held profound and persuasive meaning for some viewers, others faced difficulties in assimilating the lessons provided by those images, particularly when material conditions limited the impact of any given representation. No matter how appropriately feminist, visually interesting, or progressive an image was, other dynamics could contravene in the conversion process. This proved true even when women were not antagonistic to or apathetic about feminism.

As journalistic state-of-feminism reports emerged in the early 1970s, they frequently looked to "Middle America" to identify the effects of feminism in areas presumed to be outside the reach of women's liberation groups. While not their primary intention, some of these reports reveal the role television played in conveying images of feminism to women beyond the urban, coastal enclaves of movement headquarters and help explain impediments to image-based feminist outreach.[57] A woman in a small Illinois town interviewed for *Time*'s 1972 article "The New Feminism on Main Street" described the limited abilities of television to deliver a sustainable version of feminism, not because of a lack of interest or antifeminist sentiment, but because of competing demands on her labor and attention. "'I identify with Women's Lib.," she stated. "I watch one of those women on Johnny Carson and I think, 'That's me.'"[58] But although *The Tonight Show* motivated feminist identification for the housewife, its effects were short-lived. "'I get up the next day, feed the kids and clean house," she says, "and it wears off."[59] Such vacillation between identification and disidentification signaled obstacles to mediated feminism, no matter if feminists themselves articulated the politics of their movement.

While identification with televised images was not guaranteed, viewer letters to *Woman Alive!* indicate the success of the program's address and expression of televisual intimacy akin to the relationship between audience and "(tele)visions" that Pascucci describes. A former factory worker from Olivia, Minnesota, wrote in to express her thanks for the show's coverage of the overlooked topic of women's sweatshop labor and for its "wide range of programming."[60] Mrs. Phyllis Spisto from Brooklyn, New York, was a working mother whose job in her family's ice cream distribution business meant that she did "not come in contact with too many free thinking women."[61] She described the effect the program had on her as a "ray of light communicating directly with my consciousness."[62] "I feel very close to you in your efforts to change social awareness," wrote a twenty-two-year-old married college student from Salt Lake City, Utah, who assured producers, "Your program is encouraging to me in my own struggles to break dead end patterns."[63] A social worker from Terre Haute, Indiana, expressed a "growing enthusiasm" for the program over the course of viewing its first four episodes.[64] Georgia O'Donnell from Mesa, Arizona, enthused, "I feel more an individual today after watching your show!"[65] One viewer, an unmarried secretary, wrote to producers about the show's affective impact. "You have given me a half-hour of dignity once a week," she wrote. "Dignity, hope, and the feeling of not being alone."[66]

The outpouring of appreciation from viewers was remarkable, not least because of the show's impact in a variety of locations across America. Responses from Utah to Brooklyn, from urban areas and small towns, demonstrated the success of *Woman Alive!*'s sensitivity to regionalism, a foundational part of the show's production plans. "We are familiar with what's happening on the island of Manhattan," producers wrote in their proposal for the program. But with a production team in Texas, they were also "aware of lives and manners West of the Hudson River."[67] *Woman Alive!* expressed diversity in feminism through profiles of women rooted in regional specificity, particularly those located in areas that were assumed to be uninterested in feminist politics. The series reported on women's lives across America. From the aforementioned consciousness-raising group in Des Moines, Iowa, and Crystal Lee Jordan's attempts to unionize a factory in her small North Carolina town to a Massachusetts woman trying to create an equitable marriage with her husband, the pilot episode placed feminist concerns squarely

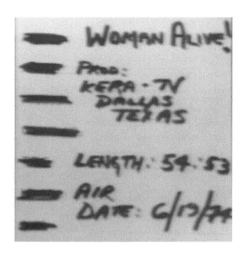

FIGURE 16. Slate for *Woman Alive!*'s
pilot episode indicates central role of
Dallas-Fort Worth's KERA in production.
PBS, June 19, 1974. (Schlesinger Library,
Vt-30)

within regions that were assumed, in typical media representations, not to have been affected by feminism.

Locating feminism in unexpected places shaped production efforts for *Woman Alive!* Producer Joan Shigekawa emphasized the type of work she undertook as she "filmed the world" in which feminists lived, both in their homes and in "the broad, flat stretches of midwestern countryside with freight trains moving regularly across the horizon, passing the endless fields of corn and soybeans."[68] In telling women's stories that "reflected the changes going on in the middle of the country," Shigekawa took particular care in conveying the particular landscapes of these areas, as her extended and detailed description of the Illinois countryside indicates.[69] Awareness of location also affected decisions about where to locate *Woman Alive!*'s production. The choice of Dallas–Fort Worth's KERA as initial coproducers underscored regard for regions that were not proximate to sites of major feminist organizations. With "facilities and personnel in Dallas capable of matching (at least) the television production standards of either coast," working in the major Texas city offered the *Woman Alive!* production team benefits, both pragmatic and experiential: lower production costs and "the Dallas ways of producing," which were deemed "less crazy-making than elsewhere."[70]

The combined resources of *Ms.* magazine and a Texas public television station promised to deliver a high-impact program, to safeguard against accusations of elitism within the women's movement, and to protect the show from ideologically suspect agendas of commercial television. The proposal to the CPB for *Woman Alive!* emphasized the professional skills that *Ms.* and KERA, respectively, would bring to television production. *Ms.* had already proven its ability to reach a "target audience" of women, while KERA employed "staff capable of producing a quality national product." KERA's obligation to the public meant that it was "free from commercial pressure that would water down content."[71] The trustworthiness of the station overtly referenced the commercial drives of the television industry and indirectly signaled the commercialization that critics felt *Ms.* had introduced into the women's movement. As the two media institutions worked in tandem to ensure different modes of media acumen, KERA operated as a counterbalance to the stigma attached to *Ms.* and its leadership, even as the production benefited from the magazine's expertise as a feminist enterprise.

Although *Ms.* and cofounder Gloria Steinem's involvement in the production of *Woman Alive!* provided all-important feminist credentials, their relationship to capitalism was a potential liability that required careful management. Steinem's celebrity status in the women's movement was perceived by some as alienating to so-called Middle American women and radical feminists alike. At best, Steinem and *Ms.* proved simply ineffective in connecting to some women. At worst, they functioned as corrupting forces within the women's movement. To understand *Woman Alive*'s unusual decision to minimize the media-savvy resources it had in Steinem and *Ms.*, a brief contextualization is in order.

To radical feminists, Gloria Steinem's media-friendly version of feminist politics was troubling, if not downright dangerous for the women's movement. In 1975, Redstockings accused Steinem of connections with the CIA and intimated that her prominence in popular media coverage of feminism was tied to this relationship. Charging that Steinem had been "meteorically installed into her current position as leader of the women's liberation movement through the efforts of the mass media" and that her past activities had been covered up, Redstockings declared Steinem a serious threat to the integrity of the movement.[72] In less extreme criticism, other feminist critics understood the media's characterization of Steinem as the singular leader of the movement to be a necessary evil. *off our backs* identified mainstream media as the force that had installed Steinem as the celebrity face of feminism, yet acknowledged the strategic usefulness of this position. A recognizable feminist offered women a figure to emulate and the media a compelling story to represent. In its pragmatic assessment of Steinem's value to the movement, *off our backs* proclaimed, "With superstardom there is the realization of what a woman can do (NOW THERE'S A WOMAN THE PRESS CAN'T IGNORE)."[73]

Regardless of the concerns feminists had about Steinem's celebrity, Steinem's influence over a national audience was not guaranteed. Paradoxically, despite its much-vaunted media appeal, Steinem's impact was often lost in translation for women who did not identify with Steinem precisely *because of* her mediated presence. The numerous state-of-feminism reports published in women's magazines in the early 1970s reveal women's complex reception of Steinem and help explain the lack of a unified political alliance with feminism. Women who lived in regions beyond major urban coastal regions had meaningful and valid reasons, beyond simple internalized sexism, for rejecting the tenets of feminist leadership conveyed from afar through popular media.

In a 1975 article, "Women's Lib Plays in Peoria," *Saturday Review* reporter Susan Jacoby found that televised images of feminists did not always operate as a lifesaver that connected women to the movement. In their geographic isolation from centers of the women's liberation movement, Peorian women forged their own state of feminism predicated on their own particular realities and the material conditions of day-to-day living. Just as they clipped coupons, they sought improved economic conditions in their hourly wage jobs. Just as they exchanged casserole recipes, they banded together to change conditions in their workplaces. When, for example, a local company who employed an all-female workforce to answer customer service calls failed to heed health and safety complaints, the workers took action. Wearing earphones on the job led to perpetual ear infections, but both the union and the company's management did nothing to change these conditions for customer service workers. In response, the women organized an in-house Women's Group to represent their interests collectively and to agitate more effectively for improved labor conditions.

Feminist role models for these Peorian women came from within their community. Jacoby interviewed a young woman who had overcome her resistance to feminism through the influence of her female coworkers. The young woman recounted how she had supported a feminist union representative in a recent election once she realized the candidate was "just like us."[74] Part of being "like us" was a matter of a conventional white femininity and heteronormativity, as the union representative possessed "beautiful silvery-blonde hair" and could "get a man."[75] These qualities were ones that Gloria Steinem herself famously possessed, yet Steinem was a figure of failed identification for the Peorian women who supported their feminist union representative. Even with her heterosexual appeals and conventional beauty (down to her very own signature blonde hair), Steinem was not an agent of feminist conversion for them. If Steinem was "'only a streaky mane of hair on a network television program,'" and "doesn't seem like a real person," then her appeal, for some, did not transmit across the remove of celebrity and the mediation of television.[76]

Given the potential liabilities Steinem brought with her to *Woman Alive!*, her appearances on the program were carefully managed. In a promotional interview that was published in WNET-13's magazine for station members, Joan Shigekawa noted that Jordan, the labor organizer from North Carolina who was profiled in the pilot episode, "didn't even know what Gloria Steinem looked like before we brought her to New York."[77] Much like the feminism of the women profiled in journalistic accounts of Middle America, Jordan's feminism stood apart from Steinem's influence. Jordan's unconventional path to feminist consciousness aligned with the ways *Woman Alive!* wished to convey feminism: as intuitive and commonsensical, complexly expressed and experienced, and adaptable to suit the conditions of any woman's life. Despite—or perhaps because of—Jordan's ignorance of women's movement leaders, she personified

Woman Alive!'s mission, which, according to Shigekawa, was to illustrate "how much more powerful and appealing 'woman alive' and in action can be rather than in mere self-contemplation."[78]

Steinem did appear in *Woman Alive!*'s first episode, but in ways that minimized her own celebrity persona in favor of emphasizing the collective aspects of the women's movement. In three, relatively brief segments scattered throughout the episode, Steinem relates her own experiences with internalized sexism, expresses her racial and class solidarity with others, positions herself as but one member of a larger group, and acknowledges the effective political activism of other women. In the first segment, Steinem describes her struggles with male authority and the need for women to define themselves apart from male approval in personal and professional relationships. The show then cuts to a group discussion about a three-day conference for Black feminists in New York City. Steinem participates in the group, which includes Margaret Sloan-Hunter and Jane Galvin-Lewis, both of the National Black Feminist Organization. Sloan-Hunter and Galvin-Lewis are more central to the discussion than Steinem and provide critical assessments of feminism and racism. Sloan-Hunter and Galvin-Lewis recount the painful experience of witnessing racist media representations of Black women or the "lack of it" altogether. This long-standing marginalization shaped representations that were beginning to emerge with the women's movement; according to Sloan-Hunter, "a lot of Black feminists were very dissatisfied with the press image of the women's movement and their relationship to the women's movement." During this discussion, Steinem is sidelined in favor of Black feminists who tell their own stories. Steinem's final appearance comes with the journalistic duty of providing a brief, contextual setup for a story of Jordan's unionization efforts in Rock Rapids, Virginia.

Steinem and *Ms.*'s director of special projects, Ronnie Eldridge, "were most closely involved in the production," yet Steinem's presence on the program was restricted.[79] This may have sidestepped the controversy Steinem brought with her, yet her minimized presence had negative consequences. While *Variety* felt *Woman Alive!* was "blessed" with a lack of a host or spokesperson, the *New York Times* noted that the "fear of elitism" and the management of a "superstar" feminist "translates as careless production."[80]

Much like Steinem's, *Ms.*'s involvement in *Woman Alive!* was a mixed blessing. While the magazine offered professional media resources and name recognition, it was also beset by criticism and mistrust from some feminist quarters. *The Lesbian Tide* charged *Ms.* with heterosexism and "gross neglect" of lesbians as well as with "perpetuating anti-feminist attitudes and politics" of "elitism, professionalism, classism, superstardom, and dollarism."[81] Redstockings was concerned that the "creation of *Ms.* magazine ha[d] put Steinem in a strategic position in the women's movement—a position from which feminist politics can be influenced, but also a position from which information can be and is being gathered on the personal and political activities of women all over the world."[82]

FIGURES 17, 18 & 19. A group discussion of the first conference of the National Black Feminist Organization (NBFO) involved Jane Galvin-Lewis (top) and Margaret Sloan-Hunter (middle) and decentered Gloria Steinem (bottom). PBS, June 19, 1974. (Schlesinger Library, Vt-30)

Ms.'s ties to commercial interests also raised suspicion. Katherine Graham, president of the Washington Post company—whose holdings included the *Washington Post, Newsweek*, and Warner Communications—was a stockholder in the magazine. Warner's ownership of Wonder Woman, who famously appeared on the cover of magazine's first issue, Graham's appearance on a 1974 cover of *Ms.* as "the most powerful woman in America," and *Newsweek*'s supportive coverage of Steinem led Redstockings to identify *Ms.* as "an area in which commercial interests and politics coincide."[83] *Ms.*'s involvement with public television further created "confusion" about the magazine's business and about whether *Ms.* was a "political or commercial venture."[84] This confusion, according to Redstockings, "led women to submit political information about themselves which they would not have sent a magazine publishing simply for profit" and "led women writers to expect better treatment from *Ms.* than from other magazines, when in fact the treatment has often been worse."[85] Amid such speculation, *Woman Alive!* downplayed the contributions of *Ms.* Although *Ms.* supplied the pilot episode with "information, provided contacts and debated ideas," the program's affiliation with *Ms.* merited just a single mention in a credit.[86]

Even though the magazine's commercial ties threatened to discredit *Woman Alive!*, *Ms.*'s "heavy involvement," as the *New York Times* noted, was "central to the program's success." *Woman Alive!* producer Joan Shigekawa credited the magazine as "the best resource center" for women's issues and as the site of all the program's preproduction work. In addition to its material resources, *Ms.* provided a template for a feminist workplace. The practice of "anti-hierarchical" relationships among workers was something *Ms.* adapted from the women's movement, which Shigekawa then adopted for *Woman Alive!* Every woman involved in a meeting for the show could contribute, which created a "network of women constantly exchanging information."[87]

The composition of *Woman Alive!*'s production team made a public-facing feminist statement. Women were employed as the show's executive producer, associate producer, writers and reporters, editor, assistant editor, field producer, film crew, title design, sounds, research, and production assistant. While their employment helped correct the industry-wide underemployment of women working in television, it did more than serve as statistical correction to gender imbalances in employment. Women working in such large numbers introduced meaningful changes to the organization and dynamics of the television workplace. "There's nothing like it—when the producer is a woman and the decisions are made by women," enthused Shigekawa, who noted that everyone was permitted to provide input, regardless of job title. This arrangement created an "open forum" for pitching ideas as well as "camaraderie and rapport within the crew."[88] Regardless of job title, women who worked on *Woman Alive!* were authorized by their gendered knowledge to contribute to a television program about and for women.

Working in such an environment and on such a project alleviated the alienating effects of wage labor. As writer and associate producer Susan Lester said, "To all of us, it was not just a job, but a project integrated into our lives." The blurred boundaries between workers' lives and their jobs attested to both the political and personal importance of the production. Film editor Sarah Stein found that working on the program fulfilled "a real desire to finally work on something meaningful to us as women."[89] The hiring of women for the program thus not only challenged the imbalance of women working in production but also transformed the work of making television for women in front of and behind the cameras.

FIGURE 20. Promotional photo for *Woman Alive!* features producer Joan Shigekawa and union organizer Crystal Lee Jordan (later known as Crystal Lee Sutton) in "a light moment." (PBS/Schlesinger Library MC 421)

For all the positive effects women brought to and experienced at *Woman Alive!*, the production team also faced uniquely gendered pressures while making the program. As a producer, Shigekawa felt obligated to refute sexist assumptions about women's inabilities to work in television. To do so, she pushed herself to exceed expectations for a successful production. Shigekawa was compelled to finish work ahead of schedule and to come in under her $500,000 budget to prove that, despite cultural biases to the contrary, women could get work done efficiently and manage the business side of production appropriately. "We felt it was especially important for us to do so," Shigekawa noted, "because men in television have held the myth too long that 'women don't know how to handle money.'"[90]

Although Shigekawa and her team successfully managed the logistical issues involved in making *Woman Alive!*, the realities of limited resources constrained them. Transforming women's television required "the total concentration of creative energy," which was impossible to sustain. But rather than mystifying the creative process and positioning herself as an artist whose artistic inspiration alone would see her through, Shigekawa emphasized the material support that focused creativity required. Creating revolutionary television required "time to think, and time to rest," a condition that necessitated financial backing. "Money makes that possible," Shigekawa argued. "Money buys you an extra day or two to rejuvenate, the time to confront the next creative problem with fresh eyes."[91] Without the necessary resources, *Woman Alive!* suffered, as did its workers. In Shigekawa's assessment, the compromised vision of the ambitious production was brought about by the realities of budgets and scheduling rather than the abilities of the production team.

Shigekawa used the thwarted potential of *Woman Alive!* and her platform as the show's producer to illustrate the problems of television work for women. To her, problems with the show originated with the industry's shortchanging of women. *Woman Alive!* was hampered by a modest budget, as expected for a public television production. As a feminist-oriented, woman-centered and woman-run program—atypical within the television industry, commercial or public—*Woman Alive!* faced additional issues of a male-dominated industry in which women were not afforded respect, power, or autonomy. From her experience working on *Woman Alive!*, Shigekawa concluded that women who wanted to work in television at any level and on any program faced additional labor that hampered their productivity and innovation. Nothing short of ending structural inequality would reform this problem. "Until women in television are totally integrated into the decision making process," Shigekawa argued, "responsible women, at whatever level they exist, must bear the additional burden of disproving a deeply ingrained set of attitudes and prejudices held by a primarily male administration."[92] Nonetheless, she held out hope for women who persisted in these inequitable circumstances and stressful labor conditions. Women succeeded in making *Woman Alive!* because, according to Shigekawa, they could rely upon their "professional best" to see them through.[93]

Notwithstanding the difficulties Shigekawa and her crew faced in making *Woman Alive!*, the program proved a significant contribution to public television and to television for women. Notable as a "full-blown vid tape and film production," *Woman Alive!* offered a rare exception to what *Variety* considered the "bleak" PBS lineup of fall 1974.[94] Its quality, measured by its "true national tv production values," set *Woman Alive!* apart from its public television contemporaries.[95] Other assessments proved equally positive and hailed the program as, among other things, "technically flawless."[96] The cultural value of the program was validated by the inclusion of three of its episodes in the Museum of Modern Art and the New York Public Library's 1976 series on "new social documentary film."[97]

After its initial pilot episode made at Dallas–Fort Worth station KERA-TV, *Woman Alive!*'s production relocated to New York City's WNET. This move marked the end of the program's regional experimentation in production location and staffing, but its dedication to diverse stories of women across the country remained a priority. An episode from season 2 titled "A Time of Change," for example, explored how the women's movement "permeated the everyday lives of women throughout the United States," even for women "who did not think of themselves as feminists in the activist sense." Program topics for the second season included reproductive freedom and the unequal terms of sterilization for women, the ERA, the impact of the women's liberation movement, and "Women and

Work," all of which promised to build on the program's initial investment in telling women's stories across regions that reflected diverse political outlooks, relationships to feminism, and identities. By the end of the season, producers guaranteed that the program would "have visited many different parts of the country" and that the ten-episode series would "present a view of women in all of their diversity."[98]

On the basis of audience research conducted by the CPB's Qualitative Research Survey, *Woman Alive!* expanded its half-hour format to an hourlong program in 1977, its second and final season. The program also moved from a magazine format with short segments to a single theme for an entire program. This shift allowed the program to develop a "documentary film around an investigation of a single topic," which afforded viewers a "deeper understanding of the issues."[99] At their March 1976 meeting, the CPB earmarked up to $554,000 for continued support of the series, but with the CPB's rejection of proposed sponsorship from Ortho Pharmaceutical, the maker of women's contraception, the program continued to lack external funding necessary to sustain it.[100]

When *Woman Alive!* was canceled in 1977, viewers wrote in to protest the cancellation. Their letters cited the program's consciousness-raising effect and the ongoing need for feminist media programming, particularly with the ongoing fight to pass the Equal Rights Amendment. Just as they had throughout the series run, letters from viewers attested to the political impact and educational outreach of the program, particularly for women who might not otherwise have connection to feminist organizations and to other feminists. Some viewers understood the cancellation as symptomatic of structural problems within the television industry. As one viewer wrote in January 1976, "Please don't cancel it because of lack of interest. Men, who run things, aren't interested in women, as whites who run things aren't interested in blacks, generally. But education is necessary."[101]

YES, WE CAN: THE DAY WOMEN TOOK OVER TELEVISION

Yes, We Can, the local Boston television production described at the top of this chapter, proved a unique experiment in television for women. Its daylong format, funding from state government and local commercial television, and volunteer efforts on the part of local women's groups and businesses resulted in a day of television for women with connections to public outreach and civic issues and a robust reimagining of the generic parameters of women's television. The production validated the importance of challenging typical commercial programming. It also raised concerns about who should be responsible for expressing feminist ideas on commercial television; the sources of labor, financial support, and creative input for a community-oriented but commercially operated event; and the political ramifications of translating feminism to a commercial television venue.

Yes, We Can ran on WBZ from 7:00 a.m. to 11:00 p.m. on Thursday, January 18, 1974, with a one-hour prime-time special that had aired the previous night. Both days' programming blended entertainment and celebrity with viewer education and civic concerns. The prime-time special featured musical performances by Liza Minnelli, Helen Reddy, and Ann Murray, between which members of the Governor's Commission on the Status of Women previewed the next day's events. The guests on the daylong show included high-profile feminist leaders (Betty Friedan, Gloria Steinem, and Florynce "Flo" Kennedy), authors (Phyllis Chesler, who wrote *Women and Madness*), and politicians (Representative Margaret Heckler), who appeared alongside entertainers and television personalities (celebrity chef Julia Child and actor and singer Kitty Carlisle) and leaders of nonprofit organizations (Maggie Kuhn, founder of the Gray Panthers).

The program was tied to a women's fair, which provided content for the live broadcast and operated as a public service to women in the Boston area. The fair was free and provided attendees with resources and information about "all aspects of womanhood from education, health, and child care to exercise" from local government groups, women's organizations, and businesses. WBZ interviewed fair sponsors and attendees alike, with panel discussions and demonstrations rounding out the program. The live broadcast of January 18 concluded with portions of multiday state hearings on sex discrimination commissioned by the governor of Massachusetts. This final segment featured "televised documentation of sex discrimination" that highlighted structural inequalities facing women in the workplace, government, and society. The segment intercut taped excerpts from the January 10 hearings instigated by the Governor's Commission on the Status of Women with live on-set discussions by women experts on the matters of concern raised in the hearings.

Yes, We Can originated with the formation of the Governor's Commission on the Status of Women in June 1971. The Commission was a fact-finding and advisory committee initially comprising thirty-five women whose goal was twofold: (1) to "survey and evaluate all statutes" of the state and "all governmental programs and practices" that involved the "employment, health, education and welfare" of women; and (2) to "investigate the need for new and expanded services that may be required for women as wives, mothers and workers."[102] The Commission was empowered to make recommendations to the governor based on their investigations, which they did in their annual report. These wide-ranging recommendations included abortion rights, sex education, availability of childcare, job opportunities, the ERA, state restrictions on women performing jury duty, and prison reform.

Over the course of seven days throughout late 1973 and early 1974, the Commission conducted a series of hearings on sex discrimination in three of Massachusetts's major cities.[103] These hearings were intended to provide women an opportunity to consider and act on the question "What can and should be done regarding needed legislation in the above areas?" Designed to set the agenda for the Commission in the following year, the hearings and their media coverage, which included *Yes, We Can*, were meant to inform viewers and prompt them to political action. Broadcasting the hearings situated *Yes, We Can* in liberal activist principles and a public service framework, but the use of commercial television to do so complicated matters. Airing the hearings on WBZ promised greater exposure to problems facing Massachusetts women, and the Commission's retrospective assessment of the event found that this strategy was "quite successful in arousing the interest of the people of the Commonwealth on women's issues."[104] The event, however, was seen by some feminists as unhelpful to women. Its relationship to commercialized media watered down feminist politics that could affect real change in women's lives and appropriated women's talent and labor for capitalist ends.

With its goal "of examining women in today's society and television programming," *Yes, We Can* was as much of a reform of women's television as it was of anything else.[105] Producers operated under the assumption that women viewers were a public underserved by commercial television. The daylong program expanded women's television to include issues beyond those designed for the imagined consumerist-housewife-mother viewer. *Yes, We Can* challenged traditions of women's television with program content debating a range of feminist issues, including financial planning, reproductive health care and abortion, and instructions on running for political office. When domestic tasks, so typically part of the consumerist cultivation of viewers of women's television, were part of the agenda, they were redefined in accordance with feminist principles: "Ms. Fix-It" encouraged women's self-sufficiency in appliance repair, plumbing, and electrician work; childcare concerns expanded to include adoption and foster care as well as guidance for raising a child in nonsexist fashion; and "Body Tone" included judo and karate demonstrations.

Yes, We Can acknowledged numerous facets of women's concerns and intersectional identities of gender, class, age, and race. The day started with "Programming for the Working Woman" from 7:00 to 9:00 a.m. Topics included discrimination and employment, day care, "women working with women," finance and money management, and "the plight of being poor and a woman." The next segment, "Programming for the Woman-at-Home," featured Elizabeth Hubbard, the current Miss Black America; Dorothy Height, president of the National Council of Negro Women and a "forerunner of the black women's liberation movement"; and various feminist authors. Topics in this segment included "examination of roles played in marriage," pregnancy, and "the changing role of women today."[106] The 4:00–6:00 p.m. time slot, "Programming for the Younger Woman," focused on abortion, birth control, consciousness-raising, and careers for young women.

To support such a large-scale production, WBZ solicited sponsorship from area businesses (Cabinet Lumber & Supply, Inc. and Westinghouse Electronic Co.)

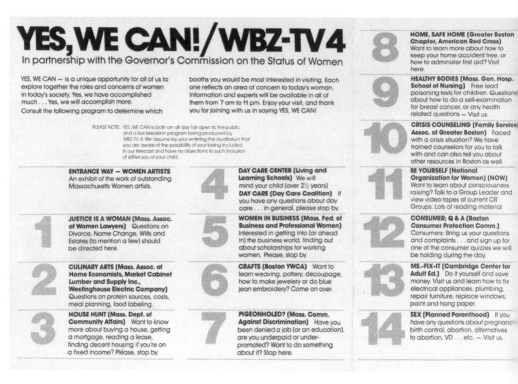

YES, WE CAN!/WBZ-TV 4

In partnership with the Governor's Commission on the Status of Women

YES, WE CAN — is a unique opportunity for all of us to explore together the roles and concerns of women in today's society. Yes, we have accomplished much . . . Yes, we will accomplish more. Consult the following program to determine which

booths you would be most interested in visiting. Each one reflects an area of concern to today's woman. Information and experts will be available in all of them from 7 am to 11 pm. Enjoy your visit, and thank you for joining with us in saying YES, WE CAN!

PLEASE NOTE: YES, WE CAN is both an all day fair open to the public and a live television program being produced by WBZ-TV 4. We assume by your entering the auditorium that you are aware of the possibility of your being included in our telecast and have no objections to such inclusion of either you or your child.

ENTRANCE WAY — WOMEN ARTISTS
An exhibit of the work of outstanding Massachusetts Women artists.

1 JUSTICE IS A WOMAN (Mass. Assoc. of Women Lawyers) Questions on Divorce, Name Change, Wills and Estates (to mention a few) should be directed here.

2 CULINARY ARTS (Mass. Assoc. of Home Economists, Market Cabinet Lumber and Supply Inc., Westinghouse Electric Company) Questions on protein sources, costs, meal planning, food labeling.

3 HOUSE HUNT (Mass. Dept. of Community Affairs) Want to know more about buying a house, getting a mortgage, reading a lease, finding decent housing if you're on a fixed income? Please, stop by.

4 DAY CARE CENTER (Living and Learning Schools) We will mind your child (over 2½ years)
DAY CARE (Day Care Coalition) If you have any questions about day care . . . in general, please stop by.

5 WOMEN IN BUSINESS (Mass. Fed. of Business and Professional Women) Interested in getting into (or ahead in) the business world, finding out about scholarships for working women, Please, stop by.

6 CRAFTS (Boston YWCA) Want to learn weaving, pottery, decoupage, how to make jewelery or do blue jean embroidery? Come on over.

7 PIGEONHOLED? (Mass. Comm. Against Discrimination) Have you been denied a job (or an education), are you underpaid or under-promoted? Want to do something about it? Stop here.

8 HOME, SAFE HOME (Greater Boston Chapter, American Red Cross) Want to learn more about how to keep your home accident free, or how to administer first aid? Visit here.

9 HEALTHY BODIES (Mass. Gen. Hosp. School of Nursing) Free lead poisoning tests for children. Questions about how to do a self-examination for breast cancer, or any health related questions — Visit us.

10 CRISIS COUNSELING (Family Service Assoc. of Greater Boston) Faced with a crisis situation? We have trained counselors for you to talk with and can also tell you about other resources in Boston as well.

11 BE YOURSELF (National Organization for Women) (NOW) Want to learn about consciousness raising? Talk to a Group Leader and view video tapes of current CR Groups. Lots of reading material

12 CONSUMER; Q & A (Boston Consumer Protection Comm.) Consumers: Bring us your questions and complaints . . . and sign up for one of the consumer quizzes we will be holding during the day.

13 MS.-FIX-IT (Cambridge Center for Adult Ed.) Do it yourself and save money. Visit us and learn how to fix electrical appliances, plumbing, repair furniture, replace windows, paint and hang paper.

14 SEX (Planned Parenthood) If you have any questions about pregnancy, birth control, abortion, alternatives to abortion, VD . . . etc. — Visit us.

FIGURE 21. Directory for the booths at *Yes, We Can* women's fair, which include legal advice on divorce, birth control, mortgages and home ownership, and career planning. (Schlesinger Library 77-M13—96-M48)

and the state government (Massachusetts Commission Against Discrimination), as well as from nonprofit and educational organizations that participated in the women's fair (Boston YWCA, Red Cross, Simmons College, and Massachusetts General Hospital Nursing School). Some organizations struggled to assume this financial burden. The Eastern Massachusetts NOW chapter wrote to WBZ after the fair to voice its concerns about smaller, underfunded groups. It was "unrealistic to expect," they wrote, that a nonprofit organization like theirs with little financial latitude could "pay for and find labor to construct a booth."[107] They suggested that it would be better if the station would "provide space for non-profit groups which serve women and advocate women's rights at such an event" instead of charging these groups the same rate as for-profit participants.[108]

Other feminist criticisms of *Yes, We Can*'s commercialization of the women's movement were more pointed. A group of around fifty women, in *Variety*'s report, "described as 'left-wing militants,'" arrived at the fair at 12:30 p.m. to disrupt the fair and its televised coverage.[109] They distributed flyers critiquing

15 IN FASHION (DuPont) Five fashion shows will be presented during the day. Personal consultation also available, courtesy Mildred L. Albert, Dean, Academie Moderne, Modeling and Finishing School.

16 IT'S TO OUR CREDIT (Amer. Assoc. of Women Accts.) How to: Get a loan, credit, insurance, invest or manage money, collect benefits.

17 BODY TONE (Cambridge YWCA) Want to learn some exercises, or how to protect yourself? Want to know more about women in sports? Stop by.

18 NATURE'S OWN (Erewhon) Want to learn more about natural foods, or talk about their costs, or pick up some recipes? Come on over.

19 WHO NEEDS A $20 TOY! (Children's Museum) We'll show you how to make your own. Demonstrations include: How to make stuffed toys, how to recycle foam and plastic and make toys out of them.

20 VOLUNTEERING? (Civic Center Clearing House, ucpc-VAC) If you think you'd like to be a volunteer but don't know the wheres, hows or pitfalls. . . . Please come and talk with us.

21 GOING BACK TO SCHOOL (Simmons College) If you are interested in finding out more about adult and continuing education programs or in talking to some women involved with them, please stop by.

22 PLANT LIFE (Mass. Horticultural Soc.) Green Thumb . . . or all thumbs, we have information and experts here for you to talk to.

23 BEAUTIFUL (Breck, I Natural) Make-up tips, make-over demonstrations, skin care treatments you can make at home . . . for all women, all colors, all ages.

24 SENIOR WOMEN (Council of Elders) Over 62 and want to know more about what you are entitled to . . . and how to get it? Come visit us.

25 CAREER DESIGN (Mass. Assoc. of Women Deans, Administrators and Women Counselors) For all women: Under 20, over 40, over 65. Need help in picking the right school, getting job training, we can help.

26 MEDIA WOMEN (Women in Communications, Inc.) Stop by and meet some of Boston's Media Women . . . Whether you are interested in becoming one yourself or just want to chat.

27 CULTURAL EVENTS IN BOSTON (American Assoc. of Univ. Women) We have information on all the cultural events going on in Boston.

28 . . . AND MAY THE BEST MAN WOMAN WIN! (League of Woman Voters) Interested in getting involved in a political campaign, or starting your own . . . Would you like information on pending legislation?

29 WOMEN IN GOVERNMENT (Women's Oppor. Comm. Bost. Fed. Exec. Board) Interested in a career in Government . . . Federal, State or Local . . . Come and talk to us about it.

30 CALL FOR ACTION (WBZ) Have a complaint about anything and want some action? Come here.

31 BREAKING BARRIERS THROUGH SPEECH (Women's Training and Resources Corp.) Interested in career promotion and mobility? Visit our communications workshop. Videotaping throughout the day.

32 WOMEN'S YELLOW PAGES (W. Y. P., Boston Women's Collective) Want more information about people, organizations and agencies who can help you meet your needs. We can help.

33 LOVE A CHILD (Boston Children's Services) Interested in adoption or foster care? Please stop by. The children will love you for it.

34 BEYOND EVE (Middlesex College Div. of Cont. Ed) Want to learn more about women in U.S. History? Who they were, when they were, what they did . . . and where you can learn even more? This is the place

35 THE FILM BOX (Polaroid Corp) An excellent selection of films by Women Filmmakers of Massachusetts will be shown throughout the day. Admission is free. Check the listing which follows for titles and times.

the commercial aspects of the event and advocating for collective action and anticapitalist politics as a viable alternative. The protest generated a spontaneous exercise in feminist praxis. The program manager came over to host Sonya Hamlin during the broadcast to tell her that protesters were outside and were threatening to come in and destroy the cameras, which amounted to all the cameras WBZ owned and were worth millions of dollars. In Hamlin's recollection of the event, the manager threatened to call the riot squad, but Hamlin created another, less confrontational situation. Hamlin told the manager, "Wait, wait, wait. If this is a day for women, why don't we look at one option: why don't you tell them to elect two people to come in and talk to me? And I will put them on the stage with me and I'll find out what this is about. And give them full voice and hear and try to answer or discuss at least. . . . Just give us a chance."[110] The women came en masse and sat on and surrounded the stage for a while but ultimately chose a few women for Hamlin to interview.

The exchange that ensued was televised live as an impromptu addition to the scheduled panel discussion. The liveness of the broadcast and the feminist ethos of inclusivity and open exchange of ideas afforded at-home viewers vigorous debate among feminists and complex and conflicting perspectives within the movement.

FIGURE 22. Feminist protesters interrupt the broadcast and fair of *Yes, We Can* before being invited to join the program. (Photo by Jack Connolly/The Boston Globe via Getty Images)

The protesters objected to, among other things, a fashion show segment, which they saw as perpetuating stereotypical notions about women's interests. Hamlin explained that the inspiration for the show came from viewer mail. Women with sewing skills wrote to her expressing their interest in starting their own business. The fashion show featured clothing they made for an audience of local business owners and fashion critics who could help the women to transform their home sewing into a business. Attorney and activist Flo Kennedy, who was one of the guests on the program, responded to the protesters by invoking the notion of "horizontal hostility," a concept that feminist historian Rebecca J. Sheehan describes as "violence enacted by one oppressed group against another, an effect of a system that divides and conquers groups who might otherwise be allied."[111] Kennedy suggested that the protesters empathize with the burgeoning awareness of some women and consider the chilling impact of the protest on other potential feminists attending the event and watching at home. Hamlin recalls a productive outcome to the exchange: "And of course we went into a large discussion after that, the essence of which was to recognize where women really are, and recognize, if you are ahead of them, open doors, show them how, be a helper not a fighter. And it was enormously successful."[112]

Invited participants also offered critical assessments about *Yes, We Can*, particularly about its awareness of racism. Sarah-Ann Shaw of WBZ's *Eyewitness*

News, and the first Black woman hired as a television news reporter on Boston television, hosted a panel to discuss the relationship between Black women and feminism. The panel, which included guests Miss Black America, Arniece Russell; Dr. Dorothy Hyde of the National Council of Negro Women; and Kennedy, quickly turned to an appraisal of the day. When Russell voiced concerns about the exhibitions and the "standpoint" they represented, Shaw asked her, "What would be of more interest. Say if you were planning a fair like this. What kinds of things would you include?"

Shaw's solicitation of feedback and critique provided an opportunity for the panel to debate how Black feminist perspectives were and could have been included in *Yes, We Can*. Both Russell and Hyde spoke about the interconnectedness of racism and sexism and cautioned against universalizing women's experiences and needs. Russell pointed out that something as generalized as childcare, a major concern of the fair, was also a racially specific experience. Hyde framed the moment as an "opportunity for white women, women of all races to be concerned with racial discrimination." She also called attention to the achievements of the day by acknowledging the government's changing stance on women's issues and noted that the Commission seemed to "take seriously those problems." Kennedy weighed in positively, if not pragmatically, on the progress the day made toward Black feminist consciousness. "It's true that there may be a basis for criticism of this event in terms of its lack of sensitivity to Black people," she acknowledged, but went on to point out the presence of Black businesswomen and "at least three booths that deal with racism as well as sexism" at the fair. Kennedy went on to voice her stance on critiquing other women, saying, "I always think before I criticize my friends I want to confront my enemies."

Of all the panelists, Kennedy focused most clearly on *Yes, We Can* as a television event. The significance of the day, to Kennedy, could best be understood within the broader cultural and economic context of commercial television. While acknowledging the value of criticizing the production, Kennedy tempered wholesale dismissal of WBZ's efforts with its relative progressiveness in comparison to television's typical endeavors. Producing an all-day event for women and undergoing "all the necessary preparation for doing what they never do except for frivolous concerns like sports or some octogenarian's funeral or the astronauts or something that's totally irrelevant to all oppressed people" was laudable. Unlike the "total waste of money" spent on large-scale spectacles, *Yes, We Can*, to Kennedy, seemed "such a large step away from that tendency to ignore women and Black people" that she pronounced that she was "delighted" by television production.

The producers of *Yes, We Can* understood that the contributions the program could make to the state of television were as much about women's roles in making the show as about its content. In a December 31, 1973, press release, executive producer Stephanie Meagher foregrounded the labor and skills that women— including television professionals, activists, business owners, and community

members—brought to the planning and execution of the fair and television program. Meagher claimed the event as a victory for women as a collective labor force:
"For one thing, a myth has been put to rest . . . the myth that women can't work
together. The dedication and selflessness, the level of professionalism and creativity, displayed not only by the women at WBZ-TV and the women on the Governor's commission on the Status of Women, but also by the women representing
the various sponsors of our booths has made our theme even more meaningful."[113]

However ideal the notion of disparate groups of women working together to
create *Yes, We Can* was, it was also potentially exploitative. Feminist critic and
journalist Janet Stone wrote to WBZ to voice a complaint along these lines. In
her letter, Stone established her multiple credentials as a lesbian feminist with
memberships in NOW, the Women's Equity Action League, and the Daughters of
Bilitis, and as a working journalist and consultant for fair employment practices
for racial minorities and women. Stone also self-identified as a "private citizen
and viewer."[114] By calling attention to these identities, Stone asserted the authority of her feedback to WBZ in several ways: as a part of the public to whom the
station was responsible, as a political activist well versed in media reform tactics
of the groups to which she belonged, and as an industry worker who understood
the labor logistics of media productions and the need for worker protections.

Stone cautioned that television should not expect women to continue to offer
their labor, energies, and creativity for free, as they had done for *Yes, We Can*,
particularly when a production was a commercial enterprise. Stone's critique,
grounded in a radical feminist perspective on capitalism, argued that women's
"volunteerism" was something that should be utilized only for "the political
arena"; otherwise it was "antithetical to the aims of the women's movement." Stone
asserted that "women, who are at the bottom of the economic ladder, are not
responsible for providing free expertise, and/or manual labor for Westinghouse,"
even if they had done so on this one-time production. For the company to expect
otherwise "deprive[d] women of jobs," reduced their volunteer efforts in other service capacities, and "reinforce[d] the myth that women's work isn't worth much."[115]

Despite her concerns, Stone lauded how *Yes, We Can* involved women
behind and in front of the cameras. In her letter to WBZ, Stone commended
"the most positive aspects" of the program, which were the "extraordinary talent, time, dedication and high level of professionalism" of the women working
on the production. The show's success "prov[ed] that women are fully capable
of pulling off a major media coup," and, given this this success, "the experiment
should be repeated."[116] Stone's assessment of *Yes, We Can*'s strengths aligned with
WBZ's hopes for the production. Employing women in extraordinary numbers
in the production of *Yes, We Can*, helped the station demonstrate its accountability to women workers and viewers. With "virtually all the women working
at WBZ-TV" coordinating to produce the special, WBZ hoped that their valuation of women would translate in public relations.[117] Program manager Paul Coss

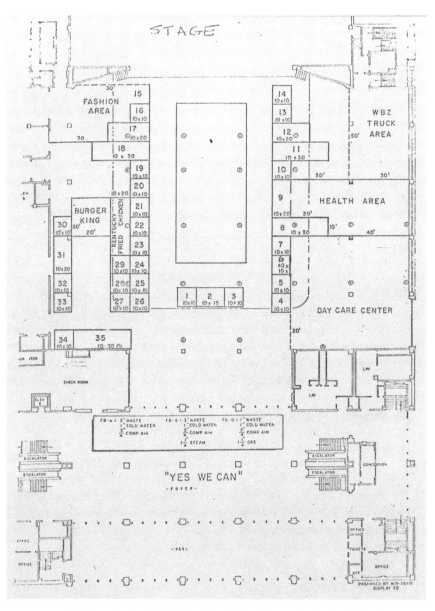

FIGURE 23. The floor plan for *Yes, We Can* fair and television production includes the main stage, areas for health and fashion, and free childcare facilities available to fair attendees. (Schlesinger Library 77-M13—96-M48)

boasted, "There will be no doubt at the completion of this complex programming commitment that WBZ-TV is intimately and significantly concerned with the role of women in contemporary society."[118]

While WBZ used *Yes, We Can* as a public relations tool, feminists seized upon its promotional value to advocate for further progress for women at the station. Instead of using the widely touted number of women working on the production to sing WBZ's praises, as Coss did, feminists used the event to leverage equal employment and promotion of women. Feminist critics and activists asserted that this one-time event should demonstrate to WBZ that, in Janet Stone's words, "women in non-professional capacities at the station have abilities that have been underutilized in day-to-day operations."[119] They converted WBZ's self-promoting, positive assessment of *Yes, We Can* to proof of women's underemployment in the television industry as a result of the industry's sexism rather than a reflection of women's talent.

In their annual report, the Governor's Commission on Women judged *Yes, We Can* and the Women's Fair to be unevenly successful. Citing strong turnout to the fair as a clear positive, Commission members still felt that they had failed to "reach all the people that we wanted to—people with the real needs for day care services, part-time jobs, better health care and credit."[120] Yet some of the day's shortcomings, ironically, were due to the tremendous interest women had in fair. Women overwhelmed the fair, and Sonya Hamlin remembers that the mayor of Boston had to come on the air at noon to ask that no more women come into Boston because there was no room to park and no more room inside the auditorium. With an estimated sixty thousand women attending the fair, the Commission concluded that "there were very real problems at the fair, none of which we could account for because of the numbers of women attending. In all, it must be judged a success on many counts."[121]

Yes, We Can called into question commercial television's programming, funding structure, and relationship to government. Unfortunately, it proved to be an exception rather than a rule in television for women. Although there were plans to recreate and to incorporate the lessons of the broadcast and to produce a series of similar programs across the nation, there are no records of such productions.[122] This single production did, however, create other outcomes: it introduced viewers to feminist ideas in welcoming and accessible ways, connected women across local organizations and government bodies, created a community of female media makers, and furthered women's careers in television.

THE FEMINIST LEGACIES OF THE "SERIOUS SISTERS"

Although each of the programs discussed in this chapter ended before their production staff and viewers wished them to, they bore lasting effects. Workers involved in the programs found communities of like-minded women trained in media production. They learned lessons about the pitfalls of public and regional television leadership, funding, and infrastructure. They experienced a different way of creating television that redefined their labor and their relationship to it. They successfully oversaw lean budgets and challenging logistical conditions. Creating television's "serious sisters" was stressful, underfunded, and largely unsustainable, but it furthered women's abilities to progress in the industry.

As they worked on *Yes, We Can*, women realized just how many of them were skilled in media production and what their potential was if they pooled talent and resources. After participating in the show's production and on the Governor's Commission on Women, these women "contacted each other and realized [they] had common problems." As a result, they formed the Women Filmmakers Cooperative of Boston. Forty-five members strong, the group worked collectively to acquire filmmaking equipment, share existing production equipment, and organize film festivals to showcase their work. They also applied for grant money to strengthen their resources, including "information, skills, equipment and job information," and sought control of media-making at multiple stages, including "distribution, editing, and video."[123]

Other women who were central to the production of experimental local and public television for women continued working in television into and beyond the late 1970s. Their ongoing careers reflected the feminist practices and ethics they helped establish on those productions. After the end of *Woman Alive!*, Joan Shigekawa continued to work in the public sphere in a number of arts-oriented, philanthropic organizations, most notably as the deputy chair of the National Endowment for the Arts from 2009 to 2012 and as its acting chair from 2012 to 2014. Flo Kennedy, who was a frequent guest on local programs like *For Women Today* and a panelist on *Yes, We Can*, went on to host a cable access show, *The Flo Kennedy Show*, from 1978 to 1995, which covered activist concerns ranging from apartheid to affordable housing to LGBT organizations and movements. After leaving WBZ in 1976, Sonya Hamlin helped train hundreds of speakers to travel throughout Massachusetts to raise public awareness of the Equal Rights Amendment. Patricia Mitchell identifies her role as a host for *Yes, We Can* and women's involvement in the production of the program as a turning point in her career and her feminist outlook on television. After realizing the "transformative" nature of television, Mitchell "became committed to using every media platform [she] could access to tell stories with impact," with a focus on women's stories.[124] "Frustrated with the limitations of network programs at the time," Mitchell went on to found her own production company that would enable her to control stories made for women, which manifested in her Emmy Award–winning syndicated daytime talk program *Woman to Woman* (1983–85).[125] In 2000, Mitchell strengthened her commitment to television outside network programming when she became the first woman president and CEO of PBS.

Women's interventions in local and public television in the 1970s led to communal work with other women, public service outreach, and control over media production. The legacy of television's "serious sisters," then, suggests that the impact of feminism on television exceeds a single, often short-lived, production. In addition to the innovative content it provided women viewers, these productions proved a feminist training ground for women who would go on to influence broader and longer-reaching realms of television the institutions that support them, and the culture that surrounds them.

Epilogue

*What the 1970s Can Teach Us
about Feminist Media Reform*

The women discussed throughout *Producing Feminism* created and supported groundbreaking television productions, helped keep networks running, and improved a host of workplace conditions for women in television. Yet their contributions have largely been forgotten. Attending to their labor and reform efforts therefore honors their legacies and enlarges our understanding of television and the women's movement. Along with this type of recollection, which is central to feminist historiography, considering the impact these women had on television also raises larger questions about the nature of feminist interventions in media: What do we imagine feminist media activism to be? Where and how do feminist politics manifest in media industries?

Asking these questions about the 1970s poses challenges, primarily because of our collective assumptions about the influence of the women's movement on media. During the many years that I worked on this project, when my health care providers, the person who cuts my hair, people who sat next to me on planes and trains, friends of friends at parties, and other relative strangers learned that I was writing a book about television and feminism in the 1970s, they would invariably recount a personal connection to the topic. Even if they were not born or were very young during the time of the women's movement, people were quick to name a beloved television character or program that, to them, expressed progressive gender politics.

Perhaps more than any other program, *The Mary Tyler Moore Show* and its protagonist, Mary Richards, have come to stand in for the triumph of feminism. In memorializing the actor Mary Tyler Moore at the time of her 2017 death, the *New York Times* hailed her as someone who "incarnated the modern woman," and

FIGURE 24. *Mary Tyler Moore* super-fan Oprah Winfrey interviews Moore in a replica of the WJM-TV newsroom built on the set of *The Oprah Winfrey Show*, May 29, 2008.

author Jennifer Keishin Armstrong recounted how Moore "became a feminist icon as Mary Richards."[1] Numerous high-profile TV showrunners, producers, and creators, including Oprah Winfrey, Tina Fey, Lena Dunham, and Rachel Bloom, have credited Mary Richards as the inspiration for their depictions of female independence and, in some cases, their own career achievements. Of these women, Winfrey expressed the most-pronounced fandom; over the years and as recently as in a 2020 Instagram post with Fey, Winfrey has paid homage to the program, describing Moore's depiction of Richards as "an inspiration to us all" and as a model for her own personal and professional aspirations.[2] On *The Oprah Winfrey Show*, Winfrey recreated the show's opening credits, shared photos of her own fashion choices modeled on Richards', and had a replica of the WJM newsroom and Mary's apartment constructed on set to host a cast reunion.

Such strong attachments to a program or fictional character attest to the continued circulation and staying power of representation. Recalling these images offers emotional and personal satisfactions as much as insights about television history and feminism. I suspect feminist scholars are similarly compelled as they return to hallowed television content from the era. I, for one, am not immune. My early career journal article on *Wonder Woman* (ABC/CBS, 1975–79) and *Isis* (CBS, 1975–77) was rooted in childhood associations between the programs and my own awareness of women's empowerment.[3] Yet as we continue to mine the meaningfulness of such television programs and make sense of our affective and sentimental attachments to them, linking feminist impact on television so powerfully to content overshadows other ways that women's liberation made inroads into television.

The ways we tell stories about feminism have consequences. As Clare Hemmings argues, histories and theories about feminism are filtered through "technologies of the presumed," primarily academic narratives and institutionalized means of knowledge production and dissemination. This process should not be taken to mean that certain scholars, authors, and voices are more or less correct, per Hemmings. Rather, the value of investigating "collective repetition" lies in understanding the "production and reproduction" of such repetition.[4] The prevalence of thought that correlates the influence of the women's movement on television with representation not only defines what happened in the recent past but also defines what meaningful feminist media activism is and how it registers in the present.

CONTEMPORARY FEMINIST MEDIA REFORM

Producing Feminism centers on women who challenged sexism through the workplaces of corporate network headquarters, local stations, public broadcasting centers, independent production companies, and network production departments. Their stories illustrate how institutional changes happen within historically specific conditions. They also suggest ways that feminist tactics can be adapted for different times and situations. Whether pooling material and intellectual resources, calling for more adequate reproductive health care coverage, creating mentoring relationships, building coalitions among workers, or insisting on dignity as well as economic parity in the workplace, actions represented in *Producing Feminism* tell us something about the possibilities of feminist workplace activism. At the very least they remind us that such activism is possible, and at most they model the means of achieving feminist goals within and beyond a particular industry.

A number of events have emerged since the 2010s that attest to the need for continued feminist reform of workplaces, media and otherwise. Widespread public knowledge of criminal conduct by Harvey Weinstein in 2017 amplified activist Tarana Burke's #MeToo movement. This intensification of the #MeToo movement has been identified by numerous feminists as a "watershed moment" that requires critical engagement in order to affect meaningful change. As journalist Sarah Jaffe argues, knowledge of widespread abuses potentially "unites women across a broad number of workplaces" and reorients feminism away from an "obsession with cracking glass ceilings and 'having it all,'" since even the most-powerful women are not immune from abuse.[5] Other analyses of #MeToo complement Jaffe's by emphasizing the need for collectivity and radical challenges to material and structural conditions. Shelley Cobb and Tanya Horeck contend that to counter violence and mistreatment of women workers, we must "carefully unpack the systemic and institutionalized histories that continue to produce and sustain the conditions for gendered power imbalances and oppression."[6] They also warn against misguided optimism: we should "not assume that the new visibility of feminist arguments about gendered inequality in the workplace will necessarily lead to the long-term structural changes so desperately needed."[7]

Rather than change priorities in light of #MeToo revelations, feminist media reform at the most prominent and influential levels continues to focus on visibility, generally measured by an increased presence of women on-screen and improved gender representations. These priorities are enunciated and reinforced through public-facing means: in celebrity interviews, acceptance speeches, and performative gestures at awards shows and in industry publications, reportage, and think pieces. Although not inconsequential or without value, contemporary image-based reform

FIGURE 25. A high-profile moment at the Seventy-Fourth Emmy Awards for feminist media reform: Geena Davis (center), alongside CEO and chair Madeline Di Nonno (right), accepts the Governor's Award and highlights the efforts of the Geena Davis Institute of Gender in Media. Shonda Rhimes and Sarah Paulson (left) presented the award. Television Academy/NBC, September 14, 2022.

depends on the individual actions of industry players. It assumes that media companies can and will accept responsibility for sexism. It also imagines that images, decontextualized from their means of production, rectifies the problems of the industry.

When Geena Davis took the stage at the 2022 Emmy Awards show to accept the Governors Award on behalf of her eponymous institute, she called attention to the continued sexism in the television industry and described the type of reform it required. This type of public appearance has become typical for Davis, as the work she does on behalf of the Geena Davis Institute of Gender in Media has been recognized on numerous awards stages and promoted in countless interviews and speeches Davis gives on behalf of the Institute. With its celebrity representative, corporate support, and research relationships with educational institutions and tech companies, the Institute sets the priorities of contemporary feminist media reform. Its considerable resources and the lack of other well-funded organizations focused on women in media mean that the Institute carries disproportionate weight in current conversations about gender equality in media.

Because of her celebrity and her authority as an industry insider, Davis is a foremost ambassador for feminist media reform, and she is given a platform to articulate the problems of and solutions to sexism in the media industries. As Vicky Ball and Melanie Bell argue, women's status in television and film production is "poorly understood and subjected to critical silence which is only occasionally interrupted by bouts of liberal handwringing when the *Palme d'Or* list is announced."[8] By granting Davis a forum at the Emmys, the Oscars, and other high-visibility events, the film and television industry can signal concerns about sexism. Yet typical of the flimsy self-critique described by Ball and Bell, these periodic reminders about the industry's gender problems are isolated and short-lived. By promoting easily enacted and achievable improvements to images of women and girls, the Institute assuages concerns about how the industry should deal with its sexism and offers solutions that are tolerable to it. Suggested remedies sideline complex and critical discussions of women workers; their systematic marginalization; and corrective, radical challenges to industry operations.

With its trademarked slogan, "If she can see it, she can be it," the Institute aims to achieve quantifiable gender equality in representation. It prioritizes tools ranging from relatively simple checklists that screenwriters can use to check biases to the high-tech Geena Davis-Inclusion Quotient (GD-IQ), all of which promise to measure inequalities objectively and accurately. The GD-IQ is, as the Institute boasts, a "revolutionary tool," the "first automated software tool to measure screen and speaking time in media content."[9] The precision of the automatic detection software promises to "calculate content detail to the millisecond" and excise human coding errors. The resulting data is presumed to reveal the flaws of representation in a given program, film, ad, or video game and, in turn, to prompt those responsible for such content to adapt and improve their gender politics.

The Institute's particular investment in and definition of female empowerment are built and reinforced through relationships with other institutions. Collectively, their vision of media reform stresses representation. Ties to the University of Southern California, Google, LEGO, and Procter & Gamble offer the Institute resources, authority, and technological aptitude.[10] Conversely, the contributions of scholars and software designers at these institutions are shaped by the agenda of the Institute; their research and design projects are influenced accordingly. The final point in this chain of institutional investments exists in the very media companies whose products the Institute analyzes.

The goal of image reform is intertwined with the Institute's cultivation of industry-friendly relationships with media executives and creators. In her 2019 acceptance speech for the Academy of Motion Picture Arts and Sciences' Jean Hersholt Humanitarian Award, Geena Davis characterized executives at film, television, and video game companies as sympathetic to feminist principles. According to Davis, "to a person," they thought that sexism had been "fixed."[11] "They felt a responsibility to do right by girls and they thought they were," Davis asserted, and concluded that "lack of awareness is the problem."[12] As a remedy, the Institute focuses on the product of these companies—the image—rather than production, labor, and infrastructure behind images. This focus, not coincidentally, avoids systematic critique or analysis of investments and motivations rooted in maintenance of power. Other approaches are not just off the agenda, they are actively critiqued by Institute leaders. In a presentation delivered at a faculty seminar at the Television Academy in 2019, the Institute's CEO and chair, Madeline Di Nonno, noted that, unlike "a lot of academics," "we never shame and blame."[13] The Institute shares its findings about problematic or nonexistent female representations "in a private, collegial way," as they indicate on their website.[14] The need to gain the trust of media owners and executives justifies this approach—"because if we're going to talk to a major studio or business unit, and they are going to reveal to us their challenges," Di Nonno argues, "we are not going to expose it in public."[15]

In the current arrangement between the Institute and the industry, negotiations and persuasive moments happen privately and among individuals. This relationship is based on a presumption that media companies want to change and that the creation of a more inclusive product is the solution to the industry's sexism. By this logic, educating industry players with power will, in turn, improve images of women. This approach calls to mind institutionalized diversity efforts that, by design, fail to provoke meaningful reform. The promise to neither shame nor blame secures the Institute's continued access to centers of power and sets expectations for change at the level of what Sara Ahmed identifies as "good practice."[16] Through "good practice," media companies, executives, and creatives can distinguish their efforts from the bare necessity of "compliance" with legal protections against discrimination and unequal opportunities; they instead enact a "set of practices that enable an organization 'to look good.'"[17] In the Institute's approach, "good practice" corresponds with not just the performative nature of diversity work (i.e., looking good) but also an effective outcome (i.e., feeling good). Simply encouraging media executives to do better replaces actionable, accountable critique and structural change with what Ahmed calls the "performance of good feeling."[18] When Davis urged the audience at the 2019 Academy Awards to convert supporting and ensemble characters from male to female by simply crossing out and revising their names in scripts, she cheerfully promised them, "It's simple. It's fun."[19]

Compared to media reform efforts of women production workers in the 1970s, the Institute's efforts lack robustness, complexity, and efficacy. First, the Institute does not occupy the relationships women had and exploited with men in power, as the women's network groups and other "borers-from-within" did. Instead, as a nonprofit company situated outside media companies, the Institute operates with less insider knowledge and influence. This means more tenuous contact with media executives, less proximity to them, and fewer points of contact with them. Second, the private nature of negotiations shields industry leaders from critique, unlike the very public ways that women's groups aired the problems of the industry. Actions taken by the women's committee of the Writers Guild of America (WGA) in 1973 demonstrate the impact of insider knowledge and industry accountability. The committee gathered and analyzed protected guild information on women's employment figures and provided trade publications with the results, which then became public. In doing so, the women of the WGA produced indisputable evidence of sexist hiring practices that "publicly shamed networks and production companies, establishing a template that would be used by other industry professionals, particularly those organizing within their guild, for generations to come."[20] Finally, the Institute's reform goals focus on images, while the worker-oriented reform of the 1970s holistically dealt with hiring practices as well as representation and concerned itself with the experiences of work for women on sets and in writers' rooms, offices, and boardrooms.

The limitations of the Institute's approach to media reform bear summation here. Merely seeing something does not translate to access or lack of institutional barriers. Emphasizing improved representations as the panacea for sexism in media overlooks media workplaces as spaces of exploitation, disempowerment, disrespect, and danger for women and other marginalized workers. Privileging discussions of contact with executives and high-level creators imagines that production workers on the whole and, more specifically, those at less visible levels bear no influence over images or could not be helpful allies. Postulating that powerful media players merely need educating about sexism uncritically assumes that they are not invested in maintaining a system of inequality. Overall, the Institute fails to heed feminist guidance in the aftermath of #MeToo: that meaningful solutions to gender inequalities must contend with structural and historical conditions of oppression and exclusion rather than visibility alone.

WORKER-ORIENTED REFORM: WAYS FORWARD

In 2021, seventeen years after it was founded, the Geena Davis Institute started to pay attention to workers in the form of a report, *Behind the Scenes: State of Inclusion and Equity in TV Writing*. The Institute partnered with the Think Tank for Inclusion and Equity (TTIE), an offshoot of Women in Film (WIF), which had been publishing this report annually since 2019. TTIE advocates for inclusion of and improved working conditions for historically marginalized and underrepresented writers in the industry, and the organization itself is composed of queer, BIPOC, disabled, and women writers. Partnering with TTIE is a crucial step in enlarging and complicating the Geena Davis Institute's univocal approach to reform. TTIE offers the Institute a way to tether their priorities of representation to media workforces and to consider how the conditions of media work could afford more meaningful and diverse representations. TTIE lobbies for the importance of "creating more opportunities for accurate and authentic storytelling" along with the goal of "increasing inclusion and improving working conditions for all TV writers, in particular those from underrepresented communities."[21]

Significantly, TTIE's reports do not rely solely on demographic employment statistics. When they do call upon statistical data, they foreground its limitations and the ways it can be manipulated or misinterpreted. In their 2021 *Behind the Scenes* report, TTIE indicated that data "seems" to reflect increased employment for underrepresented workers in television writing, but this information is "somewhat skewed by 'clustering,' where shows that focus on underrepresented communities are staffed primarily with writers from that community." This report also notes that "many rooms still do not include any Disabled, Deaf, LGBTQIA+, or age 50+ lower-level writers."[22]

TTIE's reports also provide evidence offered by workers to illustrate intolerable conditions and structural problems within workplaces. For example, the 2021 report indicates, in the wake of #MeToo, a rise in "covert forms of harassment and bullying" that "are creeping into the workplace, especially with the shift to virtual rooms."[23] Exclusionary practices are also understood as historically and context specific. Since the start of the Covid pandemic in 2020, TTIE found that hiring decisions have been "risk-averse" (i.e., stories that feature white leads and are written by "proven" overrepresented writers). Finally, the reports include concrete action plans to rectify workplace exploitation, abuse, and hostility. They describe what allyship for overrepresented workers looks like; how unpaid work involved in development and competitive pitching ("bake-offs") thwarts inclusivity; and the dynamics of gaslighting and microaggressions, tokenism, lack of agency, and lack of retention efforts in workplace cultures. The 2022 report broke down these action items for specific industry players: Networks/Studios/Streamers/Production Companies, Showrunners, Agents/Managers, and Guild/Unions.[24]

TTIE's emphasis on workers' experience and their cautionary outlook on data echoes concerns of feminist reform efforts that are threaded throughout *Producing Feminism*. This resonance suggests that media reform efforts of the 1970s offer valuable lessons for the present and could enrich current reform approaches. The Women's Advisory Council at CBS, for example, tracked real and experiential on-the-job changes for women to guard against inflated and misleading statistics on women's employment gains in television. Secretaries and researchers pointed out inaccuracies in claims about women's placement in jobs, and vice presidents raised concerns about the decreased value of executive titles once women earned them in significant numbers. These issues, raised in the early 1970s, resonated with other women's groups and their ongoing investigations into employment, including AWRT's 1972 study and the WGA Women's Committee's 1974 report, described in chapter 3. Organized efforts and observational evidence by and about women workers gauged what employment actually meant for women. Their challenges to industry claims of equal employment opportunities presaged other reports, including *Window Dressing on the Set*, conducted by the US Commission on Civil Rights in 1977, which investigated inflated and misleading statistical employment gains for women.

RETURNING TO THE FEMINIST PAST

In her exploration of the feminist past, Victoria Hesford asks, "How has the history of women's liberation been produced; what stories have been constructed and disseminated as memories of women's liberation, in the mass mediated public sphere as well as the subcultural worlds of feminist and queer studies?"[25] Other feminist scholarship augments received histories to, as Anne Enke describes it, "admit a broader set of actors and agendas into the history of the movement."[26] When we challenge perceptions that reduce the feminist past to "two parallel movements of white middle-class women that culminated in the founding of NOW and in the rise of the radical women's liberation movement," Susan Hartmann argues that "different narratives emerge."[27] As I hope to have shown in *Producing Feminism*, the role women media workers played in expressing the ideas of the movement adds further complexity to its history.

Looking to the past, as Annie Berke does in her study of women television writers in the 1950s, complicates notions of progress for women. By figuring how "earliness" in many media industries, television included, involved periods of time before women and people of color were expelled from the ranks of workers, Berke challenges "a broader cultural fallacy of liberalism and perpetual progress: things must be better for women *now*, because it was worse *before*."[28] It is tempting to think that the impediments women television workers faced in the 1970s originated in a prefeminist era, as an artifact of the times. Dress codes forbade them from wearing pants, and policies dictated that they ask permission to use the bathroom. Requests to take on prestigious producing projects were presumed to be "greedy" and unprofessional. Their presence raised questions of how writers' rooms should be run, how scripts were created and edited, and whose voices were suitable for broadcasting. Their health care coverage and support for parenting were inadequate, and their reproductive status created financial burdens and occupational precarity for them. It is remarkable that women changed these conditions for the better in the 1970s. Equally remarkable is how relevant these issues are in the present. Now more than ever, feminist reform strategies matter. At the time of writing this conclusion, the US Supreme Court has overturned *Roe v. Wade*, and major corporations like Starbucks are engaging in flagrant union-busting actions. Warehouse workers at Amazon are denied bathroom breaks and are subjected to a humiliating lack of autonomy and respect. And, of course, debates have arisen anew about women's suitability for a variety of jobs across media industries.

Returns to the past trouble presumptions of the past's disconnectedness from the present—or at the very least clear distance from it. Feminist histories of labor illuminate the conditions of the present, not least for workers themselves. As Denise McKenna points out, when someone encounters abuses of power in a system, historical knowledge counters assumptions that it is that person's responsibility or that it is an individualized issue. Instead, we can see that inequalities and exclusions are "baked into the system," and this knowledge provides us with the energy and confidence to resist, critique, and reform. Histories of workers and workplace activism counter a "flow of history" that "wants to continue on its path and collect more and more material to justify the understanding of it in a certain kind of way."[29]

Producing Feminism works to interrupt that flow by expanding histories of the women's liberation movement to include activism in television production. This mode of scholarship does not just add to what we think we know about the feminist past and its viability in the present, it reorients it. Behind representations are corresponding and co-constitutive infrastructures and systems, material circumstances and everyday practices of production, and resistant strategies that emerge in all of these contexts. Feminists were there, doing that work and contending with those circumstances. Their legacies are largely absent from histories of television and from current conversations about how to best reform media. This book attempts to amend that.

ACKNOWLEDGEMENTS

Women's work, in its many iterations, is both the subject of this book and the means by which it came into existence. Women helped me navigate my way to and through academia. When I arrived at the point at which I could write a book, they provided me with intellectual energies and expertise and sustained me emotionally and physically. *Producing Feminism* is a small indicator of all of that work.

Several years ago, Shelley Stamp and I met in a bathroom at a Society for Cinema and Media Studies conference, where she introduced herself and asked about my research. From there, she encouraged me at many more conferences to see that my research was worthy of publication. I am proud to be part of her Feminist Media Histories series. At the University of California Press, Senior Editor Raina Polivka and Editorial Assistant Sam Warren patiently addressed my many questions about the complicated things that happen after a book contract is signed. Elisabeth Magnus copyedited the manuscript, and Amron Lehte indexed it; I appreciate their professionalism and keen eye for detail. Three reviewers—Annie Berke and two anonymous readers—carefully read and provided revision suggestions for this book and changed it for the better. Lynn Spigel provided feedback for an earlier, considerably different manuscript and kindly and wisely helped reorient it.

Virginia Carter, Sonya Hamlin, and Judy Hole were three of the many women who brought the women's movement to television in creative, daring, and strategic ways. In sharing their stories of that time with me, they brought to life not just the facts of a feminist past but its energy and personality as well. I am grateful to them and to all of the women who introduced feminism into their workplaces. Women of my generation are direct beneficiaries of their efforts.

There is something uniquely thrilling about a conversation with an archivist who knows more about a topic than a researcher does and is just as invested in it. I had many such encounters, which enriched the questions I asked in my research, uncovered materials

I did not know existed, and led the project down new paths. Archives, of course, exist only because of the labor, time, and resources that go into sustaining, preserving, and organizing their materials. I thank the many people who do this work and ensure that historical materials remain available to us. I acknowledge in endnotes and the bibliography the full slate of archives and libraries that grounded my research in primary documents and television footage not available elsewhere. I identify here ones that were particularly rich sources of information: the American Heritage Center, the Howard Gotlieb Archival Research Center, the Library of American Broadcasting, the Schlesinger Library, and the Sophia Smith Collection. Sadly, since the time of my research there, the CBS News Reference Library is no longer open, and it is unclear what will happen to the invaluable materials housed there. I am beyond lucky that Cryder Bankes allowed me access to it before it closed and he retired.

My employer, Fordham University, granted me a Faculty Fellowship and a Faculty Research Grant for this project, which afforded me time to research and write in uninterrupted fashion. As at many colleges and universities, women at Fordham fulfill administrative roles and volunteer for service at every level of the institution. As such, they provided support for this project by reading funding applications and writing recommendation letters for them, serving on selection committees for awards and grants, and helping me navigate the bureaucracy of identifying sources of funding and filing for compensation once funding had been awarded. As I moved into a new administrative role the same year I finished this book, Michelle O'Dwyer, Claudia Rivera, and Marie Trombetta, the administrative assistants of my department, provided me with much guidance and support.

Colleagues in the Department of Communication and Media Studies, past and present, who overlapped with the long arc of this project made a difference in what it felt like not just to work on the book but to show up for work, period. I thank them all. Jesse Baldwin-Philippi, Margot Hardenbergh, Beth Knobel, Alice Marwick, Linde Murugan, and Margaret Schwartz sent me gifts and encouraging notes, invited me to celebrations for their many accomplishments, took me to lunch, and built community through grading sessions and writing groups. Amy Aronson understood the time it took me to finish this book. As a scholar, she modeled intensive and careful research of women's histories; as a colleague and department chair, she provided consistent support without heightening my anxiety about the project's timeline to completion.

I cannot thank friends and family enough or in the right way. Over the years that I worked on this book, Meg Leder and I traveled together to eight different countries, some of them more than once. In all that time and over all of those miles, I don't believe we talked once about the book, which was exactly what I needed. Vimala Pasupathi hung in there with me for just as many years. Our time together was intensely focused on our respective scholarship and spanned hours, days, weekends, and summers in libraries, coffee shops, rented houses in upstate New York, and, in these pandemic times, virtual writing sessions. She helped me stick to the work and alleviated its pressures with extraordinary humor, true sympathy and empathy, and plenty of cat-based entertainment. Nelda Williams and Bob Williams welcomed me into their home for countless hours of recuperation and rest, invigorating conversations, and excellent food and parties, to be part of the beautiful family life they had built together. Their daughters, Randy Fitzgerald and Cristy McCay, did the same. As one of the most patient listeners I know, John Marshall never tired of asking me what I was working on and hearing the (very long) answer. Since childhood, Kristi

Clark has been a sounding board and someone with whom I could be completely honest. I could be this way confident in the knowledge that she would call again, plan another visit, and see the better parts of who I am. Although his profession could not be more dissimilar to mine, Ronald Clark learned, along with me, about the long, complicated steps of seeing an academic book to completion. The whole time, his positivity about me and the project never flagged. Phyllis Clark sent me quarts of homegrown canned food, talked to me about her seven-thousand-square-foot garden, shared news of bird sightings, and reminded me of another kind of work beyond writing and a world outside an office. Not least, by any measure, Bill Dunks deserves tremendous thanks. He has read every single word of this book in its many versions and, more importantly, has agreed to be in my life before, during, and after this project.

NOTES

INTRODUCTION

1. Carolyn Wean to Jeff Schiffman (executive producer) and Peter Sloan (general services director), memo, December 27, 1971, #782, Box 69, Jeff Schiffman folder, Sonya Hamlin Collection, Howard Gotlieb Archival Research Center, Boston University (hereafter Hamlin Collection).

2. M. Bernstein to W. Hillier et al., December 22, 1970, #782, Box 69, Paul Coss folder, Hamlin Collection.

3. Raysa Bonow, Claire Carter, Carolyn Wean, and Connie Sanders to M. Bernstein et al., December 22, 1970, #782, Box 69, Paul Coss folder, Hamlin Collection.

4. Bonow et al. to Bernstein et al.

5. Bonow et al. to Bernstein et al.

6. Bonow et al. to Bernstein et.al.

7. Sonya Hamlin, interview with the author, September 20, 2018.

8. Bryan Marquard, "Raysa Bonow, Pioneering Producer of Feminist TV Shows; at 80," *Boston Globe*, July 12, 2011, B12.

9. Hamlin, interview.

10. Lucinda Smith, "Sonya's Sayonara," *Boston Globe*, January 18, 1975, 8.

11. List of shows sent to Paul Coss, June 20, 1972, #782, Box 69, Paul Coss folder, Hamlin Collection.

12. "The Women at Home Also Are Getting a New Shake from Television," *Broadcasting*, August 7, 1972, 40.

13. "Women at Home," 40.

14. Terry Ann Knopf, *The Golden Age of Boston Television* (Hanover, NH: University of Press of New England, 2017).

15. Laurel Stempel Mumford, "Feminist Theory and Television Criticism," in *The Television Studies Book*, ed. Christine Geraghty and David Lusted (New York: St. Martin's Press, 1998), 118.

16. Daphne Spain, *Gendered Spaces* (Chapel Hill: University of North Carolina Press, 1992), 11.

17. See Erin Hill, *Never Done: A History of Women's Work in Media Production* (New Brunswick, NJ: Rutgers University Press, 2016); Elizabeth Nielsen, "Handmaidens of the Glamour Culture: Costumers in the Hollywood Studio System," in *Fabrications: Costume and the Female Body*, ed. Jane Gaines and Charlotte Herzog (New York: Routledge, 1990), 160–79; Miranda Banks and Lauren Steimer, "The Heroic Body: Toughness, Femininity and the Stunt Double," *The Sociological Review* 63, no. 1 (May 2015): 144–57.

18. Miranda Banks, "Production Studies," *Feminist Media Histories* 4, no. 2 (Spring 2018): 160.

19. See Natalie Wreyford and Shelley Cobb, "Data and Responsibility: Toward a Feminist Methodology for Producing Historical Data on Women in the Contemporary UK Film Industry," *Feminist Media Histories* 3, no. 3 (Summer 2017): 107–32; Banks, "Unequal Opportunities"; Vicky Ball and Melanie Bell, "Working Women, Women's Work: Production, History, Gender," *Journal of British Cinema and Television*, 10, no. 3 (July 2013): 547–62.

20. Lauren Rabinovitz, "Ms.-Representation: The Politics of Feminist Sitcoms," in *Television, History, and American Culture: Feminist Critical Essays*, ed. Mary Beth Haralovich and Lauren Rabinovitz (Durham, NC: Duke University Press, 1999), 146.

21. For discussion of the manipulation of data and recategorization of jobs in hiring reports for the FCC, see US Commission on Civil Rights, *Window Dressing on the Set: Women and Minorities in Television* (Washington, DC: US Government Printing Office, 1977); "TV Hires Minorities and Women, But Are the Numbers Hyped?," *Variety*, December 4, 1974, 40, 49. Miranda Banks discusses the lack of diversity in staffing for groundbreaking programs of the 1970s and the precarious and low-paying employment behind the increased hiring of women writers. Miranda Banks, "Unequal Opportunities: Gender Inequities and Precarious Diversity in the 1970s US Television Industry," *Feminist Media Histories* 4, no. 4 (Fall 2018): 109–29. See chapter 1 of this book for an interview with Anne Nelson, a vice president at CBS, regarding the degraded value of vice president status at the networks.

22. Gayle Wald, *It's Been Beautiful: Soul! and Black Power Television* (Durham, NC: Duke University Press, 2015), 20.

23. Wald, 20–21.

24. Julie D'Acci, *Defining Women: Television and the Case of Cagney & Lacey* (Chapel Hill: University of North Carolina Press, 1994), 147.

25. D'Acci, 147.

26. Jennifer Keishin Armstrong, *Mary and Lou and Rhoda and Ted: And All the Brilliant Minds Who Made The Mary Tyler Moore Show a Classic* (New York: Simon and Schuster, 2013), 154.

27. Bonnie J. Dow, *Prime-Time Feminism: Television, Media Culture, and the Women's Movement since 1970* (Philadelphia: University of Pennsylvania Press, 1996); Katherine J. Lehman, *Those Girls: Single Women in Sixties and Seventies Popular Culture* (Lawrence: University Press of Kansas, 2011).

28. Patricia Bradley, *Mass Media and the Shaping of American Feminism, 1963–1975* (Jackson: University of Mississippi Press, 2003), 284.

29. Rabinovitz, "Ms.-Representation," 146.

30. Kathryn C. Montgomery, *Target: Prime Time: Advocacy Groups and the Struggle over Entertainment Television* (New York: Oxford University Press, 1989), 25.

31. Bonnie J. Dow, *Watching Women's Liberation, 1970: Feminism's Pivotal Year on the Network News* (Urbana: University of Illinois Press, 2014), 46.

32. Montgomery, *Target*, 25.

33. Allison Perlman, "Feminists in the Wasteland: The National Organization for Women and Television Reform," *Feminist Media Studies* 7, no. 4 (2007): 415.

34. Bernadette Barker-Plummer, "News as a Political Resource: Media Strategies and Political Identity in the U.S. Women's Movement, 1966–1975," *Critical Studies in Mass Communication* 12, no. 3 (September 1995): 306–24.

35. Women's Coalition Strike Headquarters broadside, August 26, 1970, Women and the American Story Collection, New York Historical Society, accessed January 26, 2022, https://wams.nyhistory.org/growth-and-turmoil/feminism-and-the-backlash/women-strike-for-equality/.

36. Mary Ann Johnson, Rebecca Sive, Christine Riddiough, Anne Ladky, and Joan Hall, "Activists' Panel," *Frontiers: A Journal of Women's Studies* 36, no. 2 (2015): 7.

37. "Women Strike for Equality," Women and the American Story Collection, New York Historical Society, accessed January 26, 2022, https://wams.nyhistory.org/growth-and-turmoil/feminism-and-the-backlash/women-strike-for-equality/.

38. "Women Strike for Equality."

39. Barbara Walters, *Audition: A Memoir* (New York: Knopf, 2008), 185.

40. Bradley, *Mass Media*, 199.

41. As demeaning as these representations were, CBS and NBC were more subtle in their visual rhetoric than ABC's "egregiously sexist" coverage. Dow, *Prime-Time Feminism*, 148.

42. Dow, *Watching Women's Liberation*, 154.

43. Bradley, *Mass Media*, 210.

44. "Schneider on Lib: 'Serious Business,'" *Broadcasting*, August 31, 1970, 29.

45. Hayden Lorimer, "Cultural Geography: The Busyness of Being 'More-Than-Representational,'" *Progress in Human Geography* 29, no. 1 (February 2005): 84.

46. Lorimer, 85.

47. Maya Montañez Smukler, *Liberating Hollywood: Women Directors and the Feminist Reform of 1970s Cinema* (New Brunswick, NJ: Rutgers University Press, 2019), 12.

48. Sara M. Evans, *Born for Liberty: A History of Women in America* (New York: Free Press, 1989), 287. Although feminism had already consolidated as an organized political movement—in 1968, according to most accounts—1970 was the date feminist historians often identify as the emergence of a mainstream, publicly acknowledged movement.

49. "Feminist Yearbook," *Newsweek*, November 16, 1970, 113.

50. Alice Echols, *Daring to Be Bad: Radical Feminism in America, 1967–1975* (Minneapolis: University of Minnesota Press, 1989), 198.

51. LNS and Bobbie Goldstone, "Ladies Home Journal," *off our backs* 1, no. 3 (April 11, 1970): 6.

52. Dow, *Watching Women's Liberation*, 3.

53. Script for *Women's Liberation*, Marlene Sanders Papers, A/S194, Box 1, Folder 1, Schlesinger Library, Radcliffe Institute, Harvard University.

54. Dow, *Watching Women's Liberation*, 26.

55. Bradley, *Mass Media*, xi.

56. Portions of chapter 1 were previously published as "'Feminist Borers from Within': The CBS Women's Advisory Council and Media Workplace Reform in the 1970s," *Journal of Cinema and Media Studies* 63, no. 1 (Fall 2023): 10–29.

57. Edith Efron, "Is Television Making a Mockery of the American Woman?," *TV Guide*, August 8, 1970, 9.

58. "Women at Home," 40.

59. Efron, "Is Television Making a Mockery," 9.

1. WOMEN'S GROUPS AND WORKPLACE REFORM AT NETWORK TELEVISION'S CORPORATE HEADQUARTERS

1. Marylin Bender, "Pants-Ban Tempest at C.B.S.," *New York Times*, January 21, 1970, 42.

2. Bender, 42.

3. The archival documents I refer to throughout this chapter are part of an unprocessed collection in the CBS News Reference Library, located at the CBS Broadcast Center (524 West Fifty-Seventh Street) in New York City (hereafter CBS Library). I gained access to this collection, which is intended for research internal to CBS, through the permission of Cryder Bankes, the library manager (now retired).

4. Michele Hilmes and Shawn VanCour, "Network Nation: Writing Broadcasting History as Cultural History," in *NBC: America's Network*, ed. Michele Hilmes (Berkeley: University of California Press, 2007), 308–22; Michael J. Socolow, "The C.B.S. Problem in American Radio Historiography," *Journal of Radio and Audio Media* 23, no. 2 (2016): 323–34.

5. The NBC archive, housed at the Wisconsin Center for Film and Theater Research, is "the only accessible archive of a major network in the US." Wisconsin Center for Film and Theater Research, "About: History," accessed July 10, 2023, https://wcftr.commarts.wisc.edu /index.php/history. The following represents just a small sample of the significant scholarship it has helped generate: Christine Becker, *It's the Pictures That Got Small: Hollywood Film Stars on 1950s Television* (Middletown, CT: Wesleyan University Press, 2008); Michele Hilmes, *Network Nations: A Transnational History of British and American Broadcasting* (New York: Routledge, 2012); Elana Levine, *Wallowing in Sex: The New Sexual Culture of 1970s American Television* (Durham, NC: Duke University Press, 2007); Susan Murray, *Bright Signals: A History of Color Television* (Durham, NC: Duke University Press, 2018); Lynn Spigel, *Make Room for TV: Television and the Family Ideal in Postwar America* (Chicago: University of Chicago Press, 1992).

6. Timothy Havens, Amanda D. Lotz, and Serra Tinic, "Critical Media Industry Studies: A Research Approach," *Communication, Culture and Critique* 2, no. 2 (June 2009): 238.

7. "Spokeswomen for Equal Rights Groups in Networks List Demands," *Ad Beat*, WHN, October 28, 1973, transcript, CBS Library.

8. "Spokeswomen for Equal Rights Groups."

9. Jeannine Baker, "'Once a Typist Always a Typist': The Australian Women's Broadcasting Co-operative and the Sexual Division of Labor at the Australian Broadcasting

Commission," *Feminist Media Histories* 4, no. 4 (Fall 2018): 160–84; Jeannine Baker and Jane Connors, "'Glorified Typists in No-Man's Land: The ABC Script Assistants' Strike of 1973," *Women's History Review* 29, no. 5 (2020): 841–59; Marama Whyte, "'The Worst Divorce Case that Ever Happened': The *New York Times* Women's Caucus and Workplace Feminism," *Modern American History* 3, nos. 2–3 (November 2020): 153–74; Anne O'Brien "'A Fine Old Time': Feminist Print Journalism in the 1970s," *Irish Studies Review* 25, no. 1 (2017): 42–55.

10. Judith Hole, interview by author, New York, November 10, 2016.

11. "Spokeswomen for Equal Rights Groups."

12. "Spokeswomen for Equal Rights Groups."

13. "Spokeswomen for Equal Rights Groups."

14. "Spokeswomen for Equal Rights Groups."

15. "CBS and Its Women: A Dialogue," *Columbine*, Special Supplement, September 1, 1973, 1, CBS Library.

16. Louise McPherson, "Communication Techniques of the Women's Liberation Front," *Today's Speech*, Spring 1973, 33. The Women's Liberation Front was an umbrella term used by "those outside the movement" to identify an "amorphous organization consisting of many small cells averaging about ten to fifteen women per group" that lacked membership rosters and were "often nameless" (33). Well-known WLF cells included New York Radical Feminists, W.I.T.C.H. (Women's International Terrorist Conspiracy from Hell), and the Female Liberation Movement.

17. Robert A. Wright, "CBS Sees Recovery," *New York Times*, April 22, 1971, 59.

18. "Ten Women Disrupt CBS Meeting, Assert Daytime Network Shows Turn Them Off," *Wall Street Journal*, April 16, 1970, 7.

19. "'Liberation' Women Explode at CBS Meet in Frisco, Finally Get Bounced," *Variety*, April 22, 1970, 38.

20. "Ten Women Disrupt CBS Meeting," 7.

21. "CBS Strides into the 70's," *Broadcasting*, April 20, 1970, 87.

22. "'Liberation' Women Explode," 38.

23. "'Liberation' Women Explode," 38.

24. Ironically, *Variety* and Paley himself were, at this point, imperceptive to the solutions women would bring to the loss of revenues brought about by these new regulatory restrictions. The networks reversed some of these losses through experimental formats in their local news outlets that included "bantering on the set" as well as "an unapologetic emphasis on stories that would bring in viewers, such as the weather, with a jocular weatherman, and the use of television field reporters involved in the story in flashy ways." Bradley, *Mass Media*, 227.

25. "CBS Strides," 87.

26. "'Liberation' Women Explode," 38.

27. "CBS Tips Hat to Women's Lib at Rally's Eve," *Variety*, August 26, 1970, 1.

28. "Schneider on Lib: 'Serious Business,'" *Broadcasting*, August 31, 1970, 29.

29. "Schneider on Lib," 29.

30. National Organization for Women, "About," accessed July 3, 2021, https://now.org /about/.

31. Anne W. Branscomb and Maria Savage, "The Broadcast Reform Movement at the Crossroads," *Journal of Communication* 28, no. 4 (December 1978): 25–34; Bradley, *Mass Media*; Montgomery, *Target*; Alison Perlman, *Public Interests: Media Advocacy and Struggles over U.S. Television* (New Brunswick, NJ: Rutgers University Press, 2016).

32. Whyte, "'Worst Divorce Case,'" 155.

33. Katherine Olstein, "History through Female Eyes," review of *Rebirth of Feminism*, by Judith Hole and Ellen Levine, *New Leader* 55, no. 20 (October 16, 1972): 19.

34. Myra Marx Ferree and Patricia Yancey Martin, "Doing the Work of the Movement: Feminist Organizations," in *Feminist Organizations: Harvest of the New Women's Movement*, ed. Myra Marx Ferree and Patricia Yancey Martin (Philadelphia: Temple University Press, 1995), 13.

35. Yvonne Benschop and Mieke Verloo, "Feminist Organization Theories: Islands of Treasure," in *The Routledge Companion to Philosophy in Organizational Studies*, ed. Raza Mir, Hugh Willmott, and Michelle Greenwood (New York: Routledge, 2016), 101.

36. Rosemarie Tong, *Feminist Thought: A Comprehensive Introduction* (Boulder, CO: Westview Press, 1989), 29.

37. Marlene Sanders and Marcia Rock, *Waiting for Prime Time: The Women of Television News* (Urbana: University of Illinois Press, 1988), 135.

38. Sanders and Rock, 136.

39. Montgomery categorizes these strategies as open-door policy, ongoing relationships, input, and assimilation. See the chapter "Managing Advocacy Groups" in *Target*, 51–74.

40. "CBS and Its Women: A Dialogue," *Columbine* Special Supplement, September 1, 1973, 1, CBS Library.

41. Sanders and Rock, *Waiting for Prime Time*, 135.

42. "NBC, Related Groups Hit by Women's Suit," *Broadcasting*, February 12, 1973, 44.

43. "Broadcasting: The Issue of Influence," *Columbine*, February 1975, 4, CBS Library.

44. "Initial Presentation by the CBS Women's Group to CBS President Arthur R. Taylor, Thursday, July 19, 1973," *Columbine*: Special Supplement, September 1, 1973, 7, CBS Library.

45. "CBS and Its Women," 1.

46. "Broadcasting," 4.

47. Kylie Andrews, "Don't Tell Them I Can Type: Negotiating Women's Work in Production in the Post-war ABC," *Media International Australia* 161, no. 1 (November 2016): 29.

48. Kiki Levathes, "Art Taylor, Activist Executive," *New York News*, August 25, 1974.

49. Lynn Spigel, *TV by Design: Modern Art and the Rise of Network Television* (Chicago: University of Chicago Press, 2008), 81.

50. David W. Ewing, "Who Wants Corporate Democracy?" *Harvard Business Review* 49, no. 5 (September-October 1971): 13.

51. Ewing, 24.

52. Arthur Taylor, interview by Margot Hardenbergh, TV Oral History Project, McGannon Center, Fordham University, New York, NY, September 21, 2004, http://digital.library.fordham.edu/digital/collection/ORALHIS/id/50/rec/29.

53. Ethel Winant, interview by Sunny Parich, Television Academy Foundation, North Hollywood, CA (hereafter Television Academy), August 7, 1996, https://interviews.televisionacademy.com/interviews/ethel-winant#interview-clips.

54. Anne Nelson, interview by Henry Colman, The Interview: An Oral History of Television, Television Academy, July 25, 1999, https://interviews.televisionacademy.com/interviews/anne-nelson?clip=97995#interview-clips.

55. Molly Gregory, *Women Who Run the Show: How a Brilliant and Creative New Generation of Women Stormed Hollywood* (New York: St. Martin's Press, 2002), 100.

56. "CBS Aims High on Equality Side: Taylor to Women, *Variety*, July 25, 1973, 21; "2 Women Get Mgt. Posts at CBS Inc.; Editor Job for Third," *Variety*, August 29, 1973, 21; "CBS Orders Women to Be Given Even Break," *Broadcasting*, February 19, 1973, 28, 30; "CBS Records Takes Women's Lib Seriously," *Variety*, May 16, 1973, 109; "On The Women's Equity Front: CBS Woman Counselors," *Variety*, April 11, 1973, 38; "Taylor Says CBS Will Add Woman's Angle to Management Bonus Plan," *Variety*, August 29, 1973, 2, 46.

57. "CBS and Its Women," 1.

58. Winant, interview.

59. Arthur Taylor to the Organization, "Social Service Leave Program," November 11, 1975, CBS Library.

60. Taylor, "Social Service Leave Program."

61. Arthur Taylor to the Organization, July 23, 1975, CBS Library.

62. Arthur Taylor to New York Officers and Department Heads of CBS, Groups, Divisions and Subsidiaries, October 10, 1975, CBS Library.

63. Hole, interview.

64. "Initial Presentation by the CBS Women's Group."

65. "Initial Presentation by the CBS Women's Group."

66. "CBS Response to Women's Group Presentation, August 17, 1973," *Columbine*: Special Supplement, September 1, 1973, 4, 11, CBS Library.

67. CBS cited an "overall union turnover" of 8 percent in New York and a 4 percent turnover "among technicians" ("CBS Response to Women's Group Presentation," 6).

68. "CBS Response to Women's Group Presentation."

69. "CBS Response to Women's Group Presentation."

70. "Initial Presentation by the CBS Women's Group."

71. "Initial Presentation by the CBS Women's Group."

72. "Initial Presentation by the CBS Women's Group."

73. "CBS Response to Women's Group Presentation."

74. Sheldon M. Wool to Corporate Staff, CCG, CRG, CEP, and Division Organizations, January 1, 1974, CBS Library.

75. Joan Kent, Broadcast Group, began working as a secretary for CBS and then worked as coordinator of community relations for WBCS-TV and manager of audience services; Judith Yellen, Education & Publishing Group, was a merchandise product manager; and Nancy Wendt, Records Group, worked as a project manager and then became senior information systems associate in Management Information Systems.

76. "CBS Names Three Femme Counselors," *Variety*, January 16, 1974, 95.

77. "Changing Times," *The Open Eye: A Publication of the CBS Women's Joint Steering Committee*, Fall 1974, 1, CBS Library.

78. "CBS Women's Joint Steering Committee Presentation to Arthur Taylor," July 11, 1974, CBS Library.

79. "CBS Women's Joint Steering Committee Presentation."

80. Kathy Ferguson, *The Feminist Case against Bureaucracy* (Philadelphia: Temple University Press, 1984), 7.

81. Bender, "Pants-Ban Tempest," New York Times, January 21, 1970, 42.

82. Judith Hole describes the antihierarchical nature of their leadership as directly modeled after Students for a Democratic Society (SDS) and other "left-wing" political activist groups. Hole, interview.

83. "Spokeswomen for Equal Rights Groups."

84. "Spokeswomen for Equal Rights Groups."

85. Banks, "Production Studies," 158, 159.

86. Hill, *Never Done*, 9.

87. Winant, interview, 81:34.

88. Arlie Russell Hochschild, *The Managed Heart: Commercialization of Human Feeling*, Twentieth Anniversary ed. (Berkeley: University of California Press, 2003), 165.

89. Hill, *Never Done*, 15.

90. Hill, 128.

91. "Initial Presentation by the CBS Women's Group."

92. "CBS Women's Joint Steering Committee Presentation."

93. "CBS Women's Joint Steering Committee Presentation."

94. Winant, interview.

95. Winant, interview.

96. "Spokeswomen for Equal Rights in Networks List Demands: Part Two," *Ad Beat*, WHN, November 4, 1973, transcript, CBS Library.

97. Joint Women's Steering Committee to CBS Women, "Re: July 11, 1974 Meeting with Arthur Taylor," September 11, 1974, CBS Library.

98. "Learning Session," *Billboard*, October 3, 1981, 38.

99. Wreyford and Cobb, "Data and Responsibility," 114.

100. Diane Nilsen Westcott, "Blacks in the 1970's: Did They Scale the Job Ladder?," *Monthly Labor Review* 105, no. 6 (June 1982): 29–38, https://stats.bls.gov/.

101. US Commission on Civil Rights, *Window Dressing*, 120.

102. Dorothy Sue Cobble, "'A Spontaneous Loss of Enthusiasm': Workplace Feminism and the Transformation of Women's Service Jobs in the 1970s," *International Labor and Working-Class History*, no. 56 (Fall 1999): 25.

103. Ellen Davis, "CBS Women/Minority Training Programs: Opening Doors to a New Career," *Columbine*, June 1976, 1, CBS Library.

104. "Changing Times," 1–2.

105. Davis, "CBS Women/Minority Training," 2.

106. Davis, "CBS Women/Minority Training," 1+.

107. Davis, "CBS Women/Minority Training," 8.

108. "Spokeswomen for Equal Rights Groups."

109. Joan Acker, "The Future of 'Gender and Organizations': Connections and Boundaries," *Gender, Work and Organization* 54, no. 4 (October 1998): 201.

110. Acker, 200.

111. "CBS Women's Joint Steering Committee Presentation."

112. "Sterilization or Abortion," 42 U.S.C. § 300a-7, 1973.

113. Jeannye Thornton, "Anti-abortion Pressures Building in Some States," *Christian Science Monitor*, August 7, 1973, 11.

114. Karen E. Leslie, "Abortion Hearings: When Life Begins," *off our backs* 4, no. 7 (June 1974): 9. These hearings were held over the course of eleven days in 1974: March 6 and 7, April 10 and 25, May 7, June 4 and 26, July 24, August 21, September 12, and October 8.

115. Drew Q. Brinckerhoff, memo to All CBS Women–New York, November 5, 1974, CBS Library.

116. "CBS Women's Joint Steering Committee Presentation."

117. "CBS Women's Joint Steering Committee Presentation."

118. "CBS Women's Joint Steering Committee Presentation."

119. Leslie, "Abortion Hearings," 9.

120. "CBS Women's Joint Steering Committee Presentation."

121. "CBS and Its Women."

122. "CBS Women's Joint Steering Committee Presentation."

123. "On or Off Camera, Women Move Up in TV Jobs," *Milwaukee Journal*, May 30, 1974, 7.

124. "TV Hires Minorities & Women, But Are the Numbers Hyped?," *Variety*, December 4, 1974, 40.

125. "Ed. Note: What Progress Women at CBS?" *Columbine*, February 1975, CBS Library.

126. Judith Hennessee, "What Progress Women at CBS?" *Columbine*, February 1975, 1, CBS Library.

127. Hennessee, 2.

128. Hennessee, 1.

129. Hennessee, 1.

130. Hennessee, 2.

131. Hennessee, 2.

132. Hennessee, 1.

133. Hennessee, 4.

134. Hennessee, 5.

135. "Spokeswomen for Equal Rights Groups."

136. Sanders and Rock, *Waiting for Prime Time*, 134.

137. Sanders and Rock, 138.

138. Sanders and Rock, 138. There is no evidence of a clear endpoint of WAC. The last mention of the group I could locate in the CBS Library archives was in 1985 ("CBS Employee Organization and Management: The Dialogue Continues," *Columbine*, 14). News of WAC's activities suggests that by this point the group had morphed into a social group that helped women "make contacts and friends of faces seen fleetingly on an elevator or voices heard over the phone" and that hosted speaker series including Gloria Steinem, Alice Walker, attorneys and judges, and an "assertiveness trainer." Lee Chiaramonte, WAC Chair to All Women at CBS, early 1985 (no month or day indicated), CBS Library.

139. Sanders and Rock, *Waiting for Prime Time*, 138.

140. For instance, Elizabeth Nielsen documents the effect of generational disconnection on union participation and leadership in costume design at the start of the 1990s; Erin

Hill sees the continuation of working conditions for studio-era secretaries in modern-day Hollywood assistants through unregulated, gendered abuses; Jeannine Baker and Justine Lloyd argue for understandings of contemporary "devaluation of professional work cultures" and precarity of employment through "legacies of the devaluation of women's work within media." Elizabeth Nielsen, "Handmaidens of the Glamour Culture: Costumers in the Hollywood Studio System," in *Fabrications: Costume and the Female Body*, ed. Jane Gaines and Charlotte Herzog (New York: Routledge, 1990), 160–79; Hill, *Never Done*, 215; Jeannine Baker and Justine Lloyd, "Gendered Labor and Media; Histories and Continuities," *Media International Australia* 161, no. 1 (November 2016): 7.

141. Frances Galt, *Women's Activism behind the Screens: Trade Unions and Gender Inequality in the British Film and Television Industries* (Bristol: Bristol University Press, 2021), 2.

2. FROM "JOCKOCRATIC ENDEAVORS" TO FEMINIST EXPRESSION: BILLIE JEAN KING, ELEANOR SANGER RIGER, AND WOMEN'S SPORTS ON TELEVISION

1. Susan Ware, *Game, Set, Match: Billie Jean King and the Revolution in Women's Sports* (Chapel Hill: University of North Carolina Press, 2011), 154.

2. Oedipussy Tuddé, "Fashion Politics and the Fashion in Politics," *off our backs* 4, no. 5 (July 1974): 19.

3. Tuddé, 19.

4. Tuddé, 19.

5. Ware, *Game, Set, Match*, 155.

6. Ware, 153.

7. Ware, 148.

8. Ware, 149.

9. Leslie Heywood and Shari L. Dworkin, *Built to Win: The Female Athlete as Cultural Icon* (Minneapolis: University of Minnesota Press, 2003), xxi.

10. Heywood and Dworkin, xxiv.

11. Jennifer Hargreaves, *Sporting Females: Critical Issues in the History and Sociology of Women's Sports* (New York: Routledge, 1994), 115.

12. Hargreaves, 115.

13. Mark Asher, "Abortion Made Possible Mrs. King's Top Year: Tennis Star Speaks Out for Women's Rights," *Washington Post*, February 22, 1972, D1.

14. "Billie Jean King," *American Masters*, PBS, September 10, 2013.

15. Billie Jean King, Twitter post, July 29, 2019, 3:56 p.m., https://twitter.com/billiejeanking /status/1155930015059419137; Billie Jean King, "Billie Jean King Plays to Win," interview by Shonda Rhimes, *Shondaland*, September 19, 2017, www.shondaland.com/change-makers /a12270931/billie-jean-king-shonda-rhimes-tennis-interview/#; Fiona Sturges, review of *All In: An Autobiography*, by Billie Jean King with Johnette Howard and Maryanne Vollers, *The Guardian*, September 4, 2021, www.theguardian.com/books/2021/sep/04/all-in-by-billie -jean-king-review-game-set-and-match.

16. Curry Kirkpatrick, "The Ball in Two Different Courts," *Sports Illustrated*, December 25, 1972, 32–33.

17. Ware, *Game, Set, Match*, 2.

18. Ware, 43–44.

19. Ware, 48. Title IX, Section 901(a) of the Educational Amendments Act states that "no person in the United States shall, on the basis of sex, be excluded from participation in, be denied the benefits of, or be subjected to discrimination under any education program or activity receiving federal assistance." US Department of Education, Office for Civil Rights, "A Policy Interpretation: Title IX and Intercollegiate Athletics," December 11, 1979, http://www2.ed.gov/about/offices/list/ocr/docs/t9interp.html.

20. Ware, *Game, Set, Match*, 50.

21. Named for Senator John Tower (R-Texas), who proposed it, the Tower Amendment "suggested that revenue-producing sports should be excluded from compliance with Title IX." "Tower Amendment," in *Encyclopedia of Title IX and Sports*, ed. Nicole Mitchell and Lisa A. Ennis (Westport, CT: Greenwood Press, 2007), 104.

22. Ware, *Game, Set, Match*, 43–44.

23. King testified on November 9, 1973, less than two months after the September 20 match with Riggs.

24. "Hustling a Hustler's Game," *Broadcasting*, July 23, 1973, 35.

25. "Riggs-King $1-Mil Lob for Tandem; ABC's Fast Sale," *Variety*, August 8, 1973, 26.

26. "ABC Aims for Biggest TV Remote in History," *Broadcasting*, September 16, 1968, 64C.

27. Travis Vogan, *ABC Sports: The Rise and Fall of Network Sports Television* (Berkeley: University of California Press, 2018), 3.

28. "Billie Gives Hustler the Hustle, But Where Was the ABC of Yesteryear?" *Variety*, September 26, 1973, 34.

29. "Billie Gives Hustler the Hustle," 34.

30. "Top of the Week: Tennis Everyone," *Broadcasting*, September 24, 1973, 5.

31. "Top of the Week," 5. Audience measurements were based on a "special 26-city" Trendex report. Viewership for the match declined from a 34 rating to 19 once CBS aired *Bonnie and Clyde*.

32. Vogan, *ABC Sports*, 3.

33. Given the unusual word choice, "makes" is likely a typographical error for "males." However, the error could be seen as symptomatic of gender anxiety, considering how much the remainder of the article struggles to interpret King through a heteronormative lens.

34. Scott Vernon, "Billie Jean King: New Sex Images Pose No Problem," *Boston Globe*, October 13, 1974, A12.

35. Vernon, A12.

36. "How Green Was Her Volley," *Variety*, December 25, 1974, 22.

37. "Syndication Story," *Back Stage*, December 27, 1974, 3.

38. "How Green Was Her Volley," 22; Phil Elderkin, "Billie Jean King Courts Fat TV Contract," *Christian Science Monitor*, December 27, 1974, 9.

39. "How Green Was Her Volley," 22.

40. "Biography," ABC Public Relations, 1981–1982, Box 5, unprocessed collection, SSC. MS.00286, Eleanor Sanger Papers, Sophia Smith Collection of Women's History, Smith College, Northampton, MA (hereafter Sanger Papers).

41. "Biography," Box 5, Sanger Papers.

42. Riger to Michael Phenner, March 5, 1979, Box 5, Sanger Papers.

43. Hargreaves, *Sporting Females*, 29.

44. *Maribel* script outline, Box 4, Sanger Papers.

45. Eleanor Riger, "Women in TV Sports," in *TV Book: The Ultimate Television Book*, ed. Judy Fireman (New York: Workman, 1977), 138.

46. Riger, 140.

47. Riger to Roone Arledge, memo, November 13, 1973, Box 3, Sanger Papers.

48. Riger to Arledge, memo, November 13, 1973.

49. "Byliner," 1974, box 1, Sanger Papers. The document's author is unclear, as is its publication status. Eleanor Sanger Riger's name appears at the end of the typed document. "Pam Rangno, Mainliner Magazine" also appears, in handwriting, at the bottom of the document. It is possible that both Riger and Rangno coauthored the document, or that Rangno profiled Riger. *Mainliner Magazine* was the in-flight magazine for United Airlines, but I could not confirm if this document was published in the magazine and, if so, when.

50. Sally O'Brien, "Monday Memo: Colgate Looks with a New Eye at Women," *Broadcasting*, October 7, 1974, 13.

51. "Byliner."

52. "Byliner."

53. Vogan, *ABC Sports*, 3.

54. Frank Beermann, "Dawning Era of TV's Gimmick Sports," *Variety*, September 12, 1973, 51.

55. Beermann, 51.

56. Rosemarie Putnam Tong, *Feminist Thought: A More Comprehensive Introduction* (Boulder, CO: Westview Press, 2008), 50.

57. Neil Admur, "Ellie Riger," *Smith Alumnae Quarterly*, November 1968, 32.

58. Admur, 32.

59. Admur, 32.

60. Riger résumé, undated, Box 5, Sanger Papers.

61. Admur, "Ellie Riger," 32.

62. "Byliner."

63. "Byliner."

64. The working title for the proposed sponsored show was *That Girl Athlete*, and it was to be hosted by Marlo Thomas. This proposed show seems to be the rudimentary version of what would eventually become the Colgate Special. "That Girl Athlete: A Prime Time Television Special Created for Colgate-Palmolive Company," undated treatment, Box 3, Sanger Papers.

65. Riger to Dennis Lewin, memo re: Film Supplement for Show Jumping Championship, July 19, 1978, Box 3, Sanger Papers.

66. Riger to Lewin, memo, July 19, 1978.

67. Riger to Lewin, memo, July 19, 1978.

68. Riger to Lewin, memo, July 19, 1978.

69. Typed draft of Riger profile from Pam Rangno, *Mainliner Magazine*, Box 1, Sanger Papers.

70. "Women's Action Committee Newsletter," January 1976, Box 3, Sanger Papers.

71. Admur, "Ellie Riger," 32.

72. Riger to Phenner, March 5, 1979.

73. Riger, "Women in TV Sports," 140.

74. Riger to Chuck Howard, memo re: World Series of Women's Tennis, January 10–11, 1976, dated November 17, 1975, Box 5, Sanger Papers.

75. Riger to Chuck Howard, memo, May 21, 1976, Box 5, Sanger Papers.

76. Riger to Roone Arledge, memo, August 26, 1976, Box 5, Sanger Papers.

77. Riger to Arledge, memo, August 26, 1976.

78. Riger to Chuck Howard, memo, November 8, 1976, Box 5, Sanger Papers.

79. Riger to Roone Arledge, memo re: Women's Superstars, January 7, 1977, Box 5, Sanger Papers.

80. Riger to Arledge, memo, January 7, 1977.

81. Riger to Chuck Howard, memo, April 7, 1977; Riger to Chet Forte, memo, April 7, 1977; Riger to Chuck Howard, memo re: Kentucky Derby/Preakness April 26, 1977; Riger to Dennis Lewin, memo re: NCAA Football and Pro Bowler's Tour August 9, 1977; Riger to Chet Forte, memo re: NCAA Football and Pro Bowler's Tour August 9, 1977; Riger to Chuck Howard, memo re: NCAA Football and Pro Bowler's Tour, August 9, 1977, Box 5, Sanger Papers.

82. Riger to Roone Arledge, March 28, 1978, Box 5, Sanger Papers.

83. Riger to Arledge, March 28, 1978.

84. Riger to Arledge, March 28, 1978.

85. Riger to John Martin, January 10, 1978, Box 5, Sanger Papers.

86. Riger to Martin, January 10, 1978.

87. Riger to John Martin, January 11, 1978, Box 5, Sanger Papers.

88. Riger, undated report on women's sports, Box 3, Sanger Papers.

89. Galen Clavio, "Play-by-Play Announcer," in *Encyclopedia of Sports Management and Marketing*, ed. Linda E. Swayne and Mark Dodds (Thousand Oaks, CA: Sage Publications, 2011), http://proxy.library.nyu.edu/login?url=https://search.credoreference.com/content/entry/sagesports/play_by_play_announcer/0?institutionId=577.

90. Minkyo Lee, Daeyeon Kim, Antonio S. Williams, and Paul M. Pedersen, "Investigating the Role of Sports Commentary: An Analysis of Media-Consumption Behavior and Programmatic Quality and Satisfaction," *Journal of Sports Media* 11, no. 1 (Spring 2016): 161.

91. Michael A. Messner, Margaret Carlisle Duncan, and Kerry Jensen, "Separating the Men from the Girls: The Gendered Language of Televised Sports," *Gender and Society* 7, no. 1 (March 1993): 131.

92. Riger to Chuck Howard, memo re: European gymnastics, April 29, 1975, Box 5, Sanger Papers.

93. Riger to Howard, April 29, 1975.

94. Foundational scholarship includes Michele Hilmes, *Radio Voices: American Broadcasting 1922–1952* (Minneapolis: University of Minnesota Press, 1997); Lana F. Rakow, *Gender on the Line: Women, the Telephone, and Community Life* (Urbana: University of Illinois Press, 1992); and Amy Lawrence, *Echo and Narcissus: Women's Voices in Classical Hollywood Cinema* (Berkeley: University of California Press, 1991). Subsequent work further complicates the gendering of voices and sound technologies, as in the "mismatching of voices" to gender and embodiment. See, for example, Jennifer Fleeger, *Mismatched Women: The Siren's Song through the Machine* (New York: Oxford University Press, 2014), and

Allison McCracken, *Real Men Don't Sing: Crooning in American Culture* (Durham, NC: Duke University Press, 2015).

95. Lawrence, *Echo and Narcissus*, 10.

96. Charles Maher, "Women Move in on Sports Mike: Whether Male Chauvinists Like It or Not, the Feminine Touch Appears Here to Stay," *Los Angeles Times*, January 20, 1975, E1.

97. Maher, E1.

98. Riger to Roone Arledge, memo re: ABC's First Staff Woman Commentator, June 8, 1973, Box 5, Sanger Papers.

99. Riger to Arledge, memo, June 8, 1973.

100. Riger to Mickey Dwyer, July 30, 1981, Box 4, Sanger Papers.

101. It is unclear what this future programming was going to be. Riger suggested putting together an outside program to demonstrate what she and Nyad were proposing but provides no additional details in this or any other correspondence included in her archived papers. Riger to Mickey Dwyer, November 3, 1982, Box 4, Sanger Papers.

102. Riger to Mickey Dwyer, April 29, 1983, Box 4, Sanger Papers.

103. Riger to James Spence, October 31, 1983, Box 5, Sanger Papers.

104. Riger to Herb Granath, President ABC Video Enterprises, November 14, 1984, Box 5, Sanger Papers.

105. Riger to Roone Arledge, April 18, 1977, Box 5, Sanger Papers.

106. Riger to Phenner, March 5, 1979.

3. WORKING IN THE LEAR FACTORY: ANN MARCUS, VIRGINIA CARTER, AND THE WOMEN OF TANDEM PRODUCTIONS

1. Ann Marcus to Charles B. Block, August 29, 1976, #9287-80-06-30, Box 16, Correspondence, 1976 folder, Ann Marcus Papers, University of Wyoming, Heritage Center (hereafter Marcus Papers).

2. Clarke Taylor, "Paddy May Have a Hit on His Hands," *Los Angeles Times*, November 21, 1976, M50.

3. Wilfred Altman, "Exclusive! Wilfred Altman Cables from New York This Outspoken Interview with Paddy Chayefsky, America's Leading Television Playwright," *The Stage*, December 27, 1957, 6.

4. Taylor, "Paddy May Have a Hit," M50.

5. The *Los Angeles Times* writer interviewing Chayefsky agreed to this assessment of Lear's innovation and described *Mary Hartman, Mary Hartman* as "stylistically similar" to *Network*. Taylor, "Paddy May Have a Hit," M50.

6. Kirsten Marthe Lentz, "Quality versus Relevance: Feminism, Race, and the Politics of the Sign in 1970s Television," *Camera Obscura* 15, no. 1 (2000): 57.

7. Todd Gitlin, *Inside Prime Time* (New York: Pantheon Books, 1985), 209.

8. For further elaboration about these distinctions, see Lentz, "Quality versus Relevance," 44–93.

9. Harry F. Waters, "The Mary Hartman Craze," *Newsweek*, May 3, 1976, 63.

10. Waters, 63.

11. Henry Geller and Gregg Young, "Family Viewing: An FCC Tumble from the Tightrope?," *Journal of Communication* 27, no. 2 (June 1997): 193.

12. Liz Ewen and Stu Ewen, "Mary Hartman: An All-Consuming Interest," *Seven Days*, July 26, 1976, 29, 30.

13. Waters, "Mary Hartman Craze," 54.

14. Waters, "Mary Hartman Craze," 54.

15. Norman Lear, interview with Mike Wallace, *60 Minutes*, CBS, April 11, 1976.

16. Lorraine Davis, "The Soaperstar," *Vogue*, June 1976, 157.

17. "Dialogue on Film: Norman Lear," *American Film*, June 1, 1977, 40.

18. Barbara Ehrenreich, "*Mary Hartman*: A World Out of Control," *Socialist Revolution*, October-December 1976, 136.

19. See Tania Modleski's "The Rhythms of Reception: Daytime Television and Women's Work," in *Regarding Television: Critical Approaches—An Anthology*, ed. E. Ann Kaplan (Frederick, MD: University Publications of America, 1983), 67–75, for foundational feminist analysis of soap opera narratives.

20. Stephanie Harrington, "Mary Hartman: The Unedited, All-American Unconscious," *Ms.*, May 1976, 53.

21. Harrington, "Mary Hartman," 53.

22. Waters, "Mary Hartman Craze," 55.

23. Harrington, "Mary Hartman," 53.

24. Letter from Susan Rogan, Chico, CA, undated, #9287 Box 16, Correspondence, 1976, Fan Mail for Mary Hartman, Mary Hartman file, Marcus Papers.

25. Shelley Fields to Channel 44, Oakland, CA, January 22, 1975, #9287 Box 16, Correspondence, 1976, Fan Mail for Mary Hartman, Mary Hartman file, Marcus Papers.

26. Letter from Kathy Short, Brooklyn, NY, February 1976, #9287 Box 16, Correspondence, 1976, Fan Mail for Mary Hartman, Mary Hartman file, Marcus Papers.

27. Mary Ruth Casey to WDBD-TV, Silver Springs, FL, January 25, 1976, #9287 Box 16, Correspondence, 1976, Fan Mail for Mary Hartman, Mary Hartman file, Marcus Papers.

28. Lear, interview with Wallace.

29. Levine, *Wallowing in Sex*, 22.

30. Levine, 23.

31. "*Mary Hartman* as Synd. Rhodes Show from Lear," *Variety*, Wednesday, October 8, 1975, 48.

32. *Mary Hartman* Press Kit, undated, Box 2, Series 8, MSS 05, Norman Lear Script Collection, Emerson College Archives, Emerson College, Boston.

33. *Mary Hartman* Press Kit.

34. Erin Lee Mock, "'The Soap Opera Is a Hell of an Exciting Form': Norman Lear's *Mary Hartman, Mary Hartman* and the 1970s Viewer," *Camera Obscura* 28, no. 2 (2013): 112.

35. Waters, "Mary Hartman Craze," 56.

36. Norman Lear, *Even This I Get to Experience* (New York: Penguin, 2014), 275.

37. Lear, interview with Wallace.

38. Lear, interview with Wallace.

39. *Mary Hartman* Press Kit. By the second season, Darling had left the production, and another woman, Nessa (Picker) Hyams, replaced her.

40. *Mary Hartman* Press Kit.

41. US Commission on Civil Rights, *Window Dressing*.

42. *Mary Hartman* Press Kit.

43. *Mary Hartman* Press Kit.

44. Harrington, "Mary Hartman," 54.

45. Gail Parent, interview with Nancy Harrington, July 16, 2013, The Interviews, Television Academy Foundation, North Hollywood, CA (hereafter Television Academy), https://interviews.televisionacademy.com/interviews/gail-parent?clip=1#interview-clips.

46. Parent, interview.

47. Parent, interview.

48. Ann Marcus, interview with Karen Herman, November 16, 2001, The Interviews, Television Academy, www.emmytvlegends.org/interviews/people/ann-marcus#.

49. "Dialogue on Film," 38.

50. Horace Newcomb, "The Television Artistry of Norman Lear," *Prospects* 2 (October 1977): 111.

51. Newcomb, 111.

52. Aaron Hunter and Martha Shearer, introduction to *Women and New Hollywood: Gender, Creative Labor, and 1970s American Cinema*, ed. Aaron Hunter and Martha Shearer (New Brunswick, NJ: Rutgers University Press, 2013), 5.

53. Marcus, interview.

54. Louise Lasser, interview with Adrienne Faillace, May 16, 2017, The Interviews, Television Academy, https://interviews.televisionacademy.com/interviews/louise-lasser?clip=92900#interview-clips.

55. Lasser, interview.

56. Lasser, interview.

57. Marcus, interview.

58. Writers' meeting transcript for episode #42, #9287, Box 16, Production Files, Mary Hartman 1975–1976, Marcus Papers.

59. Writers' meeting transcript for episode #103, April 12, 1976, #9287, Box 17, Production Files, Mary Hartman 1975–1976, Marcus Papers.

60. Writers' meeting transcript, December 22, 1975, #9287, Box 16, Production Files, Mary Hartman 1975–1976, Marcus Papers.

61. Marcus to Block, August 29, 1976.

62. Mary Hartman, Mary Hartman Writers Meeting Notes, December 30, 1975, #9287-80-06-30, Box 16, Mary Hartman, Mary Hartman Production Files, 1975–76 folder, Marcus Papers.

63. "Writers Meeting Notes, Mary Hartman, Mary Hartman, Long Story—Tape 3," January 20, 1976, #9287-80-06-30, Box 16, Mary Hartman, Mary Hartman Production Files folder, 1975–76, Marcus Papers.

64. "Writers Meeting Notes, Mary Hartman, Mary Hartman, Long Story—Tape 3."

65. "Writers Meeting Notes, Mary Hartman, Mary Hartman, Long Story—Tape 3."

66. Ann Marcus to Gloria Steinem, September 27, 1977, SCC.MS.00237, Box 185, folder 9, Gloria Steinem Papers, Sophia Smith Collection, Smith College.

67. Marcus, interview.

68. Marcus, interview. Lear identifies in multiple ways with feminism in interviews and in his autobiography, in which he writes, "Frances and I had become close to Betty Friedan,

Gloria Steinem, and Eleanor Smeal, the head of the National Organization for Women, so we wound up in the loathed list just behind *Maude*." Lear, *Even This*, 260–61.

69. *Norman Lear: Just Another Version of You*, directed by Heidi Ewing and Rachel Grady (2016; Loki Films, Thirteen/WNET), DVD.

70. *Norman Lear: Just Another Version of You.*

71. Mary Hartman writers' meeting transcript, April 12, 1976, #9287, Box 17, Production Files 1975–76, Mary Hartman, Mary Hartman file, Marcus Papers.

72. Taylor, "Paddy May Have a Hit," M50.

73. The hysteric, as Didi-Huberman's title suggests, was a cultural construction that emerged in the late nineteenth century and signaled a "great fear for everyone," primarily in the unrestrained emotions, desires, and physicality of women. Although hysteria was a historically specific phenomenon, Didi-Huberman argues that it retains currency in contemporary society as a condition that "everyone still knows." Georges Didi-Huberman, *Invention of Hysteria: Charcot and the Photographic Iconography of the Salpêtrière*, trans. Alisa Hartz (Cambridge, MA: MIT Press, 2003), 68.

74. Although it does not name Chubbuck, the *Los Angeles Times* makes a parenthetical aside that uses Chubbuck's suicide as proof of Chayefsky's remarkable abilities to address the cultural unrest of the day: "(A Florida newscaster did commit suicide on the air last season.)" Taylor, "Paddy May Have a Hit," M50.

75. Sally Quinn, "Christine Chubbuck: 29, Good-Looking, Educated, a Television Personality. Dead. Live and in Color," *Washington Post*, August 4, 1974, F8–F9.

76. Quinn, F9.

77. Robert Edward Balon, "Prelude to Big Brother? Measuring Broadcast Audiences in the Year 2000," *USA Today*, November 1978, 53, 54.

78. Harry F. Waters, "TV: Do Minorities Rule?," *Newsweek*, June 2, 1975, 78.

79. Waters, 78.

80. "Forms for Femmes, Etc., Now Required by FCC," *Variety*, December 22, 1971, 48.

81. "WREC-TV Target of First Equal Opportunity Suit," *Broadcasting*, July 23, 1973, 8; "EEOC Upholds Charges against WRC Stations," *Broadcasting*, February 5, 1973, 36.

82. "AWRT Seeks Profile for Women's Jobs," *Broadcasting*, December 18, 1972, 34.

83. "Suggested Mailing to Prospective Members," undated, AWRT Collection, Series 1, box 4, folder 3, Library of American Broadcasting, University of Maryland, College Park (hereafter Library of American Broadcasting).

84. AWRT's support for any cause would have been considerable. They arguably were and are the most visible and powerful organization of women in broadcasting, with award winners (Peabody, Emmy, and AP awards); officeholders in the National Association of Broadcasters, National Association of Educational Broadcasters, and state broadcasters' associations; honorary doctoral holders at multiple, highly regarded universities; delegates to White House conferences; and membership on university boards of trustees.

85. "AWRT, Inc. Presents 'Women in Broadcasting,'" report to members, 1967, AWRT Collection, series 1, box 4, Library of American Broadcasting.

86. "AWRT, Inc. Presents 'Women in Broadcasting,'" 1967.

87. "AWRT, Inc. Presents 'Women in Broadcasting,'" 1967.

88. "AWRT Looks for Emphasis: Professionalism or Feminism or Both?," *Broadcasting*, May 5, 1975, 18.

89. "American Women in Radio and Television: A Profile of the Membership, 1978," AWRT Collection, series 1, box 4, Library of American Broadcasting.

90. "American Women in Radio and Television."

91. Banks, "Unequal Opportunities," 118.

92. Lee served as FCC commissioner from 1953 to 1981.

93. "Lee Comes on Strong for Equal Employment," *Broadcasting*, October 27, 1975, 27.

94. "Lee Comes on Strong," 27.

95. "First Meeting" transcript, #9287-80-06-30, Box 25, Scripts and Related Materials, 1976, *All That Glitters* folder, Marcus Papers.

96. Lear, *Even This*, 444.

97. Helen Dyer, "The Surprising Career of Virginia Carter," *MaGill News, Alumni Quarterly*, Fall 2002, https://mcgillnews-archives.mcgill.ca/news-archives/2002/fall/carter/index.html.

98. Robert S. Alley and Irby B. Brown, *Women Television Producers: Transformation of the Male Medium, 1948–2000* (Rochester, NY: University of Rochester Press, 2001), 79.

99. Carter replaced Marian Rees, who describes the event as unexpected and "terribly hurtful." Rees was given two weeks' notice after working at Tandem for fifteen years. She saw the decision as one that was "engineered" by Frances Lear, who "wanted to redesign the company and hire someone with a feminist viewpoint." Rees makes it clear that Carter had no knowledge of this decision-making process and that only after meeting for lunch were the two women able to reconstruct what had transpired (Alley and Brown, 63).

100. Virginia Carter, interview with author, April 30, 2019.

101. Carter, interview.

102. Carter, interview.

103. Carter, interview.

104. Dyer, "Surprising Career of Virginia Carter."

105. Carter, interview.

106. Carter, interview.

107. Alley and Brown, *Women Television Producers*, 81, 90.

108. Alley and Brown, 78.

109. Alley and Brown, 78.

110. Alley and Brown, 78.

111. Waters, "TV: Do Minorities Rule?," 78.

112. Waters, 78.

113. Waters, 78.

114. "CORE vs. Lear on Blacks, Jobs," *Variety*, January 29, 1975, 47.

115. "CORE vs. Lear," 47.

116. Carter, interview.

117. Virginia Carter to Rod Parker, Gene Marcione, Woody Kling, and Norman Lear Re: "George & Gordon" screening for Gay Community, February 24, 1975, #9287, Box 17, Production Files, Mary Hartman 1975–76 folder, Marcus Papers.

118. Carter, interview.

119. Carter, interview.

120. Kalish remembers turning to newspaper stories about abortion as "where we went for inspiration." Gregory, *Women Who Run the Show*, 26.

121. Alley and Brown, *Women Television Producers*, 157.

122. Montgomery, *Target*, 41.

123. "Chatter: Hollywood," *Variety*, December 30, 1975, 45.

124. "ADL Raps 'Hartman' Segment," *Variety*, August 18, 1976, 45.

125. "ADL Raps 'Hartman' Segment," 45.

126. "ADL Raps 'Hartman' Segment," 45.

127. "Minority Programming Fails to Capture Majority's Attention at NAB Workshop," *Broadcasting*, March 29, 1976, 56.

128. "Minority Programming," 57.

129. "Minority Programming," 57.

130. *Variety* mentions Carter's promotion as one of several that came with Tandem's 1977 "expansion into theatrical production" and "formalization of its tv syndication sales division." These new business plans prompted a corresponding "burst of promotions and new hirings in a broad executive realignment." "Exec Shuffle Cues Promotions, Hirings at Tandem & TAT," *Variety*, January 26, 1977, 58. See also "Fates & Fortunes: Programming," *Broadcasting*, January 31, 1977, 65.

131. "First Meeting" transcript.

132. "First Meeting" transcript.

133. "Frontloaded with Sexual Titters, Glitters Could Bother Carson," *Variety*, April 13, 1977, 46.

134. "Knight 'Glitters' Prod.," *Variety*, February 2, 1977, 72.

135. Don Shirley, "Norman Lear Plots Sex-Role Swap," *Washington Post*, April 10, 1977, 105.

136. "All That Glitters," *Variety*, April 20, 1977, 102.

137. "'All That Glitters' Dies," *Variety*, Wednesday, June 15, 1977, 49.

138. "Title Tells It," *Broadcasting*, November 1, 1976, 5.

139. These figures are based on the reported costs for New York station WNEW. "Title Tells It," 5. WPIX paid a "strapping" price of $30,000 for the rights fee for the show. "Lear Finds 'All That Glitters' Is Not Gold, but He Still Hopes to Strike It with Off-Network Series," *Broadcasting*, June 20, 1977, 49.

140. Family Viewing Hour was found to be in violation of the First Amendment and was no longer in effect in fall 1977. Although no longer official policy, networks generally continued to carry out the policy with "family-friendly" prime-time programming.

141. "Frontloaded with Sexual Titters," 46. Although *Variety* reported that Lear dictated back-to-back programming, in his *American Film* interview Lear suggested that his ability to dictate such terms to stations was limited. "Dialogue on Film," 42.

142. New York's WPIX viewership started with a 5.1 rating and a 16 share in the show's first week; in the second week, it fell to a 4.1 rating and a 12 share. By the third week, it garnered a 3.3 rating and a 9 share. Los Angeles fared similarly with an initial 8 rating and an 11 share, a 6 rating and a 9 share, and a 4 rating and a 6 share in the first three weeks of airing on KCOP. In comparative terms, *The Tonight Show* averaged at this point a 13 rating and a 27 share in Chicago, whereas *All That Glitters* brought in an 8 rating and a 16 share, a 5 rating and an 11 share, and a 5 rating and a 10 share in its first three weeks on Chicago's WFLD. "'All That Glitters' Falters in Ratings," *Broadcasting*, May 16, 1977, 50–51.

143. "The Post-NATPE Program Marketplace," *Broadcasting*, March 7, 1977, 49.

144. *All That Glitters* distinguished itself even further in being one out of the two shows, along with *Front Page Feeney*, that made this cut of twenty-one particularly successful shows at NATPE that year. "Post-NATPE Program Marketplace," 49.

145. Robert McLean, "'All That Glitters' Premiers on Ch. 56," *Boston Globe*, March 24, 1977, 75.

146. Carol Burton Terry, "All That Glitters Strikes Ratings Gold," *Newsday*, April 30, 1977, 34A.

147. Gerald Clarke, "Eve's Rib and Adam's Yawn," *Time*, April 25, 1977, 82.

148. Carter, interview.

149. "Frontloaded with Sexual Titters," 46.

150. Don Shirley, "In the Wake of *All That Glitters*," *Washington Post*, April 19, 1977, B3.

151. Clarke, "Eve's Rib," 82.

152. Shirley, "In the Wake," B3.

153. Shirley, B3.

154. Shirley, B3.

155. Novick was "troubled" that women in power would simply reflect the same behaviors as men in power. She "like[d] to think that having been oppressed, we would have more insight into what it means to be oppressed." Shirley, B3.

156. Don Shirley, Kay Gardella, Fran Breslin, Katie Kelly, Jim O'Brien, Bill Mandel, and Bill Granger, quoted in advertisement: "The Critics Speak Out about *All That Glitters*," *Broadcasting*, May 2, 1977, 45.

157. "First Meeting" transcript.

158. Marcus to Steinem, September 27, 1977.

159. "Monitor," *Broadcasting*, June 4, 1979, 70.

160. Marcus, interview.

161. Marcus, interview.

162. "Monitor," 70.

163. Marcus, interview.

164. Marcus, interview.

165. John Dempsey, review of *The Life & Times of Eddie Roberts*, *Variety*, January 16, 1980, 73.

166. Gail Williams, review of *The Life & Times of Eddie Roberts*, *Hollywood Reporter*, January 7, 1980, 6.

167. John O'Connor, "TV: Two Late-Night Arrivals," *New York Times*, January 7, 1980, C17.

168. Marcus, interview.

169. Elana Levine, *Her Stories: Daytime Soap Opera and US Television History* (Durham, NC: Duke University Press, 2020), 43.

170. The Morgan Cox award was presented each year to a guild member whose "vital ideas, continuing efforts and personal sacrifice best exemplify the ideal of service to the guild." David Robb, "Marcus to Get WGA's Cox Nod," *Hollywood Reporter*, December 16, 1999, 4, 50.

171. "Candidate Statements: Board of Directors," *Journal: Writers Guild of America, West*, September 1990, 11.

172. "Candidate Statements," 11.

173. "Candidate Statements," 11.

174. Lee Grant directed her first feature film, *Tell Me a Riddle*, in 1980; Nessa Hyams directed *Leader of the Band* (1987) and continued working as a casting director for feature films; among her many television and film credits, Gail Parent was a co-executive producer for *The Golden Girls* (NBC, 1985–92) and a supervising producer for *Tracey Takes On* (HBO, 1996–99).

175. Horace Newcomb, "Susan Harris," in *Encyclopedia of Television*, ed. Horace Newcomb, 2nd ed. (New York: Routledge, 2004), 1064.

176. Lee Grant, interview with Henry Coleman, May 10, 2000, The Interviews, Television Academy, https://interviews.televisionacademy.com/interviews/lee-grant#interview-clips.

177. Alley and Brown, *Women Television Producers*, 159.

178. Grant, interview.

179. Grant, interview.

180. Grant, interview.

181. Lear, *Even This*, 223, 471.

182. WGA Women's Committee, "Women's Committee Statistics Report," November 7, 1974, Archives, Writers Guild Foundation Shavelson-Webb Library, Los Angeles, in Miranda Banks, *The Writers: A History of American Screenwriters and Their Guild* (New Brunswick, NJ: Rutgers University Press, 2015), 181.

183. WGA Women's Committee, "Women's Committee Statistics Report."

184. WGA Women's Committee, "Women's Committee Statistics Report."

185. Banks, *Writers*, 180.

186. Dave Kaufman, "Women Are on the Rise in Television's Executive Suites," *Variety*, February 4, 1981, 99.

4. TELEVISION'S "SERIOUS SISTERS": EXPERIMENTS IN PUBLIC AND REGIONAL TELEVISION FOR WOMEN

1. A thirty-two-minute compilation tape of the *Yes, We Can Entertainment Special* and *Yes, We Can*, which was submitted for consideration for the Peabody Awards, is available for viewing in the Paley Archive, the Paley Center for Media, New York, catalog ID: 107099.

2. Marsha F. Cassidy, *What Women Watched: Daytime Television in the 1950s* (Austin: University of Texas Press, 2005), 5.

3. *In Her Own Right* and *Woman Alive!* aired at 8:30–9:00 p.m. and 8:00–9:00 p.m., respectively.

4. "Tomorrow Is Liberated," *Back Stage*, Friday, March 24, 1972, 3. Audiotapes of *In Her Own Right* and episodes of *Woman, Alive!* are housed in the Schlesinger Library collections, Radcliffe Institute, Harvard University (hereafter Schlesinger Library). *Woman Alive!* Collection, 1974–1977, MC 421: Vt-30; Papers of Katharine S. Kinderman, 1969–1970, MC 253: T31.

5. "The Women at Home Also Are Getting a New Shake from Television," *Broadcasting*, August 7, 1972, 40.

6. Joan Shigekawa, "The American Woman—*Alive* and Well," *Public Communications Review* 4 no. 5 (September/October 1976): 48.

7. Shigekawa, 48.

8. Shigekawa, 48.

9. Rachel Moseley, Helen Wheatley, and Helen Wood, "Introduction: Why 'Television for Women'?," *Screen* 54, no. 2 (Summer 2013): 238.

10. Foundational inquiry into women's television focuses on soap operas and game shows in daytime programming. See, for instance, Tania Modleski, "The Search for Tomorrow in Today's Soap Operas: Notes on a Feminine Narrative Form," *Film Quarterly* 33, no. 1 (Autumn 1979): 12–21; Charlotte Brunsdon, "*Crossroads*: Notes on a Soap Opera," *Screen* 22, no. 4 (December 1981): 32–37.

11. Moseley, Wheatley, and Wood, "Introduction," 239.

12. Moseley, Wheatley, and Wood, 238.

13. DuMont's New York City–owned and –operated station, WABD, reported "Daytime Tele as Profit Maker," *Variety*, October 27, 1948, 2.

14. Cassidy, *What Women Watched*, 27.

15. "Daytime Television," *Broadcasting*, March 29, 1954, 78.

16. "Daytime Television," 76.

17. Cassidy, *What Women Watched*, 75.

18. "Women at Home," 40.

19. "Women at Home," 40.

20. NBC's Paul Klein, in his role as vice president of programming, is credited with coining this term. It reflects a programming philosophy based on the assumption that viewers "will watch anything unless they are offended into changing channels." Horace Newcomb, "Programming," in *Encyclopedia of Television*, ed. Horace Newcomb, 2nd ed. (New York: Routledge, 2004), 1835.

21. "Women at Home," 40.

22. "Women at Home," 40.

23. Eileen Shanahan, "Public TV Said to 'Overlook' Women," *New York Times*, November 19, 1975, 85.

24. Shanahan, 85.

25. Montgomery, *Target*, 25.

26. Lucinda Smith, "Yes, We Can, 20,000 Are Told at Women's Fair," *Boston Globe*, January 19, 1974, 1.

27. "CPB Says Its Efforts in Hiring Women, Minorities Are Improving," *Broadcasting*, May 2, 1977, 34.

28. John J. O'Connor, "Programming for Women—Time for Reevaluation," *New York Times*, April 24, 1977, D39.

29. O'Connor, D39.

30. Devorah Heitner, *Black Power TV* (Durham, NC: Duke University Press: 2013), 153.

31. Heitner, 153–54.

32. Wald, *It's Been Beautiful*, 5.

33. Wald, 23.

34. WGBH program order: "How to Make a Woman's Show," MC 253, Box 1, Folder 1, Papers of Katharine S. Kinderman, 1969–1970, Schlesinger Library.

35. "Inventory," MC 253, Box 1, Folder 1, Papers of Katharine S. Kinderman, 1969–1970, Schlesinger Library.

36. "Brothers and Sisters," *Newsweek*, September 7, 1970, 57.

37. "Television," *The Spokeswoman*, October 30, 1970, 8.

38. Quoted in Michael Kenney, "Ch. 2 Cancels Women's Program," *Boston Globe*, August 27, 1970, 28.

39. Kenney, 28.

40. Kenney, 28.

41. "Television," 8.

42. "Brothers and Sisters," 57.

43. "Brothers and Sisters," 56.

44. "Brother and Sisters," 56.

45. Douglas Bailey, Director, KERA-TV, "A Proposal for [An Untitled] Series of Public Television Programs for Women," undated first draft, SSC.MS.00237, Box 166, Folder 18, Gloria Steinem Papers, Sophia Smith Collection, Smith College (hereafter Steinem Papers).

46. Bailey.

47. Bailey.

48. Bailey.

49. Bailey.

50. Publicity packet for *Woman Alive!*, 1976, SSC.MS.00237, Box 167, Folder 4, Steinem Papers.

51. KERA-TV, "Woman Alive Focuses on Crystal Lee Jordan," news release, undated, MC 421, Box 1, Folder 18, *Woman Alive!* Collection, Schlesinger Library.

52. KERA-TV, "National Broadcast of *Woman Alive!*," news release, undated, MC 421, Box 1, Folder 17, *Woman Alive!* Collection, Schlesinger Library.

53. Ernest Pascucci, "Intimate (Tele)visions," in *Architecture of the Everyday*, ed. Steven Harris and Deborah Berke (New York: Princeton Architectural, 1997), 46.

54. Dow, *Prime-Time Feminism*, 5.

55. Fran Pollner, "Turn On, Tune In, and Take Over," *off our backs* 3, no. 2 (October 1972): 4.

56. Lucy Komisar, "The National Organization for Women Press Handbook," June 1970, 6, National Organization for Women Records, 1959–2002, MC 469, Box 29, Schlesinger Library.

57. It is worth noting that the reports identified here were not hit pieces on the women's movement; they were written by women who identified as feminist (Susan Jacoby) or were sympathetic to progressive political and humanitarian causes (Marguerite Michaels). Their work, in many ways, presages scholarship like Judith Ezekiel, *Feminism in the Heartland* (Columbus: Ohio State University Press, 2002) and Nancy Whittier, *Feminist Generations: The Persistence of the Radical Women's Movement* (Philadelphia: Temple University Press, 1995).

58. Marguerite Michaels, "The New Feminism on Main Street," *Time*, March 20, 1972, 32.

59. Michaels, 32.

60. Susan Redman to *Woman Alive!*, December 11, 1975, SSC.MS.00237, Box 167, Folder 4, Steinem Papers.

61. Phyllis Spisto to *Woman Alive!*, November 28, 1975, SSC.MS.00237, Box 167, Folder 4, Steinem Papers.

62. Spisto to *Woman Alive!*

63. Catherine Cox to *Woman Alive!* (Dear Sisters), undated, SSC.MS.00237, Box 167, Folder 4, Steinem Papers.

64. Barbara Cox to *Woman Alive!*, November 12, 1975. SSC.MS.00237, Box 167, Folder 4, Steinem Papers.

65. Georgia O'Donnell to *Woman Alive!*, undated, SSC.MS.00237, Box 167, Folder 4, Steinem Papers.

66. Sharon to *Woman Alive!*, undated, SSC.MS.00237, Box 167, Folder 4, Steinem Papers.

67. Bailey, "Proposal."

68. Shigekawa, "American Woman," 43.

69. Shigekawa, 43.

70. Bailey, "Proposal."

71. Bailey.

72. "Redstockings Challenge Steinem & *Ms.*: Redstockings' Statement," *off our backs* 5, no. 6 (July 1975): 8.

73. Georgia Jones, "Twinkle, Twinkle . . . The Great Superstar Fiasco," *off our backs* 3, no. 3 (September 1972): 3.

74. Susan Jacoby, "Women's Lib Plays in Peoria," *Saturday Review*, February 8, 1974, 11.

75. Jacoby, 11.

76. Quoted in Jacoby, 10, 11.

77. Myrna Blyth, "*Woman Alive!*: The New Feminism in Action," *Image: The Membership Magazine of WNET-13*, June 1974, 20, MC 421, Box 1, Folder 18, *Woman Alive!* Collection, Schlesinger Library.

78. Blyth, "*Woman Alive!*" [*Image*], 20.

79. Myrna Blyth, "*Woman Alive!*," *Primetime: Channel 13*, June 1974, 8, MC 421, Box 1, Folder 18, *Woman Alive!* Collection, Schlesinger Library.

80. "Television Reviews: *Woman Alive!*," *Variety*, June 26, 1974, 42; Ellen Cohn, "Two TV Shows That Reflect the Changing Role of Women in Society," *New York Times*, July 16, 1974, 38.

81. "Indykement against *Ms. Magazine*," *Lesbian Tide*, August 1974, 5.

82. "Redstockings Challenge Steinem," 9.

83. "Redstockings Challenge Steinem," 29.

84. "Redstockings Challenge Steinem," 30.

85. "Redstockings Challenge Steinem," 30.

86. Blyth, "*Woman Alive!* [*Primetime*], 8.

87. Cohn, 38.

88. KERA-TV, "*Woman Alive!*' Is Not Just for Women—It's by Women," news release, undated, MC 421, Box 1, Folder 18, *Woman Alive!* Collection, Schlesinger Library.

89. KERA-TV, "*Woman Alive!*.

90. Shigekawa, "American Woman," 42.

91. Shigekawa, 46.

92. Shigekawa, 42.

93. Shigekawa, 46.

94. Television Reviews: *Woman Alive!*," 42.

95. Television Reviews: *Woman Alive!*," 42.

96. Marvin Kitman, "The Two Sexes View a Sexist Magazine," *Newsday*, October 22, 1975, 58A.

97. William Sloan, Film Librarian, NYPL, to Ronnie Eldridge, January 19, 1976, SSC. MS.00237, Box 167, Folder 4, Steinem Papers.

98. *Woman Alive!* promotional packet, SSC.MS.00237, Box 167, Folder 4, Steinem Papers.

99. *Woman Alive!* promotional packet.

100. "Open CPB Meeting Hears Criticisms by Minorities and by Proponent of Decentralization," *Broadcasting*, March 22, 1976, 83.

101. Flo Piclette to *Woman Alive!*, January 21, 1976, Steinem Papers.

102. Commonwealth of Massachusetts, *Report of the Commissioners, Governor's Commission on the Status of Women, 1972–73* (Boston: The Commission, 1973), iv.

103. Hearings were held in Worcester on November 17, 1973; in Boston on January 10, 1974; and in Springfield on February 4–8, 1974.

104. Commonwealth of Massachusetts, *Report of the Commissioners, Governor's Commission on the Status of Women, 1975–76* (Boston: The Commission, 1976), 4.

105. WBZ-TV and Massachusetts Governor's Commission on Women, press release for *Yes, We Can*, December 31, 1973, MC 684, Box 2, Folder 6, Eunice P. Howe Papers, Schlesinger Library.

106. WBZ-TV and Massachusetts Governor's Commission on Women, press release for *Yes, We Can*.

107. Carol Cote, President, Eastern Massachusetts NOW Chapter, to Paul Coss, Program Manager, WBZ-TV, January 22, 1974, 77-M13—96-M48; T-187, Box 2, Folder 80, Records of Boston N.O.W., Schlesinger Library.

108. "WBZ-TV's All-Fair for Women—On the Air & At Aud.," *Variety*, January 23, 1974, 34.

109. Sonya Hamlin, interview with the author, September 20, 2018.

110. Hamlin, interview.

111. Rebecca J. Sheehan, "Intersectional Feminist Friendship: Restoring Colour to the Second-Wave through the Letters of Florynce Kennedy and Germaine Greer," *Lilith: A Feminist History Journal* 25 (November 2019): 87.

112. Hamlin, interview.

113. WBZ-TV and Massachusetts Governor's Commission on Women, press release for *Yes, We Can*.

114. Janet Stone to Paul Coss, Program Manager, WBZ-TV, January 29, 1974, 77-M13—96-M48; T-187, Box 13, Folder 457, Records of Boston N.O.W., Schlesinger Library.

115. Stone to Coss.

116. Stone to Coss.

117. WBZ-TV and Massachusetts Governor's Commission on Women, press release for *Yes, We Can*.

118. WBZ-TV and Massachusetts Governor's Commission on Women, press release for *Yes, We Can*.

119. Stone to Coss.

120. Massachusetts Commonwealth, *Report of the Commissioners, 1975–76*, 19.

121. Executive Committee Meeting Minutes, January 29, 1974, GO30/1372, Advisory Committee meeting minutes, 1976–1989, Commonwealth of Massachusetts State Archive, Boston.

122. The *Boston Globe* reported "mulling the future shock of such programming" at other Westinghouse-owned stations. If this were to happen, the next installment would take place in Philadelphia.

123. Patrick McGilligan, "Women Filmmakers Form Cooperative," *Boston Globe*, March 19, 1974, 34.

124. Pat Mitchell, "The Revolution Will Be Televised," The State of SIE, Skoll Center for Social Impact Entertainment, UCLA School of Theater, Film & Television, accessed April 1, 2022, https://thestateofsie.com/pat-mitchell-public-broadcasting-highlighting-inequality -communicating-change/.

125. Mitchell.

EPILOGUE: WHAT THE 1970S CAN TEACH US
ABOUT FEMINIST MEDIA REFORM

1. Virginia Heffernan, "Mary Tyler Moore, Who Incarnated the Modern Woman on TV, Dies at 80," *New York Times*, January 26, 2017.

2. Oprah Winfrey (@Oprah), "Mary Tyler Moore Statue," Instagram, January 10, 2020, www.instagram.com/p/B7J6QQ2BMsS/?hl=en.

3. Jennifer S. Clark, "Liberating Bicentennial America: Imagining the Nation through TV Superwomen of the Seventies," *Television and New Media* 10, no. 5 (September 2009): 434–54.

4. Clare Hemmings, *Why Stories Matter: The Political Grammar of Feminist Theory* (Durham, NC: Duke University Press, 2011), 22.

5. Sarah Jaffe, "The Collective Power of #MeToo," *Dissent* 65, no. 2 (Spring 2018): 87.

6. Shelley Cobb and Tanya Horeck, "Post Weinstein: Gendered Power and Harassment in the Media Industries," *Feminist Media Studies* 18, no. 3 (2018): 490.

7. Cobb and Horeck, 490.

8. Ball and Bell, "Working Women, Women's Work," 547.

9. Caroline Heldman et al., *See Jane 2020 TV Report*, Executive Summary, Geena Davis Institute on Gender in Media, 2020, https://seejane.org/research-informs-empowers/2020 -tv-historic-screen-time-speaking-time-for-female-characters/.

10. Google funded the GD-IQ project, and the University of Southern California's Signal Analysis and Interpretation Laboratory (SAIL) designed its software. The Institute's Spell Check for Bias tool, which codes for characters and dialogue in film, television, and advertising scripts, was also developed in relationship with SAIL. Procter & Gamble funded "Fair Play? The Triumphs and Challenges of Female Athletes in the U.S.," and LEGO sponsored research for the Ready for Girls Creativity Study.

11. Geena Davis, Academy Awards Acceptance Speech (Ray Dolby Ballroom, Hollywood & Highland Center, Los Angeles, October 27, 2019), Academy of Motion Pictures Arts and Sciences, http://aaspeechesdb.oscars.org/link/092-204/.

12. Davis, Academy Awards Acceptance Speech.

13. Madeline Di Nonno, "Intersectionality on Television: Getting It Right," paper presented at Faculty Seminar: The Conference, Saban Media Center, Los Angeles, November 5, 2019.

14. "About Us," Geena Davis Institute on Gender in Media, accessed July 27, 2022, https://seejane.org/about-us/.

15. Di Nonno, "Intersectionality on Television."

16. Sara Ahmed, *On Being Included: Racism and Diversity in Institutional Life* (Durham, NC: Duke University Press, 2012), 105.

17. Ahmed, 107.

18. Ahmed, 84.

19. Davis, Academy Awards Acceptance Speech.

20. Smukler, *Liberating Hollywood*, 69.

21. TTIE, "Think Tank for Inclusion and Equity," accessed August 8, 2022, www .writeinclusion.org/.

22. TTIE, Women in Film, and Geena Davis Institute, *Behind the Scenes: The State of Inclusion and Equity in TV Writing*, Spring 2021, https://seejane.org/wp-content/uploads /ttie-behind-the-scenes-2021-report.pdf.

23. TTIE, Women in Film, and Geena Davis Institute, "Executive Summary," *Behind the Scenes: The State of Inclusion and Equity in TV Writing*, 2021, https://seejane.org/research -informs-empowers/behind-the-scenes-the-state-of-inclusion-and-equity-in-tv-writing/.

24. TTIE, Women in Film, and Geena Davis Institute, *Behind the Scenes: The State of Inclusion and Equity in TV Writing*, 2022, https://static1.squarespace.com /static/5f8a09a4bd8bae2e8075daob/t/628c1d6d623846629a4eb9d6/1653349749205 /TTIE+BTS4+2022+Report.pdf.

25. Victoria Hesford, *Feeling Women's Liberation* (Durham, NC: Duke University Press, 2013), 6.

26. Anne Enke, *Finding the Movement: Sexuality, Contested Space, and Feminist Activism* (Durham, NC: Duke University Press, 2007), 11. Other revisions to received histories of women's liberation movements include Susan M. Hartmann, *The Other Feminists: Activists in the Liberal Establishment* (New Haven, CT: Yale University Press, 1998) and Winifred Breines, *The Trouble between Us: An Uneasy History of White and Black Women in the Feminist Movement* (New York: Oxford University Press, 2006).

27. Hartmann, *Other Feminists*, 2.

28. Annie Berke, *Their Own Best Creations: Women Writers in Postwar Television* (Berkeley: University of California Press, 2022), 14.

29. Denise McKenna, guest editor of "Labor" issue, *Feminist Media Histories*, interview with Shelley Stamp, n.d., Feminist Media Histories, accessed February 5, 2018, https://soundcloud.com/user-161032629.

BIBLIOGRAPHY

ARCHIVAL SOURCES

American Heritage Center, University of Wyoming
    Ann Marcus Papers
CBS News Reference Library, CBS Broadcast Center, New York
    Unprocessed collection
Commonwealth of Massachusetts State Archive, Boston
    Governor's Office on Women's Issues Records
Howard Gotlieb Archival Research Center, Boston University
    Sonya Hamlin Collection
Emerson College Archives, Emerson College, Boston
    Norman Lear Script Collection
Library of American Broadcasting, University of Maryland, College Park
    AWRT Collection
McGannon Center, Fordham University, New York
    The TV Oral History Project
New York Historical Society, New York
    Women and the American Story Collection
Paley Center for Media, New York
    Paley Archive
Schlesinger Library, Radcliffe Institute, Harvard University
    Boston National Organization for Women Records
    Eunice P. Howe Papers
    Katharine S. Kinderman Papers
National Organization for Women Records
    Marlene Sanders Papers
    Woman Alive! Collection

Sophia Smith Collection of Women's History, Smith College, Northampton, MA
    Eleanor Sanger Papers
    Gloria Steinem Papers
Television Academy Foundation, North Hollywood, CA
    Television Academy Interviews

PUBLISHED WORKS

Acker, Joan. "The Future of 'Gender and Organizations': Connections and Boundaries." *Gender, Work and Organization* 54, no. 4 (October 1998): 195–206.

Ahmed, Sara. *On Being Included: Racism and Diversity in Institutional Life*. Durham, NC: Duke University Press, 2012.

Alley, Robert S., and Irby B. Brown. *Women Television Producers: Transformation of the Male Medium, 1948–2000*. Rochester, NY: University of Rochester Press, 2001.

Andrews, Kylie. "Don't Tell Them I Can Type: Negotiating Women's Work in Production in the Post-war ABC." *Media International Australia* 161, no. 1 (November 2016): 28–37.

Armstrong, Jennifer Keishin. *Mary and Lou and Rhoda and Ted: And All the Brilliant Minds Who Made The Mary Tyler Moore Show a Classic*. New York: Simon and Schuster, 2013.

Baker, Jeannine. "'Once a Typist Always a Typist': The Australian Women's Broadcasting Co-operative and the Sexual Division of Labor at the Australian Broadcasting Commission." *Feminist Media Histories* 4, no. 4 (Fall 2018): 160–84.

Baker, Jeannine, and Jane Connors. "'Glorified Typists in No-Man's Land: The ABC Script Assistants' Strike of 1973." *Women's History Review* 29, no. 5 (2020): 841–59.

Baker, Jeannine, and Justine Lloyd. "Gendered Labor and Media: Histories and Continuities." *Media International Australia* 161, no. 1 (November 2016): 6–17.

Ball, Vicky, and Melanie Bell. "Working Women, Women's Work: Production, History, Gender." *Journal of British Cinema and Television* 10, no. 3 (July 2013): 547–62.

Banks, Miranda J. "Production Studies." *Feminist Media Histories* 4, no. 2 (Spring 2018): 157–61.

———. *The Writers: A History of American Screenwriters and Their Guild*. New Brunswick, NJ: Rutgers University Press, 2015.

———. "Unequal Opportunities: Gender Inequities and Precarious Diversity in the 1970s US Television Industry." *Feminist Media Histories* 4, no. 4 (Spring 2018): 109–29.

Banks, Miranda J., and Lauren Steimer. "The Heroic Body: Toughness, Femininity and the Stunt Double." *The Sociological Review* 63, no. 1 (May 2015): 144–57.

Barker-Plummer, Bernadette. "News as a Political Resource: Media Strategies and Political Identity in the U.S. Women's Movement, 1966–1975." *Critical Studies in Mass Communication* 12, no. 3 (September 1995): 306–24.

Becker, Christine. *It's the Pictures That Got Small: Hollywood Film Stars on 1950s Television*. Middleton, CT: Wesleyan University Press, 2008.

Benschop, Yvonne, and Mieke Verloo. "Feminist Organization Theories: Islands of Treasure." In *The Routledge Companion to Philosophy in Organizational Studies*, edited by Raza Mir, Hugh Willmott, and Michelle Greenwood, 100–112. New York: Routledge, 2016.

Berke, Annie. *Their Own Best Creations: Women Writers in Postwar Television*. Berkeley: University of California Press, 2022.

Bradley, Patricia. *Mass Media and the Shaping of American Feminism, 1963–1975*. Jackson: University of Mississippi Press, 2003.

Branscomb, Anne W., and Maria Savage. "The Broadcast Reform Movement at the Cross-roads." *Journal of Communication* 28, no. 4 (December 1978): 25–34.

Breines, Winifred. *The Trouble between Us: An Uneasy History of White and Black Women in the Feminist Movement*. New York: Oxford University Press, 2006.

Brunsdon, Charlotte. "*Crossroads*: Notes on a Soap Opera." *Screen* 22, no. 4 (December 1981): 32–37.

Cassidy, Marsha F. *What Women Watched: Daytime Television in the 1950s*. Austin: University of Texas Press, 2005.

Clark, Jennifer S. "'Feminist Borers from Within': The CBS Women's Advisory Council and Media Workplace Reform in the 1970s." *JCMS* 63, no. 1 (Fall 2023): 10–29.

———. "Liberating Bicentennial America: Imagining the Nation through TV Superwomen of the Seventies." *Television and New Media* 10, no. 5 (September 2009): 434–54.

Clavio, Galen. "Play-by-Play Announcer." In *Encyclopedia of Sports Management and Marketing*, edited by Linda Swayne and Mark Dodds. Thousand Oaks, CA: Sage Publications, 2011. http://proxy.library.nyu.edu/login?url=https://search.credoreference.com/content/entry/sagesports/play_by_play_announcer/0?institutionId=577.

Cobb, Shelley, and Tanya Horeck. "Post Weinstein: Gendered Power and Harassment in the Media Industries." *Feminist Media Studies* 18, no. 3 (2018): 489–91.

Cobble, Dorothy Sue. "'A Spontaneous Loss of Enthusiasm': Workplace Feminism and the Transformation of Women's Service Jobs in the 1970s." *International Labor and Working-Class History* no. 56 (Fall 1999): 23–44.

Commonwealth of Massachusetts. *Report of the Commissioners, Governor's Commission on the Status of Women, 1972–73*. Boston: The Commission, 1973.

D'Acci, Julie. *Defining Women: Television and the Case of Cagney & Lacey*. Chapel Hill: University of North Carolina Press, 1994.

"Dialogue on Film: Norman Lear." *American Film* 2, no. 8 (June 1, 1977): 33–48.

Didi-Huberman, Georges. *Invention of Hysteria: Charcot and the Photographic Iconography of the Salpêtrière*. Translated by Alisa Hartz. Cambridge, MA: MIT Press, 2003.

Dow, Bonnie J. *Prime-Time Feminism: Television, Media Culture, and the Women's Movement since 1970*. Philadelphia: University of Pennsylvania Press, 1996.

———. *Watching Women's Liberation, 1970: Feminism's Pivotal Year on the Network News*. Urbana: University of Illinois Press, 2014.

Echols, Alice. *Daring to Be Bad: Radical Feminism in America, 1967–1975*. Minneapolis: University of Minnesota Press, 1989.

Ehrenreich, Barbara. "*Mary Hartman*: A World Out of Control." *Socialist Revolution* 6, no. 4 (October-December 1976): 133–38.

Enke, Anne. *Finding the Movement: Sexuality, Contested Space, and Feminist Activism*. Durham, NC: Duke University Press, 2007.

Evans, Sara M. *Born for Liberty: A History of Women in America*. New York: Free Press, 1989.

Ezekiel, Judith. *Feminism in the Heartland*. Columbus: Ohio State University Press, 2002.

Ferguson, Kathy. *The Feminist Case against Bureaucracy*. Philadelphia: Temple University Press, 1984.

Ferree, Myra Marx, and Patricia Yancey Martin. "Doing the Work of the Movement." In *Feminist Organizations: Harvest of the New Women's Movement*, edited by Myra Marx Ferree and Patricia Yancey Martin, 3–26. Philadelphia: Temple University Press, 1995.

Fleeger, Jennifer. *Mismatched Women: The Siren's Song through the Machine*. New York: Oxford University Press, 2014.

Galt, Frances. *Women's Activism behind the Screens: Trade Unions and Gender Inequality in the British Film and Television Industries*. Bristol: Bristol University Press, 2021.

Geller, Henry, and Gregg Young. "Family Viewing: An FCC Tumble from the Tightrope?" *Journal of Communication* 27, no. 2 (June 1997): 193–201.

Gitlin, Todd. *Inside Prime Time*. New York: Pantheon Book, 1985.

Gregory, Molly. *Women Who Run the Show: How a Brilliant and Creative New Generation of Women Stormed Hollywood*. New York: St. Martin's Press, 2002.

Hargreaves, Jennifer. *Sporting Females: Critical Issues in the History and Sociology of Women's Sports*. New York: Routledge, 1994.

Hartmann, Susan M. *The Other Feminists: Activists in the Liberal Establishment*. New Haven, CT: Yale University Press, 1998.

Havens, Timothy, Amanda D. Lotz, and Serra Tinic, "Critical Media Industry Studies: A Research Approach." *Communication, Culture and Critique* 2, no. 2 (June 2009): 234–253.

Heitner, Devorah. *Black Power TV*. Durham, NC: Duke University Press: 2013.

Hemmings, Clare. *Why Stories Matter: The Political Grammar of Feminist Theory*. Durham, NC: Duke University Press, 2011.

Hesford, Victoria, *Feeling Women's Liberation*. Durham, NC: Duke University Press, 2013.

Heywood, Leslie, and Shari L. Dworkin. *Built to Win: The Female Athlete as Cultural Icon*. Minneapolis: University of Minnesota Press, 2003.

Hill, Erin. *Never Done: A History of Women's Work in Media Production*. New Brunswick, NJ: Rutgers University Press, 2016.

Hilmes, Michele. *Network Nations: A Transnational History of British and American Broadcasting*. New York: Routledge, 2012.

———. *Radio Voices: American Broadcasting, 1922–1952*. Minneapolis: University of Minnesota Press, 1997.

Hilmes, Michele, and Shawn VanCour. "Network Nation: Writing Broadcasting History as Cultural History." In *NBC: America's Network*, edited by Michele Hilmes, 308–22. Berkeley: University of California Press, 2007.

Hochschild, Arlie Russell. *The Managed Heart: Commercialization of Human Feeling*. Twentieth Anniversary ed. Berkeley: University of California Press, 2003.

Hunter, Aaron, and Martha Shearer. Introduction to *Women and New Hollywood: Gender, Creative Labor, and 1970s American Cinema*, edited by Aaron Hunter and Martha Shearer, 1–14. New Brunswick, NJ: Rutgers University Press, 2023.

Jaffe, Sarah. "The Collective Power of #MeToo." *Dissent* 65, no. 2 (Spring 2018): 80–87.

Johnson, Mary Ann, Rebecca Sive, Christine Riddiough, Anne Ladky, and Joan Hall. "Activists' Panel." *Frontiers: A Journal of Women's Studies* 36, no. 2 (2015): 3–24.

Knopf, Terry Ann. *The Golden Age of Boston Television*. Hanover, NH: University of Press of New England, 2017.

Lawrence, Amy. *Echo and Narcissus: Women's Voices in Classical Hollywood Cinema*. Berkeley: University of California Press, 1991.

Lear, Norman. *Even This I Get to Experience*. New York: Penguin, 2014.

Lee, Minkyo, Daeyeon Kim, Antonio S. Williams, and Paul M. Pedersen. "Investigating the Role of Sports Commentary: An Analysis of Media-Consumption Behavior and Programmatic Quality and Satisfaction." *Journal of Sports Media* 11, no. 1 (Spring 2016): 145–67.

Lehman, Katherine J. *Those Girls: Single Women in Sixties and Seventies Popular Culture*. Lawrence: University Press of Kansas, 2011.

Lentz, Kirsten Marthe. "Quality versus Relevance: Feminism, Race, and the Politics of the Sign in 1970s Television." *Camera Obscura* 15, no. 1 (2000): 44–93.

Levine, Elana. *Her Stories: Daytime Soap Opera and US Television History*. Durham, NC: Duke University Press, 2020.

———. *Wallowing in Sex: The New Sexual Culture of 1970s American Television*. Durham, NC: Duke University Press, 2007.

Lorimer, Hayden. "Cultural Geography: The Busyness of Being 'More-Than-Representational.'" *Progress in Human Geography* 29, no. 1 (February 2005): 83–94.

McCracken, Allison. *Real Men Don't Sing: Crooning in American Culture*. Durham, NC: Duke University Press, 2015.

Messner, Michael A., Margaret Carlisle Duncan, and Kerry Jensen. "Separating the Men from the Girls: The Gendered Language of Televised Sports." *Gender and Society* 7, no. 1 (March 1993): 121–37.

Mitchell, Nicole, and Lisa A. Ennis, eds. *Encyclopedia of Title IX and Sports*. Westport, CT: Greenwood Press, 2007.

Mock, Erin Lee. "'The Soap Opera Is a Hell of an Exciting Form': Norman Lear's *Mary Hartman, Mary Hartman* and the 1970s Viewer." *Camera Obscura* 28, no. 2 (2013): 109–49.

Modleski, Tania. "The Rhythms of Reception: Daytime Television and Women's Work." In *Regarding Television: Critical Approaches—An Anthology*, edited by E. Ann Kaplan, 67–75. Frederick, MD: University Publications of America, 1983.

———. "The Search for Tomorrow in Today's Soap Operas: Notes on a Feminine Narrative Form." *Film Quarterly* 33, no. 1 (Autumn 1979): 12–21.

Montgomery, Kathryn C. *Target: Prime Time: Advocacy Groups and the Struggle over Entertainment Television*. New York: Oxford University Press, 1989.

Moseley, Rachel, Helen Wheatley, and Helen Wood. "Introduction: Why 'Television for Women'?" *Screen* 54, no. 2 (Summer 2013): 238–43.

Mumford, Laurel Stempel. "Feminist Theory and Television Criticism." In *The Television Studies Book*, edited by Christine Geraghty and David Lusted, 114–30. New York: St. Martin's Press, 1998.

Murray, Susan. *Bright Signals: A History of Color Television*. Durham, NC: Duke University Press, 2018.

Newcomb, Horace. "Programming." In *Encyclopedia of Television*, edited by Horace Newcomb, 2nd ed. New York: Routledge, 2004.

———. "Susan Harris." In *Encyclopedia of Television*, edited by Horace Newcomb, 2nd ed. New York: Routledge, 2004.

———. "The Television Artistry of Norman Lear." *Prospects* 2 (October 1977): 109–25.

Nielsen, Elizabeth. "Handmaidens of the Glamour Culture: Costumers in the Hollywood Studio System." In *Fabrications: Costume and the Female Body*, edited by Jane Gaines and Charlotte Herzog, 160–79. New York: Routledge, 1990.

O'Brien, Anne. "'A Fine Old Time': Feminist Print Journalism in the 1970s." *Irish Studies Review* 25, no. 1 (2017): 42–55.

Pascucci, Ernest. "Intimate (Tele)visions." In *Architecture of the Everyday*, edited by Steven Harris and Deborah Berke, 39–54. New York: Princeton Architectural, 1997.

Perlman, Allison. "Feminists in the Wasteland: The National Organization for Women and Television Reform." *Feminist Media Studies* 7, no. 4 (2007): 413–31.

———. *Public Interests: Media Advocacy and Struggles over U.S. Television*. New Brunswick, NJ: Rutgers University Press, 2016.

Rabinovitz, Lauren. "Ms.-Representation: The Politics of Feminist Sitcoms." In *Television, History, and American Culture: Feminist Critical Essays*, edited by Mary Beth Haralovich and Lauren Rabinovitz, 144–67. Durham, NC: Duke University Press, 1999.

Rakow, Lana F. *Gender on the Line: Women, the Telephone, and Community Life*. Urbana: University of Illinois Press, 1992.

Riger, Eleanor. "Women in TV Sports." In *TV Book: The Ultimate Television Book*, edited by Judy Fireman, 138–40. New York: Workman, 1977.

Sanders, Marlene, and Marcia Rock. *Waiting for Prime Time: The Women of Television News*. Urbana: University of Illinois Press, 1988.

Sheehan, Rebecca J. "Intersectional Feminist Friendship: Restoring Colour to the Second-Wave through the Letters of Florynce Kennedy and Germaine Greer." *Lilith: A Feminist History Journal* 25 (November 2019): 76–92.

Shigekawa, Joan. "The American Woman—*Alive* and Well." *Public Communications Review* 4, no. 5 (September/October 1976): 41–48.

Smukler, Maya Montañez. *Liberating Hollywood: Women Directors and the Feminist Reform of 1970s American Cinema*. New Brunswick, NJ: Rutgers University Press, 2019.

Socolow, Michael J. "The C.B.S. Problem in American Radio Historiography." *Journal of Radio and Audio Media* 23, no. 2 (2016): 323–34.

Spain, Daphne. *Gendered Spaces*. Chapel Hill: University of North Carolina Press, 1992.

Spigel, Lynn. *Make Room for TV: Television and the Family Ideal in Postwar America*. Chicago: University of Chicago Press, 1992.

———. *TV by Design: Modern Art and the Rise of Network Television*. Chicago: University of Chicago Press, 2008.

Tong, Rosemarie. *Feminist Thought: A Comprehensive Introduction*. Boulder, CO: Westview Press, 1989.

———. *Feminist Thought: A More Comprehensive Introduction*. 3rd ed. Boulder, CO: Westview Press, 2008.

US Commission on Civil Rights. *Window Dressing on the Set: Women and Minorities in Television*. Washington, DC: US Government Printing Office, 1977.

Vogan, Travis. *ABC Sports: The Rise and Fall of Network Sports Television*. Berkeley: University of California Press, 2018.

Wald, Gayle. *It's Been Beautiful: Soul! and Black Power Television*. Durham, NC: Duke University Press, 2015.

Walters, Barbara. *Audition: A Memoir*. New York: Knopf, 2008.

Ware, Susan. *Game, Set, Match: Billie Jean King and the Revolution in Women's Sports.* Chapel Hill: University of North Carolina Press, 2011.

Westcott, Diane Nilsen. "Blacks in the 1970's: Did They Scale the Job Ladder?" *Monthly Labor Review* 105, no. 6 (June 1982): 29–38.

Whittier, Nancy. *Feminist Generations: The Persistence of the Radical Women's Movement.* Philadelphia: Temple University Press, 1995.

Whyte, Marama. "'The Worst Divorce Case That Ever Happened': The *New York Times* Women's Caucus and Workplace Feminism." *Modern American History* 3, nos. 2–3 (November 2020): 153–74.

Wreyford, Natalie, and Shelley Cobb. "Data and Responsibility: Toward a Feminist Methodology for Producing Historical Data on Women in the Contemporary UK Film Industry." *Feminist Media Histories* 3, no. 3 (Summer 2017): 107–32.

INDEX

Note: Page numbers in *italics* refer to illustrative matter.

Founded in 1893,
UNIVERSITY OF CALIFORNIA PRESS
publishes bold, progressive books and journals
on topics in the arts, humanities, social sciences,
and natural sciences—with a focus on social
justice issues—that inspire thought and action
among readers worldwide.

The UC PRESS FOUNDATION
raises funds to uphold the press's vital role
as an independent, nonprofit publisher, and
receives philanthropic support from a wide
range of individuals and institutions—and from
committed readers like you. To learn more, visit
ucpress.edu/supportus.